पुरातत्त्व

PURĀTATTVA

Bulletin of the Indian Archaeological Society

No. 23 1992-93

Editor
K. N. Dikshit

Jt. Editor
K.S. Ramachandran

D.K. Printworld (P) Ltd.
New Delhi

Cataloging in Publication Data — DK
[Courtesy : D.K. Agencies (P) Ltd. <docinfo@dkagencies.com>]

Purātattva : bulletin of the Indian Archaeological Society, no. 23, 1992-93 / editor, K.N. Dikshit ; jt. editor, K.S. Ramachandran.
p. cm.
Includes bibliographical references.
ISBN 8124602980

1. Archaeology — India — Periodicals. 2. India — Antiquities — Periodicals. 3. India — Civilization — Periodicals. I. Dikshit, K.N. II. Indian Archaeological Society.

First Published in 1993
First Reprinted in 2005
ISBN 81-246-0298-0
Price for volume 23 (1992-93): Rs. 800 US $ 40

Reprint authorised by
Indian Archaeological Society
New Delhi - 110 016

The Editors are not responsible for the opinions expressed by the Contributors.

Purātattva is published annually.

Manuscripts (whether in the form of articles or notes or book reviews) offered for publication should be sent to the Editor, Purātattva, Indian Archaeological Society, B-17, Qutab Institutional Area, New Delhi - 110 016.

Published and printed by:
D.K. Printworld (P) Ltd.
'*Srikunj*,' F-52, Bali Nagar
New Delhi – 110015
Phone : (011) 2545 3975, 2546 6019 Fax : (011) 2546 5926
E-mail : dkprintworld@vsnl.net
www. dkprintworld.com

PURATATTVA

CONTENTS

PURATATTVA

Number 23 1992-93

Editorial

The present *Purattatva*, number 23, is being placed in the hands of our readers. We have reduced the number of articles in order to print a complete Index—authorwise as well as titlewise of all the articles and notes published during the last 22-years in the *Purattatva* Nos. 1 to 22 as a separate supplement soon and will be sent to our members by post. This, we have done to facilitate our readers for easy access to their subject of choice besides indicating the range of articles and the variety of subjects that *Purattatva* carries. We hope the readers will be benefitted by this.

We are also publishing an up-to-date list of our Life Members. We invite our members to write to us, in case their names do not find place in the list in spite of having paid full amount of the life membership fee. It is also possible that some of the members have moved out from their previous addresses but have not communicated their present mailing addresses; they or others who know, are requested to inform us their present addresses so that we may incorporate them in the next issue of the *Purattatva.* This will help both the members and the organisers in keeping contact with each other.

The World Archaeological Congress will meet in New Delhi from 4th through 11th of December, 1994. Perhaps never again such an opportunity will come for our members to participate in a World meet in their home country. May we request our members to fill up the form enclosed herewith at the end and send it Dr. Makkhan Lal, Post Box No. 112, H.P.O., Aligarh. The normal fees is much higher but we are trying to find out sources to bring it down for the Indian delegates to Rs. 1500/- only. For those first one hundred in the universities whose papers we accept for presentation, the fees may be further reduced by Rs. 1000/-, a subsidy which ICHR has very generously agreed to provide Thus your burden will be only Rs. 500/-. It is in your interest to utilize the opportunity.

We request members to prepare original papers based upon new Archaeological findings, fresh Archaeological excavations, fresh interpretation, or absolutely new ideas on any subject, the list of which is given at the end. Consequently, there will be no annual conference of the Society next year i.e. 1994. The World Archaeological Congress-3 will be the next session of the Society as well.

Editors

Plant Economy of Late Harappans at Hulas

K.S. Saraswat*

The ancient mound, located in the revenue limits of the village Hulas (Lat. 28°43'N; Long. 77°22'E) in Nakur Tahsil of Sahranpur District, western Uttar Pradesh, was subjected to a largescale excavation by the Archaeological Survey of India in 1978-79, under the direction of K.N. Dikshit. The mound measured 330 × 172m in area and was found damaged by villagers who levelled down a sizable part of it for agricultural operations. On excavation, about 5 m thick deposit of ancient occupation was found. It is divisible into five distinct cultural periods. Of these, the earliest Period-I represented by 1.40 m thick deposit on the natural soil yielded Harappan red ware, alongwith non-Harappan red and thick Grey wares. Empirical study of the data available from Hulas and many other sites in Haryana and Punjab confirms that the Harappan Civilization did have substantial influence on the cultural development of the areas outside the Indus basin. Whatever be the course followed by the Harappans, the archaeological evidences at Hulas have confirmed the diffusionary process of Harappan culture through successive adaptations to the regional cultural and environmental systems.

At Hulas are witnessed new pottery, absence of cities, relatively uniform features of architecture and house plans, and some cultural items first recognized in the components of the Mature Harappan culture. The Late Harappans developed local variations by mingling with regional cultures until what was once typical Harappan was diluted to the point of non-existence. The Late Harappan phase in Period-I at this site, which has filled the cultural gap between the gradual end of the Harappan culture and the emergence of Iron Age culture (Painted Grey Ware) in the subsequent Period-II, has been dated on the basis of typological study between *Ca* 1700 and 1000 B.C.[1]

The study of Late Harappan plant economy has been taken up with an objective to assess the change in subsistence pattern during the course of Harappan migration, from the semi-arid or arid zones of Haryana and Punjab to the different climatic region of Upper Ganga-Yamuna *doab* receiving higher rainfall. Further, the study is likely to throw light on the dietary habits of the people in this region during different periods.

Materials and Methods

The majority of plant remains, dispersed in the deposits of Late Harappan culture at Hulas, turn out to be a mixture of carbonised seeds and fruits alongwith small pieces of wood charcoal. The carbonized remains represent a small fraction of plant resources utilized by ancient settlers in which food grains and fuel plants, whose processing require heating and burning, are more likely to be accidentally or deliberately charred than the plant material not exposed to fire. A few hard and woody fruit-shell and seed-coat pieces have also survived in uncarbonized state. Therefore, the archaeological record cannot be considered complete. Most of the remains are likely to have resulted from certain human activities. But the preservation of wild seeds and fruits may have been incidental. Potsherds and burnt mud-clods of plasters bearing the impressions of rice husk, which was used as *degraissant* in the clay, have also been found in the excavation.

*Bibal Sahni Institute of Palaebotany, Lucknow-226 007

Samples of soil containing botanical remains, potsherds and burnt mud-plaster pieces were collected from different horizons of Late Harappan deposits. Some larger and apparently visible remains were sorted out from the soil with the help of a forcep. In view of obvious problems in the systematic recovery of material by hand, the soil samples were immersed in water and agitated so that light carbonized remains buoyed to the surface and washed out through a standard geological sieve of 25 mesh. As a result, the seeds and other material remains, as small as 0.7 mm, could be retained on the sieve. Individually separate seeds and fruits were cleaned in acid-alcohol (Glacial Acetic Acid 10% + Ethyl Alcohol 50% in equal volumes) with the help of soft camel-hair brush. Their identification has been made on the basis of comparison with authentically identified extant material, under a stereobinocular microscope. Deformation due to over-burning an puffing in a large number of seeds and fruits, rendered their specific identification not discernible. This made considerable data loss for which no correction is possible. Only recognizable fraction of the samples of seeds and fruits have been presented in this paper, taking into account the changes in their shape, size and proportions caused by carbonization.

The study of grain and husk impressions in the matrix of potsherds and mud-plaster has also been made under a stereobinocular microscope. Cuticle remains obtained from the soil on being cleaned in 5% acetic acid and treated with 10% hydrogen peroxide revealed the cellular structure, but they disintegrated when mounted in Canada balsam. It could, however, be possible to photograph them in glycerine drop on a slide. Sectioning of wood charcoal pieces was done with rotary microtome by following the method of double embedding in celloidyin and paraffin, as suggested by Chowdhury and Ghosh[1a]. The results of botanical analysis along with the archaeological provenance of samples are given in Table 1.

Table 1. Plant Remains Recovered from Hulas (*Ca.* 1700–1000 B.C.)

Sl. No.	Archaeological Number of Samples	Nature of the Material	Results of Study
1	2	3	4
1.	HLS. 82-83 Trench: XC-9, Qdt.2 Stratum: 10 Depth: 2.05 m	Carbonized seeds and fruits	Barley (*Hordeum vulgare),* Wheat (*Triticum spaerococcum*), Field pea (*Pisum arvense*) Green-gram (*Vigna radiata*).
2.	HLS. 82-83 Trench: XG-9, Qdt. 1 Stratum: 9 Depth: 1.82 m	Carbonized seeds and fruits.	Barley (*Hordeum vulgare*), Rice (*Oryza sativa*), Lentil (*Lens culinaris*), Field-pea (*Pisum arvense*), Oat (*Avena sativa*) Wheat (*Triticum sphaerococcum*), Cotton (*Gossypium/arboreum-herbaceum*).
3.	HLS. 82-83 Trench: XG-9, Qdt. 1 Stratum : 8 Depth: 1.64 m	Carbonized seeds and fruits.	Rice (*Oryza sativa*), Wheat (*Triticum sphaerococcum, T.aestivum*), Jowar (*Sorghum bicolor*), Ragi-millet (*Eleusine coracana*) Green-gram (*Vigna radiata*), Horse-gram(*Dolichos biflorus*), Chick-pea (*Cicer arietinum*).

1	2	3	4
4.	HLS. 82-83 Trench: XG-9, Qdt.1 Stratum:7 Depth: 1.42m	Carbonized seeds and fruits	Rice (*Oryza sativa*), Chick-pea (*Cicer arietinum*), Horse-gram (*Dolichos biflorus*), Green-gram (*Vigna radiata*), Grass-pea (*Lathyrus sativus*).
		Cuticle pieces. Uncarbonized pieces of fruit shell (Endocarp) and seed-coat	Cuticle pieces of rice-husk Endocarp (shell) pieces of Almond (*Prunes amygdalus*) and seed-coat piece of Castor (*Ricinus communis*).
5.	HLS. 82-83 Trench: XJ-8, Qdt.2 Stratum:5 Depth: 0.90 m	Carbonized seed and fruits	Rice (*Oryza sativa*), Barley (*Hordeum vulgare*), Wheat (*Triticum sphaerococcum*, *T. aestivocompactum*), Field-pea (*Pisum arvense*), Grass-pea (*Lathyrus sativus*), Oat (*Avena sativa*).
		Wood charcoal pieces Fruit-shell (endocarp) pieces.	Babul (*Acacia nilotica*). *Broken* pieces of walnut (*Juglans regia*) shell.
6.	HLS. 82-83 Trench: XJ-8, Qdt. 2 Stratum: Pit 2 SB.1. Depth: 0.40-0.60m	Carbonized seeds and fruits Potsherds bearing impressions of some grains and husk.	Rice (*Oryza sativa*), Wheat (*Triticum Sphaerococcum*), Barley (*Hordeum vulgare*), *Kundru* or Ivy Gourd (*Coccinia cordifolia*). Husk impressions of cultivated rice (*Oryza sativa*).
7.	HLS. 82-83 Trench: XJB, Qdt.3 Stratum: Pit 4 S.B.1 Depth: 0.56-0.60m	Carbonized seeds and fruits.	Rice (*Oryza sativa*), Oat (*Avena sativa*), Jowar-millet (*Sorghum bicolor*), Field-pea (*Pisum arvense*), Lentil (*Lens culinaris*), A Wild Grass-Anjan (*Cenchrus ciliaris*).
8.	HLS. 82-83 Trench: XJ-8, Qdt. 2 Stratum: 3 Depth: 0. 52-0.56 m	Burnt mud-plaster bearing husk impressions.	Husk-impressions of cultivated rice (*Oryza sativa*), along with those of a wild rice comparable to *Oryza rufipogon.*
9.	HLS. 82-83 Trench: XJ-9, Qdt. 2 Stratum:3 Depth: 0.56m	Carbonized seeds and fruits.	Rice (*Oryza sativa*), Wheat (*Triticum aestivum*), Green-gram (*Vigna radiata*), Cow-pea (*Vigna unguiculata*).
		Uncarbonized broken pieces of some fruit	Fruit (Syconium in botanical sense) of Pipal-tree (*Ficus religiosa*).

1	2	3	4
10.	HLS. 82-83 Trench: XJ-9, Qdt. 2 Stratum: 3 Depth: 0.76 m	Carbonized seeds and fruits	Wheat (*Triticum sphaerococcum*), Lentil (*Lens culinaris*), Rice (*Oryza sativa*), Green-gram (*Vigna radiata*).
11.	HLS. 82-83 Trench: XJ-9, Qdt.2 Stratum: 3 Depth: 0.75 m	Carbonized seeds and fruits	Barley (*Hordeum vulgare*), Rice (*Oryza sativa*), Lentil (*Lens culinaris*), Wheat (*Triticum spherococcum*).
		Uncarbonized piece of Seed-coat	Castor (*Ricinus communis*)
12.	HLS. 82-83 Trench: XJ-8, Qdt.3 Stratum: Pit 4 S.B.1 Depth: 0.24-0.30m	Broken seeds and fruits in carbonized state	Rice (*Oryza sativa*), Barley (*Hordeum vulgare*), Wheat (*Triticum sphaerococcum/ aestivum*), Lentil (*Lens culinaris*).
		Potsherds bearing husk impressions	Husk impressions of cultivated rice (*Oryza sativa*).
13.	HLS. 82-83 Trench: XH-9, Qdt.3 Stratum: 3	Broken seeds and fruits in carbonized state	Barley (*Hordeum vulgare*) Rice (*Oryza sativa*), Lentil (*Lens culinaris*), Wheat (*Triticum aestivum aestivocompactum*).
	Depth: 0.55-0.60 m	Potsherds with husk impressions.	Husk impressions of cultivated rice (*Oryza sativa*).
14.	HLS. 82-83 Trench: XG-9, Qdt.4 Stratum: 1 Depth: 0.00-0.08 m	Burnt mud-clods and pottery bearing copious husk impressions.	Husk impression of cultivated rice (*Oryza sativa*) along with those of some wild species (cf. *Oryza rufipogon*).

Plant Remains

The plant remains comprise carbonized and uncarbonized seeds, fruits, impressions on plaster-pieces, burnt mud-clods and potsherds, epidermal peels and wood charcoals. The results of their study have been grouped as given below:

1. Rice (*Oryza* L.) (Pl.1 Figs. 1-2; Pl. 3, Figs. 28-31; Pl.4, Figs. 32-33)

All the 29 carbonized grains in this lot are without husk. The grains are elongate to oblong in shape, laterally flattened and prominently ribbed, measuring 3.30-5.30 mm in length, 2.00-2.70 mm in breadth and 1.50-2.00 mm in thickness. The position of embryo is well marked in most of the grains. The grains show close resemblance with those of rice (*Oryza* sp.). The differentiation between the cultivated and wild species of rice, only on the basis of rice kernels without husk, is difficult to untangle. The reason is that the cultivated rice (*Oryza sativa*) and its varieties grown in different geographical and climatic conditions show enormous divergence in shape, size and other diagnostic features. Among several perennial and annual wild species of *Oryza*, which grow as weeds in the swampy cultivated fields of paddy crop, *Oryza rufipogon* is a highly variable perennial species closely resembling the cultivated forms of *Oryza sativa*. Boldness of grains gives appearance of cultivated rice. This wild rice is also occasionally harvested with cultivated crop. Further, weedy forms intercross rather freely with one another, and cultivated rice as well. Cultivated characteristics are often transferred to spontanea races. The situation thus becomes genetically messy and the interactions between cultivated and wild species of rice are so extensive that the differentiation in the grains, especially in carbonized state, becomes perplexing. It is, therefore, not possible to incontestably infer whether all the grains from Hulas (Figs. 1-2) belong to cultivated taxa or represent the mixture of cultivated and wild species of rice.

Further evidence of rice has been sought in the husk or glume impressions preserved in potsherds (Figs. 29-31) and burnt mud-clods and plaster-pieces (Figs. 32-33). Pottery and burnt pieces of mud and plasters bearing rice-husk impressions were broken open and in quite a few of them copious impressions were found. The mixing of rice-husk as *degraissant* in the clay resulted in the breaking of glumes and their irregular plane. Consequently, complete impressions are less frequently met with. Firing brought shrinkage in the size of husk. The study has, therefore, been confined to the features of tissue and no allowance could be made for the amount of reduction in the size of husk pieces.

The impressions reveal detailed ornamentation pattern on the surface of glumes i.e. lemma and palea Lemma is boat-shaped with convex outerside, partially enclosing the palea. The granules present on their surface give the appearance of 'chess-board' pattern of tissue. Embracive investigations on the epidermal structure of lemma and palea of a wide range of wild and cultivated species of *Oryza* have been carried out by Savithri[2] and Sharma[3]. The impressions showing dark areas at the points where four genules unite, almost cubicular shape of granules and at places their alignment in horizontal wavy rows (Figs. 30, 33) compare closely with those of some varieties of universally cultivated *Oryza sativa* L. Quite a few impressions of the type as shown in Fig.31 reveal closely spaced rounded granules protuded from the surface and aligned in straight rows. Such type of impressions appear to be of the slender grains, which are relatively much longer than broad. Critical observations show that they resemble the features of perennial, seed propagated and highly variable wild rice—*Oryza rufipogon* Griffith. Biologically and morphologically, this species, growing as a weed, resembles *Oryza sativa* and produces fertile hybrids in cultivated rices. The occurrence of husk impressions of cultivated as well as wild rice together indubitably indicates that the wild rice growing as a weed in fields was also harvested along with the cultivated rice.

2 Dwarf Wheat (*Triticum spaerococcum* Perc.)
(Pl. , Fig. 3)

All the 33 complete grains in this lot, in spite of some puffing during carbonization, retain their broad and more or less rounded shape with broad and circular hump on the dorsal side. The cheeks along the sharp and deep ventral furrow, are puffed. Embryo is rather large The pericarp has got partly rubbed off. Grains measure 5.00-5.75 mm in length, 2.60-3.50 mm in breadth and 2.00-2.75 mm in thickness. On account of morphological features the grains are comparable to those of dwarf wheat (*Triticum sphaerococcum*).

3. Bread/Club Wheat (*Triticum aestivum* L./*T.aestivo-compactum* Schiemm.) (Pl. 1, Figs. 4, 5)

Eight grains measuring 5.00—6.00 mm in length, 2.70–380 mm in breadth and 2.20-2.75 mm in thickness are slightly narrower towards both the ends and broader in the middle. Thickest portion is near the embryo, the dorsal side is rounded, cheeks to the deep ventral furrow are also rounded, and the embryo is steeply placed. Pericarp of some grains has got partially rubbed off during their preservation in carbonized condition. On the basis of shape and other morphological features, the grains compare with those of *Triticum aestivum* (bread wheat). A few more plump grains of bread wheat-type in the collection having somewhat flattened area on smoothly rounded dorsal side appear to be similar to club wheat (*Triticum compactum*). Nevertheless, it is difficult to make such differentiation when no rachis pieces are found. Under the circumstances when the number of grains is limited, they may safely be regarded as *Triticum aestivum—aestivocompactum* Schiem. This, however, surmounts the difficulty of nomenclature, but does not unravel the problem of identification.

4. Jowar-millet (*Sorghum bicolor* (L.) Moench.)
(Pl. 1, Fig. 6)

Five carbonized grains oblong to obovate and dorsoverntrally symmetrical, measure 3.30-4.00 mm in length, 2.40-3.30 mm in breadth and 2.00-2.80 mm in thickness. Oval-round hilum scar is one-third to half as long. The morphological features indicate their resemblance with those of sorghum-millet (*Sorghum bicolor*)

5. Barley *(Hordeum vulgare* L emmend. Bowden) (Pl. 1, Figs. 7,8)

In all, there are 4 carbonized grains in the collection. They are elongated and measure 5.00-6.50 mm in length, 2.40-3.30 mm in breadth and 2.00-2.60 mm in thickness. The embryo is situated on the beak-like projection of flatfish dorsal side. Ventral furrow goes upward from the base and gradually widens towards the upper end of the grain. Glumes are attached to the surface of grains by fusion of tissues and show longitudinal striations on their surface, resulted by closely running husk-veins. Husk at places disappeared as a consequence of heat and wear. In size and shape, the carbonized grains compare with those of barley (*Hordeum vulgare*). The grains reveal mixture of straight grains showing a distinct bulge in the middle as well as comparatively smaller, asymmetrical grains showing ventro-lateral twist. In view of this fact, the barley belongs to six-row form. In this form the tough rachis bears three grains per node. Median grains are symmetrical and the lateral ones, being smaller and asymmetrical, develop ventro-lateral twisting. All the species of barley belong to the same interfertile population and are grouped under single species-*Hordeum Vulgare* L. emmnd. Bowden. The barley from Hulas has, therefore, been placed under six-row form of hulled *Hordeum vulgare*. In a burnt plaster piece (Fig 8), a hollow cast of barley grain has also been noticed.

6. Oat *(Avena sativa* L.) (Pl. 2 , Fig. 9)

Five grains in semi-carbonized state are elongated and lanceolate in shape, measuring 5.30-6.50mm in length, 2.00-2.50 mm in breadth and 1.70-2.00 mm in thickness. In general appearance they compare with the spikeles of some species of oat (*Avena*). Unlike many wild species of oat in which the spikelets separate from pedicel by abscission leaving a suckermouth basal scar, the oat caryopses from Hulas appear to be separated from pedicel by fracture. In the absence of distinct sukermouth scar the grains are thus referable to a cultivated form of *Avena sativa.*

7. Finger-millet/Ragi-millet *(Eleusine coracana* (L.) Gaertn.) (Pl. 2, Figs.10, 12)

Two subglobose to oblong carbonized grains with conspicuously broad hilum, almost half of the length of grain, measure 1.60-1.75 mm in length, 1.30-1.40 mm in breadth and about 1.00 mm in thickness. Grains have been found embedded in black tar-like material (Fig. 11), on which impressions of caryopses reveal rugose ornamentation (Fig.12). A few granules in surface ornamentation fuse together and give the appearance of wavy horizontal rows. These characteristic features of the carbonized grains compare with those of ragi-millet (*Eleusine coracana).*

8. Cow-pea *(Vigna unguiculata* (L.) Walp., Syn. V. *sinensis* Endl.) (Pl. 2, Fig. 13)

A broken piece of reniform, thick and plano-convex cotyledon is tightly enclosed by thick seed-coat (A). A piece of scraped seed-coat (B) has also been found. Seed-coat surface shows transversely oriented reticulate ornamentation. Cotyledon measures 8.00 mm in length, about 4.50 mm in breadth and 1.70 mm in thickness. In shape, size and ornamentation, the carbonized cotyledon compares with that of cow-pea (*Vigna unguiculata*).

9. Lentil *(Lens culinaris* Maedik.) (Pl. 2, Fig. 14)

Forty-one complete carbonized seeds measuring about 2.00-3.60 mm × 2.00 – 3.00 mm (L × B) are circular and flattened with keeled margins They are more or less lenticular in appearance. Hilum is acutely lanceolate in shape and very small in size. Seed-coat in a number of seeds got partly rubbed off due to carbonization. Morphologically, the seeds are comparable to lentil *(Lens culinaris).*

10. Grass-pea/Khesari *(Lathyrus sativus* L.) (Pl. 2, Fig. 15)

Six carbonized seeds, varying from triangular to wedge-shaped in appearance, measure 4.00-4.50 mm in length, 3.50-4.00 -400 mm is breadth and 2.70-3.50 mm is breadth and 2.70-3.50 mm in thickness. Seed coat is rough-textured. Small and oval hilum has been noticed at one corner of the broader end. The seeds compare with those of *khesari* (*Lathyrus sativus*).

11. Chick-pea/Gram *(Cicer arietinum* L.) (Pl. 2, Fig. 16)

A complete seed and two cotyledons have been found. Seed is semi-round with one end broad and lobed, while the other end somewhat angular and beaked. The seed-coat surface is granular and slightly roughened by raised lines. Due to carbonization the hilum could not be distinctly seen, yet there is no doubt about its situation in the depression on the pointed end. Chalazal plate on the ventral side of seed is noticeably broad. The seed measures about 5.50 mm in length, 4.00 mm in breadth and 3.30 mm in thickness. Cotyledons measure about 3.75-4.00 mm × 2.80-3.10 mm × 1.50-1.80 mm (length × breadth × thickness) and their outer surface shows undulations. On the basis of overall morphological features the seed and cotyledons have been referred to chick-pea (*Cicer arietinum*).

12. Field-pea *(Pisum arvense* L.) (Pl. 2, Fig. 17)

Six seeds are spherical to hemispherical in shape measuring about 3.50-4.70 mm in diameter. Faintly preserved oval hilum, flush with the seed surface, could be observed only in one seed. Seed-coat is blurred and broken at places due to carbonization and puffing. The seeds resemble those of field-pea *(Pisum arvense).*

13. Cotton *(Gossypium arboreum/herbaceum* L.) (Pl. 2, Fig. 8)

Single carbonized seed with one end rounded and lobed and the other end narrow and angular in cross view, measures 6.00 mm in length, 4.30 mm in breadth and 3.60 mm in thickness. Ventral side of the seed is more or less flattened and the dorsal side shows rounded bulging. Hilum is ventrally located on the narrow end of the seed. In all morphological respects, the carbonized seed compares with that of cotton.

14. Horse-gram/Kulthi *(Dolichos biflorus* L.) (Pl. 2, Fig.19)

In all there are 8 complete seeds and two cotyledons (shown in extreme left of upper and lower rows). Seeds are ellipsoid to somewhat kidney-shaped and laterally flattened, measuring 3.80-4.50 mm in length, 2.70-3.50 mm in breadth and 2.00-2.50 mm in thickness. Seed surface is smooth. The small elliptical hilum measures about 1.00-1.50 mm × 0.50 mm. The seeds resemble those of horse-gram (*Dolichos biflorus*).

15. Green-gram/Mung *(Vigna radiata* (L.) Wilczek.) (Pl. 2, Fig. 20)

Fourteen carbonized cotyledons, mostly elongated with angular to rounded ends, measure 3.00-4.00 mm in length, 2.00-2.50 mm in breadth and 1.00-1.50 mm in thickness. Under a stereobinocular microscope a few of them exhibit faint and wavy markings on their outer surface. It is difficult to ascertain the specific identity without the characteristic features of hilum. The cotyledons may also belong to black-gram (*Vigna mungo).* However, in view of the faint markings on their surface, the cotyledons are tentatively referred to green-gram (*Vigna radiata).*

16. Ivy gourd/Kundru *(Coccinia cordifolia* Cogn.) Pl. 2, Fig. 21)

Four complete and broken oblong to somewhat elongated seeds with velvetty smooth surface and compressed margins, measuring 4.00-4.40 mm in length, 1.70-2.00 mm in breadth and 1.20-1.50mm in thickness, compare with those of *kundru (Cocciniaa cordifolia).*

17. Pipal-tree fruit *(Ficus religiosa* L.) (Pl. 3, Figs. 22,23)

Three uncarbonized broken pieces (Fig. 22) are comparable to those of rounded to obviate fruits of *Ficus religiosa.* Botanically, the receptacle has by involution developed into a hollow fleshy axis (termed as syconium), bearing single-seeded fruits on the inner surface . Seeds more or less flattened and pointed at hilum (Fig. 23) have also been recovered from the inner faces of syconium pieces. The characteristic pore known as orifice or ostiole, which connects the cavity of syconium with the exterior, is also seen on the terminal end of a broken piece (middle one in Fig. 22).

18. Anjan Grass *(Cenchrus ciliaris.)* (Pl. 3, Fig. 24)

Five carbonized caryopses of a grass, oblong in shape with rougose surface, measure 1.50-2.00 mm in length, 1.00-1.20 mm in breadth and 0.70-0.80 mm in thickness. Morphologically they compare with the caryopses of *Cenchrus Ciliaris.*

19. Walnut/Akhrot *(Juglans regia* L.) (Pl. 3, Fig.25)

Four pieces of hard and stony endocarp (shell), grooved and pitted irregularly, have been found in uncarbonized state. In their characteristic features, they compare with the endocarp of walnut (*Juglans regia*) fruit.

20. Almond *(Prunus amygdalus* Batsch.) (Pl. 33, Fig. 26)

Two pieces of woody and deeply pitted fruit shell

have been found comparable to the endocarp of almond (*Prunus amygdalus*).

21. Castor (*Ricinus communis)* Two broken parts of oblong, crustaceous testa of seeds are comparable to those of castor (*Ricinus communis).*

22. Wood charcoal of Babul *(Acacia nilotica)*

A diffuse-porous wood. Vessels moderately large to small, solitary and in radial multiples of 2-3, oval to oval-round, open and occluded with gummy deposits, 7-16 per mm^2 and 50.70-170μm (av. 115.40μm) in tangential diameter. Parenchyma paratracheal, paratracheal-zonate and apotracheal; paratracheal type abundant, forming one to many seriate sheath around the vessels and also in patches which join the vessels or vessel groups and rays, or extend tangentially beyond the contiguous rays to end blindly or become confluent between the vessels as paratracheal-zonate; apotracheal parenchymaa scattered or in group of several cells. Fibres libriform, round to oblong in cross-section, aligned in radial rows, forming broad tracts between rays and vessels, non-septate.

Rays fine to moderately broad, homogenous, mostly 2-3 seriate, 48. 2-110.5 μm in width; 17-37 cells and 1.80-3.92μm in height.

Anatomically the charcoals resemble the wood of *Acacia* sp. of Leguminosae[3a]. *Acacia nilotica* (Babul) has been found commonly growing at the site and therefore, the charcoals have been referred to the same.

Discussion

The cereal and legume crop remains from Hulas include rice*(*Oryza sativa*), barley (*Hordeum vulgare*), two forms of wheat-dwarf wheat *(Triticum sphaerococcum)* and bread wheat *(T.aestivo-compactum),* jowar millet *(Sorghum bicolor),* ragi millet *(Eleusine coracana),* oat (*Avena sativa*), cow pea *(Vignaa unguiclata),* lentil *(Lens culinaris),* grass pea or *Khesari (Lathyrus sativus),* chickpea or gram (*Cicer arietinum*), fieldpea (*Pisum arvensse*), horse gram *(Dolichos biflorus)* and green gram or *mung (Vigna radiata).* Besides, a seed of cotton (*Gossypium arboreum/ herbaceum*), broken testa of oleiferous castor seeds *(Ricinus communis)* and fruit-shell pieces of walnut *(Juglans regia)* and almond *(Prunus amygdalus)* are other finds of considerable economic importance. Scrutiny of the contexts of these seed and fruit remains indicates that these were purposely brought into the site by the inhabitants. Amongst the remains of wild plants from Hulas, the seeds of ivy gourd or *kundru* (*Coccinia cordiffolia)* indicate the possible use of its fruits as a vegetable. Seeds of pipal tree appear as an accidental admixture. Charcoal remains indicate the common use of babul *(Acacia nilotica)* wood for fuel.

Wheat, barely, jowar-millet, lentil, chick pea, field pea and horse gram the staple crops of the Harappans, grown in Punjab and Rajasthan, during *ca.* 2300-1700 B.C.[4] In the recent collection from Bara culture at Sanghol in Ludhiana District, which has provided parallels with the Harappans in Punjab during *ca.* 2000-1500 B.C. similar forms of food grains alongwith grass pea or *khesari* have been found[5]. Presence of these crops at Hulas in the economy of Late Harappans, is an effect of cultural filter from the region of Punjab and Haryana. Rice and green gram have also been recorded at Sanghol, but in the subsequent phase of Painted Grey Ware culture from 1100 B.C. to 700 B.C[6]. mentioned the occurrence of blackgram *(Vigna mungo)* in the Hulas material sent to the Birbal Sahni Institute of Palaeobotany by the excavator; it is absent in my collection. The Late Harappans at Daulatpur in district Kurukshetra, Haryana also consumed blackgram[7]. It is thus apparent that blackgram was also included in the crop husbandry of the Late Harappan communities in this region. One should keep in mind that in the identification of green gram and blackgram the shape and dimensions of hilum is the principal criterion. The correlation between overall size of cotyledons and seeds without the remnant of hilum is a variable factor in both the species. Their identification is precarious when only the cotyledons are found preserved. Although, the cotyledons found at Hulas compare relatively more with those of greengram, yet the possibility of inclusion of blackgram cotyledons in the mixture, can not be ruled out.

Cultivation of rice by the Late Harappan communities in this region deserves special mention. The Harappan agriculture, based mainly on the cultivation of wheat and barely, underwent a drastic change when the rice cultivation was opted from other cultures of Ganga-Yamuna *Doab*. The use of rice straw as *degraissant* in the clay of pottery and mud-plasters at Hulas indicates that this crop was much advantageously grown and utilized by the inhabitants. Without the fortunate condition of studying the impressions of husk it would not be possible to determine with certainty the actual species of cultivated *Oryza sativa* and wild (*O.rufipogon*). Plants of perennial wild rice (*O.rufipogon*) look similar to cultivated *O.sativa*, but for a few introgressed characters of annual wild *O.nivara* and forms of *O.rufipogon*. Characteristically, this aquatic wild rice with procumbent and floating stem grows either in water or swampy places or as a weed in cultivated field. Panicles give the appearance of cultivated rice; its grains are also edible. Thus, the weedy rice (*O.rufipogon*) is occasionally harvested alongwith the cultivated crop. Evidence from Hulas indicates that rice became an important crop with the Harappans during the course of their migration towards Ganga-Yamuna *Doab* from the region of Punjab and Haryana, where they persisted at least until the beginning of the first millennium B.C. Nevertheless, this change in the subsistence pattern of the Harappans was not their cultural choice. Moreover, rice cultivation was not opted simply because it was available in this new area, but because the Harappans must have given due considerations to the ecological conditions of the area for its advantageous cultivation.

According to Fairservis[8] the final eclipse of the Harappan style of agriculture may have occurred when the knowledge of the rice cultivation opened more southerly and easterly regions to the farmers. In the southerly region of the Harappan culture area the rice-imprints in pottery have been found at Lothal, district Ahmedabad, Gujarat. But these appear to be of undomesticated species[9]. From another site, at Rangpur in Surendranagar District, Gujarat, the identification of rice-husk impressions in mud-plasters as to the wild or cultivated taxa, has remained tentative[10]. Fairservis considers that these remains represent the 'stage of incipient rice cultivation". While assuming this hypoyhesis for incipient cultivation, one should keep in mind that in the marshes, where wild varieties rice grow in abundance, the clay is densely strewn with spikelets. The clay collected from marshy places, which abound in wild rices, may also have contributed to the presence of rice-impressions in the Harappan pottery. In the absence of detailed study of rice-imprints in the pottery and mud-plasters, it has not been possible to assess the cultivation of rice in Gujarat. However, at Hulas in the Upper Ganga-Yamuna *Doab* the mixing of chaff and husk of rice with clay, prior to turning it into pottery and mud-plasters, has evidently demonstrated the cultivation or rice as a staple crop.

We have ample evidences of ragi-millet (*Eleusine coracana*) from neolithic and chalcolithic cultures in different regions of India, dating back as early as about 2500 B.C. and upto the first millennium B.C. The Harappans in Gujarat made use of ragi-millet along with other cereals and pulses. Ragi-millet has consistently been recorded at Harppan Rojdi, district Rajkot (*ca.* 2500-2000 B.C.) in the assemblage of jowar-millet, pearl-millet or *bajra*, little-millet, barely, lentil, grass pea, green gram, field-brassica, etc[11]. Other important records are from Surkotada, district Bhuj[12] and Shikarpur in the Runn of Kutch[13]. Also from the post-urban phase at Oriyo Timbo in district Bhavanagar, millets belonging to *Eleusine, Panicum* and *Setaria have* been found to be consumed by the Late Harappans[14]. The remains of ragi-millet from Hulas also furnish the contextual evidence of its consumption by the Late Harappans in the upper Ganga-Yamuna *Doab*.

The cultivated oat (*Avena sativa*) from Hulas provided the sole record of this secondary crop of Mediterranean region in India. Remains of oat from Neolithic Burzahom (*ca.* 2400-1500 B.C.) and post-Neolithic Semthan (*ca.* 1500-1000 B.C.) in the Kashmir Valley, belong to wild and weedy form of *Avena fatua*[15]. When the crops of wheat and barley diffused from Central Asia, the weed oats and other species also came along and infested the fields in Kashmir during the Neolithic times. *Avena fatua* at present is a common weed in cereal crops in much of Pakistan, particularly in the north, and adjoining Indian region of Kashmir, at an elevation between 1700 and 2200m. *Avena sativa* probably got derived from weed races of *A. sterlis* [16]. However, we do not know when it attained the status of the cultivated plant. Oat does not appear to have been important as a crop in antiquity, until much later. Probably it spread as a weed in wheat and barley crops of the Harappans and they also accepted the oat contamination in their food grains. This may have been the plausible reason why the presence of this fodder crop of minor importance could not be worked out so far. However, the accidental inclusion of *Avena sativa* in the food grains has been recorded at Hulas.

Cow pea, commonly grown in India as one of the subsidiary crops of either jowar or *bajra*-millet, was earlier known from Malwa culture (*ca.* 1600-1400 B.C.) at Daimabad in Ahmednagar District, Maharashtra[17]. More or less, its contemporaneous evidence has now been recorded from Hulas. Seeds of cow pea are used mostly as pulse and pods also as a vegetable, when they are tender.

Oleiferous seeds of castor *(Ricinus communis)* from Hulas are recorded for the first time in the economy of the Harappaan culture. Earlier record from Satavahna period (*ca.*200 B.C. –100 A.D.) at Ter in Osmanabad District, Maharashtra[18] belonged to much later times. Utility of castor seeds mentioned in the Egyptian monuments and Sanskrit literature suggests that in prehistoric times its oil was mainly used for illumination and medicinal purposes. It is well-known that the Harappans in the Indus valley grew the oleiferous crops of sesame and field-brassica. Castor seeds from Hulas have further affirmed the high value in which the seeds and oil were held by the Harappans for their varied uses in cooking, medicine, toiletry, illumination and rituals. Original home of the castor plant is uncertain; some authors favour Africa while others India, because it is found growing wild in the scrubby jungles of the outer Himalayas. The plant was, in all likelihood, cultivated by the Harappans in India.

Cotton textile of the Harappans in the Indus valley were the products of a sophisticated textile craft. Cultivation of cotton as a commercial crop for the establishment of textile industry occupied the foremost place in the Harappan agriculture during the 3rd millennium. Earlier evidences of cotton from the Indus valley civilization remained in the form of cloth-impressions from Harappa and a fibre of *Gossypium arboreum* from Mohenjodaro[19]. Now, the evidence of cotton seed from Hulas affirms that the Late Harappans continued to grow this important commercial fibre-crop, even in the later phase confronting the gradual depletion of their material economy.

The commercial and trade activities in the Late Harappan communities of the upper Ganga-Yamuna *Doab*, also brought material prosperity in the subsistence economy; otherwise how else can one explain the presence of walnut and almond at Hulas, which were very likely imported from far distant regions. Trees of walnut *(akhrot)* occur in the forests of the Himalayas, extending west to Afghanistan and Baluchistan and east to Bhutan, at an elevation of 1000-3000 m; hills of upper Burma. Cultivated extensively in the Himalayas and also in the Khasia Hills of Meghalaya[20] walnuts are also native to Central Asia, Iran, the Caucasus, Anatolia, the Balkan peninsula and southern Europe[21] and have occasionally been found from archaeological sites in Europe[22]. Similarly, almond is also indigenous to the region from Central Asia and Persia to Anatolia, cultivated in Mediterranean region and throughout southern Europe; sometimes escapes to wild. In the Indo-Pakistan region it runs wild also in Baluchistan, Kurram, Chitral, Gilgit and Astor, and cultivated in Kashmir at elevations of 760-2400 m as one of the principal crops[23]. Nuts of wild almond are reported to be sold in the market in south-west Iran, and doubtless elsewhere in the Near East. There are definite evidences from the Kashmir Valley that the ancient settlers consumed walnuts and almond and made consistent use of the quality timber of walnut trees, which is highly valued for furniture and carving work, right from the Neolithic times, as early as the third millennium and upto Kushana period i.e., 200-300 A.D.[24] Evidence of walnut and almond fruits from Hulas becomes particularly significant because these temperate zone nuts continued to be imported even in later phase when prosperous Harappan culture was facing widespread degeneration and fresh adaptation.

Kundru (Coccinia cordifolia) commonly grows as a climbing herb. Its fruits turn scarlet when ripe and eaten raw; green unripe fruits are used as vegetable. Seeds of *kundru* found at Hulas indicate that the fruits of this wild plant might have been consumed by the Late Harappans. Anjan grass or buffel-grass *(Cenchrus ciliaris)* represented by carbonized caryopses at Hulas, is a valuable fodder, especially for hay. Pipal *(Ficus religiosa)* is a large tree. Its leaves and fruit-bearing branches are lopped for fodder and ripe fruits are sometimes eaten by rural folk. The questions of the buffel grass caryopses and pipal-fruits getting into the habitational deposits remain unaccounted for. May be these were thrown about inadvertently. Charcoal pieces recovered in the ancient remains indicate the use of babul *(Acacia nilotica)* wood for fuel. Babul trees still commonly grown in the region of the site and in addition to firewood also provide valuable wood for making wheels, well-curbs, agricultural implements and tool handles. Leaves and pods are given as fodder to cattle, sheep and goats. Thorny boughs are used to fence agricultural fields. the gum is largely collected and used in native medicines. In how many ways this tree was used by the Late Harappans, it is difficult to ascertain on the factual grounds.

The plant remains collected only in one season of

excavation work represent a fraction in which food and fuel plants, which accidentally or deliberately got burnt, have survived the preservation. A few macro-remains also got chance of being preserved in the absence of conflagration. Howsoever insufficient the data are it has become apparent that the Late Harappan settlers at Hulas enjoyed rich and varied food and agricultural products. Cereals and pulses of summer and winter crops were the important source of food. Cultivation of cotton, which brought about the economic prosperity and boom in trade of cotton textile with advanced communities in Iran and Mesopotamia during *ca.* 2350-1700 B.C., was still practiced by the Late Harappans at Hulas. Profitable cultivation of rice was also undertaken by them, considering the environmental potentiality of the area. Equally important were the dry-fruits in their subsistence economy, which have furnished minor but very important nutritional complements. Evidence of walnut and almond had amply demonstrated the ingenuity of the rural Late Harappans in Ganga-Yamuna *Doab*, for wistfully acquiring through trade the quality foodstuff of patrician class. The archaeological evidence borne out by a number of sites in Haryana and western Uttar Pradesh, bears ample testimony to an overall disintegration of material economy in the nebulous settlements of the Late Harappans. The credulous evidences of botanical remains from Hulas, however, highlight that the Harappan migrants in Upper Ganga-Yamuna *Doab* still enjoyed sound economic status in their food economy and crop husbandry.

Acknowledgments

Grateful thanks are due to Shri K.N. Dikshit, the excavator of the site, for providing me an opportunity to collect the material remains from Hulas. Facilities provided by the Director, BSIP to carry out the studies are to be gratefully acknowledged. Thanks are due to Dr. J.S. Antal for his valuable help during the course of the preparation of manuscript and to Mr. P.C. Roy for his assistance in photography.

REFERENCES

1. Diskshit, K.N. 1979. The Late Harappan Culture in India in Agrawal, D.P. and Chakrabarti, D.K. (Eds.). *Essays in Indian Protohistory.* Delhi. pp. 123-33. Dikshit, K.N. 1981. The Excavations at Hulas and Further Exploration at Upper Ganga-Yamuna also Doab. *Man & Environment.* Vol. V pp. 70-76; 1982. The Distribution of Harappan Wares in Gangetic Doab. In: Sharma, R.K. (Ed.) *Indian Archaeology: New Perspectives,* pp. 113-123. Agam Kala Prakashn: New Delhi. 1984; Late Harappa in Northern India. In Lal, B.B. and Gupta, S.P. (Eds.) *Frontiers of the Indus Civilization,* New Delhi pp. 253-269.

1a. Chowdhury, K.A. and Ghosh, S.S. 1951. Plant Remains from Harappa-1946. *Ancient India,* 7: 3-19.

2. Savithri, R. 1976. Study in Archaeobotany together with its Bearings upon Socio-economy and Environment of Indian Proto- Historic Cultures. Ph. D. Thesis, University of Lucknow. (Unpublished).

3. Sharma, A. 1983. Further Contributions to the Palaeobotanical History of the Crops. Ph. D. Thesis, University of Lucknow. (Unpublished).

3a. Pearson, R.S. and Brown, H.P. 1932. *Commercial Timbers of India.* Vol. I. Govt. of India: Central Publication Branch, Calcutta. Rao Ramesh, K. and Purkayastha, S.K. 1972. *Indian Woods,* Vol. III. Dehra Dun.

4. Saraswat, K.S. 1986. Ancient Crop Economy of Harappans from Rohira, Punjab (*C.* 2,000-1700 B.C.). *Palaeobotanist,* 35(1), pp. 32-38; 1988. Pre-Harappan Crop Economy at Ancient Rohira, Punjab (*C.*2,300-2,000 B.C.) In Ramachandran, K.S. (Ed.) *Studies in Indian History and Culture,*. Ind. Hist. and Cult. Soc., New Delhi. pp. 221-240; 1990-91. Crop Economy at Ancient Mahorana, Punjab (*C.*2,100-1,900 B.C.) In Tiwari, R. (Ed.) *Pragdhara: Jour. of U.P. State Archaeol. Organization,* 1(1): 83-88 and Vishnu-Mittre and Savithri, R. 1982. Food Economy of the Harappans. In: Possehl, Gregory L. (Ed.) *Harappan Civilization,*. Oxford & IBH, New Delhi. pp. 205-221

5. Saraswat, K.S. unpublished paper.

6. Sharma 1983 *op. cit.*

7. Vishnu-Mitre and Savithri, 1982 *op. cit.*

8. Fairservis Jr., Walter, A. 1979. The Origin, Character and Decline of an Early Civilization. In: Possehl, Gregory L. (Ed.) *Ancient Cities of Indus,*. New Delhi: Vikas Publ. House. pp. 66-89

9. *ibid.*

10. Vishnu-Mittre, 1974. Palaeobotanical Evidence in India. In: Hutchinson, Sir Joseph (Ed.) *Evolutionary Studies in World Crops: Diversity and Change in the Indian Subcontinent,*. Cambridge: Cambridge Univ. Press. pp. 3-30

11. Wagner, Gaail E. 1983. Late Harappan Crops in Gujarat. Paper presented in the symposium Late Harappaan Civilization in Gujarat. The XIIth Annual Meeting, Mid-Atlantic Region of the Association for Asian Studies, Oct. 28-30, 1983. University of Pennsylvania, Philadelphia and Weber, Steven, AA. 1991. *Plants and Harappan Subsistence: An Example of Stability and Change from Rojdi.* Oxford & IBH Publ. Co. Pvt. Ltd., New Delhi, Bombay & Calcutta.

12. Chanchala, 1984. Wild Plant Remains from the Archaeological sites: A Paleobotanical, Palaeoecological and Palaeoethnobotanical Study. Ph. D. Thesis: University of Lucknow (Unpublished).

13. Chanchala, unpublished.

14. Reddy, N.S. 1991. Archaeobotanical Investigation at Oriyo Timbo (1989-90) : A Post-Urban Site in Gujarat. *Man & Environment*. Vol XVI: No.1 pp. 73-83

15. Buth, G.M. and Kaw, R.N. 1985. Plant Husbandry in Neolithic Burzahom, Kashmir, In: Agrawal, D.P., Kusumgar, S. and Krishnamurthy, R.V. (Eds.) *Current Trends in Geology : Climate & Geology of Kashmir,* No. 6: pp. 109-113. New Delhi: Today & Tomorrow Publ. Buth, G.M., Bisht, R.S. and Gaur, G.S. 1982. Investigations of Palaeoethnobotanical Remains from Semthan, Kashmir. *Man & Environment,* Vol. VI: 41-45.

15. Buth, G.M. 1983. Palaeobotanical and Pollen Analytical Investigation. In: Mitra, D. (Ed.) *Indian Archaeology–A Review* (1980-81). New Delhi.

16. Harlan, Jack R. 1977. The Origins of Cereal Agriculture in the Old World. In: Reed, Charles A. (Ed.) *Origins of Agriculture,* pp. 357-383. Mouton Publishers: The Hague: Paris.

17. Vishnu-Mittre, Sharma, A. and Chanchala 1986. Ancient Plant Economy at Daimabad. In: Sali, S.A. (Ed.) *Daimabd 1976-79,* MASI*: 83,* pp. 588-627. New Delhi: Arch. Survey of India.

18. Vishnu-Mittre, 1968. Protohistoric Records of Agriculture in India. *Trans. Bose Res. Inst.,* Vol. 31: No. 3: pp. 87-106.

19. Vats. M.S. 1941. *Excavations at Harappa,* Vols. I & II. Delhi: Govt. of India. Gulati, A.N. Turner, A.J. 1928. A Note on the Early History of Cotton. Bulletin No. 17. Tech. Ser. 12, Indian Central Cotton Committee Laboratory.

20. Gamble, J.S. 1902. *A Manual of Indian Timbers.* Reprinted 1972: Dehra Dun. Kanjilal, U. and Gupta, B.L. 1928. *Forest Flora of the Chakrata, Dehra Dun and Saharanpur Forest Divisions,* Uttar Pradesh. Third Edition (4th Reprint-1969): Dehra Dun. Stewart, R.R. 1972. An Annotated Catalogue of the Vascular Plants of West Pakistan & Kashmir. Edited by Nasir, E. & Ali, S.I. *Flora of West Pakistan.* Karachi.

21. Zukovskij, P.M. 1950. *Cultivated Plants and their Wild Relatives* (Trans. Hudson, P.S. 1962). Commonwealth Agricultural Bureau, Farnham, Bucks.

22. Renfrew, Jane M. 1973. *Palaeoethnobotany: The Prehistoric Food Plants of the Near East and Europe.* London: Methuen & Co. Ltd.

23. Gamble 1902 *op. cit.*, Zukovskij. 1950 *op. cit.* and Steward 1972 *op. cit.*

24. Chanchala, 1988. Wood Remains from Gufkral, Kashmir Valley. In: Singh, P. and Tandon, O.P. (Eds.). *Archaeological Studies,* pp. 78-87. Bharat Kala Bhavan, B.H.U. Varanasi. Lone, F.A., Khan, M. and Buth, G.M. 1988. Five Thousand Years of Vegetational Changes in Kashmir: The Impact of Biotic Factory. *Proc. Indian Natn. Sci. Acad.,* 54A (3). Lone, F.A., Khan, M. and Buth, G.M. 1993. *Palaeoethnobotany.* Oxford & IBH Publ. Co. Pvt. Ltd., New Delhi, Bombay, Calcutta.

EXPLANATION OF PLATES

PLATE-1. Fig.1. Rice (*Oryza sativa*); fig.2. Rice grains (Note the variation in their shape and size); Fig. 3. Dwarf wheat *(Triticum sphaerococcum);* Fig. 4. Bread Wheat *(T.aestivum)*; Fig. 5. Bread wheat *(T.aestivocompactum)*; Fig. 6. Jowar millet *(Sorghum bicolor)*; Fig.7. Barey *(Hordeum vulgare);* Fig. 8. An imprint of barley grain in the mud-plaster.

PLATE-2. Fig.9. Oat *(Avena sativa)*j Fig.10. Ragi millet *(Eleusine coracana)*; Fig. 11. Burnt tar-like matter in which grains of ragi millet are embedded; Fig. 12. Enlarged ornamentation of ragi millet left in the impression on black tar-like material; Fig.13. A-Cotyledon and B-Scraped seed-coat of cow pea *(Vigna unguiculata)*; Fig.14. Lentil *(Lens culinaris)*; Fig. 15. Grass-pea *(Lathyrus sativus)*; Fig. 16. Chick pea *(Cicer arietinum);* Fig. 17. Field pea *(Pisum arvense)*; Fig. 18. Cottonseed *(Gossypium arboreum-herbaceum)*; Fig. 19. Horsegram *(Dolichos biflorus);* Fig. 20. Greengram *(Vigna radiata)*; Fig. 21. Seeds of ivy gourd *(Coccinia cordifolia).*

PLATE-3. Fig. 22. Fruit-pieces of pipal tree (*Ficus religiosa*); Fig. 23 Seeds of pipal-fruit; Fig. 24. Seeds of buffel-grass *(Cenchrus ciliaris);* Fig. 25. Fruit-shell pieces of walnut (*Juglans regia);* Fig. 26. Fruit-shell pieces of almond *(Prunus amygdalus);* Fig. 27. Seed-coat pieces of castor *(Ricinus communis)*; Fig. 28. Rice-husk fragment, × 180; Fig. 29. Potsherds with rice-husk impressions; Fig. 30. Husk impression of cultivated rice *(Oryza sativa)*; Fig. 31. Husk impression of wild rice (comparable to *O.rufipogon).*

PLATE-4. Fig. 32. Mud-plaster pieces with copious husk-impressions of cultivated and wild forms of rice; Fig. 33. Husk-impression of cultivated rice *(Oryza sativa)*; Fig. 34. Babul wood *(cf. Acacia nilotica)* in cross section, × 50; Fig. 35. Babul wood in tangential longitudinal section, ×50.

An Optimal Modelling Exercise for the Harappan Civilization with Special Reference to its Regional Context in Haryana, India

Vijneshu Mohan*

Models, as explanatory devices, are fairly common to such disciplines like Geography. But, in archaeology, models have apparently gained a wider acceptance since Clarke's pioneering studies in analytical model-building[1]. Scholars, in India, too have applied the concept to the Harappan Civilization, in general[2]. The theoretical foundations behind models and model-building are, relatively recently studied by a few Indian scholars[3].

It is important to realize that without consciously and explicitly resorting to model-building, researchers have emphasized the factors of population dynamics, prevalence of antecedent conditions or resource exploitation as factors responsible for the growth of the Harappan Civilization. A considerable corpus of literature is available to this effect[4]. Besides, scholars have attempted to highlight the fundamental importance of the internal factors[5]. This is in contrast to Wheeler's[6] well known diffusionistic paradigm that emphasizes the external Mesopotamian contributions as the most important factor in the growth of the Harappan Civilization. Here, it must be recalled that an undue emphasis on a single cause or factor, is not enough or sufficient to satisfactorily postulate the growth of the complex entity of the Harappan Civilization. It is worth noting, too, that the so-called internal factors remain to be largely incomprehensible.

Multiple causes could be more safely presumed to have influenced the rise of the Harappan Civilization[7]. The respective relative importance of the causes or factors remains to be assessed in the right perspective. The present study further aims to substantiate the usefulness of multiple causes in the explanation of the archaeologically observable growth of the Harappan Civilization. However, it is possible, that at a regional level of the civilization, in Haryana, the inevitability of the multi-causal interactions is discernible only at diminished scale. This theoretical position is comparable to the "hierarchy of interaction" as propounded for China[8].

In an attempt towards the syncretical analysis of the civilization in a regional context, the single factor models are re-examined as new evidence accumulates from the proxy area. Thus, this article seeks to analyse the growth of the Harappan Civilization in its regional context in Haryana, India, in the light of the relative validity of models. New drawbacks have naturally surfaced due to the scanty nature of evidence. As the analysis proceeds, the relative importance of the causal factors emerges as self-evident, albeit at subjective level.

(a) The pressure conflict model and the limited contribution of the uninstitutionalized warfare in the present context

It is often rightfully stated that the presence of conflicts, competition or feuds is an intrinsic trait of the growing societies. This leads to the basic premise that warfare, especially institutionalized, is responsible for the growth of stratified society as one of the "prime-movers"[9]. It should be continued to be stressed that institutionalized warefare is not the only causative factor. Actually, the universal applicability of this model is no less doubtful. For example, in the pre-Hispanic context, this model is found to be inapplicable[10].

*508,Sector 13, Urban Estate, Kurukshetra-132 118

In Haryana, it is not possible, at once, to classify warfare as an institutionalized force during the Harappan period. The efficacy of copper spear-heads, daggers or knives, axes and mace-heads should remain undeniable, as weapons of offense, in the Harappan context[11]. It is all the more important that these so-called weapons are not profusely excavated from Haryana, at the present level of excavations[12]. Thus, these so-called weapons are decidedly less common from the study area. As an alternative, the fortifications, sling balls and pellets were obviously meant to be effective against incursions from wild beasts[13]. If the ethnographic parallels stand valid then the terracotta sling balls or pellets were most probably employed to scare off birds from the ripening agricultural fields[14]. The fortification walls existed from the pre-Harappan levels as evidenced at Banawali[15]. Therefore, more appropriately, it is indicative of urban expansion design instead of a purely defense mechanism against warfare. Their mere presence should not mean to suggest definite institutionalized warfare. The walled fortifications or *mahi-durga* presumably served to delineate the boundaries or *grishtti* of towns that most probably succeeded villages, of the preceding pre-Harappan levels, however, big or small[16]. The boundary walls, it is possible, were not deliberately or exclusively raised for military purposes. In the Indian state of Haryana, the present villagers protect their individual habitations by raising low enclosure walls or thorn hedges *(bhitmara)*. By extension it could safely be presumed that the mud enclosures served the purpose of *actuating identity.*

The perceived remains of a moat from Banawali[17], at the present level of knowledge, appear to be an exceptional feature from the area. The site of Rakhigarhi by its proximity to the river Apaya or Apaga may provide similar evidence on excavation[18]. Again, the moat, at Banawali, was not exclusively meant for defensive purposes. It is significant that the site of Banawali is known to be located close to the Sarasvati river. If it were so during the past then it is well nigh possible that the moat served the purpose of an escape device for the river waters during flash floods. Similar usages for moats are conceived elsewhere[19].

All these observations taken collectively provide little evidence regarding the establishment of organizational leadership of active standing armies, in this important segment of what is rightfully known as the eastern domain of the Harappan Civilization. Needless to add, of course, that petty feuds and scuffles might have continued to exist[20]. Such skirmishes are naturally bound to happen in any differentiating stratified society growing towards the level of civilization.

(b) The Validity of the hydraulic hypothesis as the latest evidence comesforth from Haryana

The model based on the concept of the hydraulic state depends on the postulated importance and related control mechanisms of the extensive irrigation networks. These are automatically associated with the prospective growth of a "body of officials to devise and administer" the irrigation facilities[21]. The rise of an administrative elite, as a natural consequence, insures the basis of a stratified society[22].

Scholars have relatively recently began to assert that artificial irrigation was practised in Haryana during the Harappan period. The Indo-French joint project or the MAFI claims to have discovered underground water channels or pipes emanating from what is, at present, known as the Chautang[23]. The geoarchaeologists[24] are of the opinion that the "excremental fabrics" and "fine fractions associated with adequate moisture", are surely indicative of the past irrigation channels. It must however, be noticed as conceded by one of the scholars that the "proxy" area of this study is very small[25]. Significantly, it falls towards the "tail-end" of the river regimes[26]. This indeed, might have considerably reduced the availability of river water for irrigation purposes. Moreover, these channels are regarded to be only sporadically functional[27]. Under these circumstances, their utility could be doubted, especially, for the more demanding *rabi* crops. These channels are not conclusively dated, as yet. Therefore, great restraint is required before they are definitely assigned to a third millennium time-bracket coinciding with the Harappan Civilization.

In fact, to give an example, the Texcoco region shows the growth of the state without the expansion of the extensive hydraulic network[28]. Similarly, urban growth linked to the intensively cultivated swamp land obviously precludes a necessity for large irrigation networks[29].

The usefulness of rainfall becomes pre-eminent in this respect[30]. It enjoys importance as *deva jal* in the now agriculturally rich state of Haryana. The village pond as of today, might have served the purpose, to some extent, of controlled storage device, genuinely meant for domestic usage. On ethnographic extrapolations, it could be postulated that such ponds were kept functional by the collective efforts of the village inhabitants. Although the art of excavating wells was not totally unknown[31] in the area, yet as Leshnik[32] has proposed, their usefulness for agricultural irrigation remains enigmatic. The possibility of irrigation by throwing dikes or *gabarbands,* across shallow river courses, is now fairly acceptable. Bisht[33] has elaborated upon the practice of damming of rivers in the Rann of Kutch, Gujarat. However, this too might have remained a supplementary measure depending upon the periodicity of the low ebb and flooding. As elsewhere, the fertile soils of the river valleys[34] were conducive to a relative ease of cultivation and might have raised the overall prospects for a better harvest. On the basis of the above observations, at the existing level of research, it is not possible to surely prove the existence of an elite class solely on the basis of its role in the maintenance of extensive irrigation networks. Francfort[35] himself warns against the need to stress the extremes of the hydraulic civilization in this context.

(c) The validity of the population pressure hypothesis in the light of the existing lack of the demographic data from Haryana for the Harappan Civilization

The model based on the population pressure opines that the "tremendous growth of population" normally encourages "technological development" which manifests itself in the stratification of society through unequal access to the technological knowhow[36]. Also, it is contended that the intensification of agricultural practices is triggered off by a certain level of population density[37].

At the present level of research, the population pressure hypothesis could not be assessed on firm grounds, in the given context. Most of the diverse methods to reach population estimations[38] are not satisfactorily applicable due to the badly disturbed archaeological evidence in Haryana. Only crude estimations, without adequate justification, are possible. The inapplicability has, thus, surfaced due to the lack of rigour of the virtually incompatible archaeological data[39]. It is more recently hypothesized that even at large scale methodical excavations, the "longevity of sturctures and family size" are purely conjectural[40] and open to criticism. Considering these elements of ambiguity in the demographic calculations, the models based on such estimations tend to be unsound, as the commonly employed unit area concept also looses its validity for correct computation of population figures.

Needless to add, the demographic estimates do not appear to be feasible in Haryana because of the extensive site destruction due primarily to agricultural intensification. It would, to the contrary, be undesirable to inadvertantly *exclude* population dynamics as one of the primemovers of growth. The eventual dispersal into large number of post-urban Late Harappan type sites, especially, in the northern Haryana points to one of the inevitable after consequences of population proliferation. In general terms, prosperity, say during the urban Mature Harappan phase, entails a supportive network to a larger population base which breaks down into smaller units after the urban decay. An exact converse is only partly true as a disproportionate increase in population is likely to induce complexity and invoke stratification.

But, archaeologically speaking, the destined optimum level of population density is unfortunately difficult, if not impossible, to accurately perceive. This so–called "unrealistic specificity"[41] is the main impediment towards the unconditional acceptance of the population pressure hypothesis[42]. It is all the more relevant to duly emphasize that simple one to one cause and effect relationship is far from conceivable between the optimal population density and agricultural growth[43].

(d) The validity of the model of differential accessibility

The differential distribution of land, raw materials and their exploiters or users is the common denominator also of the model of environmental circumscription and the concept of core and buffer zone. The model based on environmental circumscription propounds that the stratified societies emerge due to the presence of highly circumscribed arable area[44]. The need for an effective control over these constricted lands generates the ultimate growth of stratified societies. Therefore, as a corollary, social circumscription grows along with the land-based circumscription. In turn, this provides enough desired stimulus for the eventual growth of population pressure[45]. Under similar conducive conditions the resultant pressures from the anthropogenic environment lead to put constraints on the availability of cultivable land. With the result, the man–land relationships are further complicated. Thus, the human agency is naturally a "non-passive" factor[46] in this model that might be associated with that of the differential accessibility.

In the same vein the core-periphery or the core-buffer zone model, by virtue of the above mentioned common denominator, be coupled with the model of differential accessibility. Originally conceived for the Peten core area of Guatemala, this model highlights the lack of basic resources that leads to the development of exchanges with the surrounding buffer zones with ample resources[47]. A disciplined control over the resources warrants an elite class which, in turn, paves the way for social stratification.

A brief digression. Technically, when multiple causes are considered[48], the causal factors could be reduced to sets of enablers, pre-conditions and prime-movers[49]. The enablers[50] are not essential or absolutely necessary for the growth of civilization, howsoever slow or gradual. The enablers, however, stimulate growth under adequate preconditions.

As stated for the model of environmental circumscription, the model of the differential accessibility is mainly based on, for example, the differential distribution of arable land. This hastens the growth of elite class and subsequently that of the stratified urban form of the society. Not only such distribution of arable land but also that of resource material, craftsmanship or demand provides opportunity for comparable growth[51]. The growing elite are, as a rule, considered to be engaged in offensive or defensive actions[52] or their control[53]. The latter aspect seems to be present in a minimized form during the Harappan period in Haryana.

In the form of preconditions, the natural distribution of man and beast, land and minerals has differentially yet definitely preceded the emergence of the stratified society. This ordinarily satisfied the antecedent or preconditions[54]. The primemovers were as usual, functional in the form of internal socio-economic development, local and long distance trade or interactions at varying degree of intensity.

The crafts-persons of Haryana, contributed towards, at least, a semblance of a stratified society and its infrastructure. They might have compromised with an acute shortage of raw materials, especially metal ores, from within the present geographical boundaries of Haryana. There are only a few copper mines, for instance, concentrated in Singhana (28° 06′ N; 75° 04′E), Babei (27° 83′ N;75° 49′ E) and the well known Khetri[55] belt (28° 50′N; 76° 57′E)[55]. So far, no gold mines are documented for the area. It is another matter though that small scale panning was occasionally practised for gold in the ephemeral streams of Sirsa. But, the crafts-persons dared to innovate despite all odds (see below).

Incidentally at Banawali, excavations have unearthed the remains of a merchant's house[56]. This structure is associated with mercantile activity on the basis of the excavated seals, weights, gold and carnelian beads. It must be recalled that the sources for semi-precious stones, like carnelian, are rare in Haryana. There is all likelihood that a majority of such items as semi-precious carnelian beads reached centres like Banawali, as finished by-products of vigorous trade. To a large Harappan region, the lapidaries of Saurashtra are likely to be the chief exporters, significantly relying upon the rich mines of Ratnapura[57]. Thus, Banawali might also have functioned as a redistributive centre.

A singular example of an unfinished bead reported from Mithathal[58] points to be isolated practice of bead-making at a very low key. Despite this evidence it is relevant to suggest that the sites like Banawali matured due mainly to their strategic location by the inland trade routes[59]. Banawali's status becomes comparable to that of a frontier settlement[60] for this region. In India, Hajnali[61], for example, is known to have enjoyed similar peripheral location.

From Haryana metal artifacts are also excavated from Mithathal[62]. The small scale of excavations is, however, responsible for the paucity of metallurgical finds. Some metal artefacts are reported from unstratified contexts from the adjoining areas[63]. At the existing level of research, the discovery of these surface finds, although important, fails to compensate for the overall scarcity of metal objects from Haryana. With these limitations and in view of the depleted resources, it could be conjectured that though conversant with it, the metal technology was not fully exploited by the contemporary smiths. On the other hand, a class or segment of population, familiar with the technology, might certainly have helped the differential growth of civilization. Especially, the coppersmiths must have contributed to stratification from the study area.

Symbolically, metal objects are often regarded as denoting "political or social power"[64]. Their possession symbolizes a higher status, to certain extent. But, as already said, metal technology is deemed to have developed at a low key in Haryana. It, however, played a "distinctly minor role" as in pre-Hispanic Meso-America. In conclusion, the negative evidence of excavated data, remains to be properly ascertained in conjunction with studies on the relationship of deficiency and differential distribution of craft-specialization[65].

The indiscriminate expansion of towns and rapid industrialization have, in the more recent past, altered the distribution pattern of arable land. This pattern might naturally have differently obtained during the period of the Harappan civilization. However, the preponderance of archaeological sites in the present fertile zones of Haryana, raises the possibility of the correlation of the growth to the fertile patches of land.

The size-based classification of sites is now fairly acceptable[66]. It is indicative of the survival and co-existence of a strong rural element throughout the long span of the Harappan Civilization. Uninterrupted as it might seem to be, this continuum is all the more significant for the rise of the civilization in Haryana. Even with the gradual increase in modern urban pressures, the state continues to enjoy a predominantly rural ambience. Enthnographic parallels are, therefore, supportive of a bias towards the rural side of the scale.

The dense forest cover might have, in places, restricted the availability of land for settlement and agriculture. Fairservis[67] had earlier expounded that, holistically speaking, primitive and localized economies were inseparable segments of the economic system of the Harappan civilization. In the present context, the site, for example, of Kathana (29°32′23"N; 76° 23′30"E) and Singhwal (29° 45′50′′N; 76° 13′E) are located within the legendary limits of the Suraj Bhan of the Mahabharata[68]. If tradition contains truth, then the site of Balu (29° 40′15′′N; 76° 23′16′′E) could be said to belong to the stipulated domains of the Vyas Ban[69] .

Although the forests might have reduced the easy availability of land for agriculture yet they obviously substantiated the subsistence level by providing diverse dietary items. More importantly, the forest cover might have insured a higher reliability of rainfall while reducing the risk of flash floods. Consequently, a more balanced ecological cycle was favourably obtained in this part of the Harappan Civilization. As cultivable areas were situated close to the forests, it enables the researcher to depose of a dynamic relationship[70] whereby hunter-gatherers might have co-existed in a dichotomous interaction with agriculturists[71].

Concluding Remarks

It is unthinkable to pinpoint a single major cause as responsible for the rise of social stratification in Haryana during the Harappan period. Allchins have proposed three concurrent factors of local and long-distance trade, optimization of arable land and, perhaps, least importantly the stimuli from outside[72] as the factors contributive to growth of the Harappan Civilization. Fairservis[73], besides others, laid emphasis on similar factors. Thus, the threads of differential accessibility, trade or, more appropriately, interactions and exchanges have run stronger in this development. Subjectively speaking, a degree of impetus was also provided by the exploitation of irrigation (?) potential, be it through rainwater; warfare (?), be it *via* petty feuds and skirmishes; and tremendous (?) population growth seen in proliferation of sites. The active pastoral communities simultaneously co-lived with the primary agriculturists and secondary hunter-gatherers to give rise to distinct strata of society leading to the complex growth of the civilization. It is pertinent to note, here, that Haryana has typically retained a ratio of a smaller number of large towns to the rural population. There is a lack of evidence to disprove or falsify this statement in the context under study.

A word of caution before this article comes to its close. The model-building exercises are not free from limitations. It is aptly said that models are important only as "heuristic devices"[74]. Moreover, in archaeological terms, models are only rarely and exclusively conceived for the growth of civilizations[75]. Thus, models have limited value as aids towards explanations of the growth of civilizations. But, adequate revisions or modifications, surely enhance their validity level.

Acknowledgements

A significant portion of the studies for this research was undertaken at the University of Cambridge as a Cambridge Nehru Scholar. My thanks are due to the Nehru Trust, the Smutts Memorial Fund, the Magdalene College and the Ancient India and Iran Trust for financial assistance. I gratefully acknowledge the help of the Librarians and staff of Haddon and the Faculty of Oriental Studies Library in Cambridge, and the Central Library of the Archaeological Survey of India in New Delhi. I will remain indebted to Dr. F.R. Allchin, Dr. (Mrs.) B. Allchin and Dr. Ken D. Thomas for constructive criticism, constant encouragement and valuable suggestions. I thank Shri Rajiv Madan for efficiently typing the manuscript.

REFERENCES

1. Clarke, D.L. 1968. *Analytical Archaeology*, London, Methuen; 1973. Archaeology: the loss of innocence, *Antiquity* 47, pp. 6–18.
2. Gupta, S.P. 1972–73. Model for first urbanization in India, *Puratattva* 6, pp. 42–44.
3. Singh, S. 1985. *Models, Paradigms and the new archaeology*. Varanasi, Department of Ancient Indian History, Culture and Archaeology.
4. Agrawal, D.P. 1972–73. Genesis of the Harappa Culture, *Puratattva* 6. pp. 37–44. Allchin, F.R. 1982. The legacy of the Indus Civilization in Possehl, G.L. (ed.) *Harappan Civilization: a Contemporary Perspective*, Warminister, Arris and Phillips Limited. pp. 325–33. Gupta, S.P. 1974. Two urbanizations in India: a side study in their social structure, *Puratattva* 7. pp. 53–60 and Gupta, S.P. and Asthana, S. 1978. Harappan *vis–a–vis* Mesopotamian urbanism and town planning, *Man and Environment* 2. pp. 47–50. Soundara Rajan, K.V. 1982. Motivations for early Indian urbanization: an examination. In possehl, G.L. (ed.) *Harappan Civilization: a Contemporary Perspective*, Warminister, Arris and Phillips Limited. pp. 68-75. Thapar, B.K. 1982. The Harappan Civilization: some reflections of its environments and resources and their exploitation. In Possehl, G.L. (ed.) *Harappan Civilization: a Contemporary Perspective*. New Delhi, Oxford and IBH. pp. 3-13.
5. Allchin, B. and Allchin, F.R. 1982. *The Rise of Civilization in India and Pakistan*, Cambridge, Cambridge University Press. Shaffer, J.G. 1986. Cultural development in eastern Punjab in Jacobson, J. (ed.) *Studies in the Archaeology of India and Pakistan.*. New Delhi, Oxford and IBH. pp. 195-236.
6. Wheeler, R.E.M. 1953. *The Indus Civilization*, Cambridge: At the University Press.
7. Allchin and Allchin 1982 *op. cit.*
8. Chang, K.C. 1986. *The Archaeology of Ancient China*, New Haven, Yale University press.
9. Carneiro, R.L. 1970. A theory of the origin of state, *Science* 169. pp. 733–738. Webster, D. 1977. Warfare and the evolution of the Maya civilization in Adams, R.E.W. (ed.) *The Origins of Maya civilization*. Albuquerque, University of New Mexico Press. pp. 335-371.
10. Wilson, D.J. 1983. The origins and development of complex prehispanic society in the lower Santa Valley, Peru: implications for theories of state origins. *Journal of Anthropological Archaeology* 2. pp. 209-276.
11. Singh, S.D. 1965. *Ancient Indian Warfare with Special Reference to the Vedic Period.* London, E.J. Brill. Jacobson, J. 1986. The Harappan Civilization: an early state. In Jacobson, J. (ed.) *Studies in Archaeology of India and Pakistan.* New Delhi. Oxford and IBH. pp. 137–174. Rao, S.R. 1985. *Lothal: a Harappan Port Town*, New Delhi, Archaeological survey of India.
12. Suraj Bhan, 1975, *Excavations at Mitathal (1968) and Other Explorations in the Sutlej Yamuna Divide*, Kurukshetra, University, Kurukshetra. Thapar, B.K. (ed.) 1980. *Indian Archaeology: A Review*, New Delhi, Archaeological Survey of India. Yule, P. 1985. *Metal Works of the Bronze Age in India*, Munchen, Verlagsbuchhandlung.
13. Begde, P.V. 1982. *Forts and Palaces of India*, New Delhi, Sagar. Chippindale, C. 1987. Editorial *Antiquity* 61. pp. 353–363. Kesarwani, A. 1984. Harappan gateways: a functional reassessment in Lal, B.B. and Gupta, S.P. (eds.) *Frontiers of the Indus Civilization*, New Delhi, Books and Books. pp. 63–73.
14. Oswalt, W.H. Mann, G. and Satterthwait, L. 1976. *An Anthropological Analysis of Food Gathering Technology*, London, John Wiley and Sons.
15. Bisht, R.S. 1984. Structural remains and town planning of Banawali in Lal, B.B. and Gupta S.P. (eds.) *Frontiers of the Indus Civilization*, Delhi, Books and Books. pp. 89–92.
16. Bisht, R.S. 1987. Further excavation at Banawali 1983–84 in Pande, B.M. and Chattopadhyaya, B.D. (eds.) *Archaeology and History*, Delhi, Agam Kala Prakashan, Volume 1. pp. 135–56. Konsola, D. 1986. Stages of urban transformation in the early Helladic period in Hagg, R. and Konsola, D. *Early Helladic Architecture and Urbanization*, Goteborg, Paul Atroms Forlag: 9–10.
17. Bhist, 1987. *op. cit*
18. Personal observation
19. Allchin F.R. 1989. City and state formation in early historic South Asia. In *South Asian Studies* 5. pp. 1–16.
20. Possehl, G.L. 1984. Archaeological terminology and the Harappan civilization in Lal, B.B. and Gupta, S.P. (eds.) *Frontiers of the Indus Civilization*. New Delhi, Books and Books, pp. 27-36.
21. Wittfogel, K. 1957. *Oriental Despotism*, New Haven, Yale University press.
22. Kahn, M. 1984. Taro irrigation: a descriptive account from Wamira, Papua New Guinea. *Oceania* 54. pp. 204–222. and Kumar, N.K. 1982. Nature of the Harappan state in Devahuti (ed.) *Historical and Political Perspectives*, New Delhi. pp. Books and Books, 113–120.
23. Francfort, H.P. 1985. *Prospections archaeologiques au Nordo est de L'Inde.* Paris. Editions Recherche sur les civilizations, 1986. Preliminary Report (1983–84). *Man and Environment* 10. pp. 97–100: 1987.a. The Indus civilization confronts the desert.

The World Scientist 4. pp. 7; and 1987 b. Report of the Indo–French archaeological mission: summary of the 1985 field season. *Man and Environment* 11. pp. 123–125.

24. Courty, M.A. and Fedoroff, N. 1985. Micro morphology of recent and buried soils in a semi-arid region of north western India. *Geoderma* 35. pp. 287-337 also 1987. Report of the Indo–French archaeological mission: summary of the 1985 field season, *Man and Environment* 11. pp. 123.; also 1989. Integration of sediment and soil information in the reconstruction of prothistoric and historical landscapes of the Ghaggar plain (north west India) in Frifelt, K. and Soresen, P. (eds.) *South Asian Archaeology 1985*: Copenhagen, Nordic Institute of Asian Studies. 255–259.

26. Haines, A.T. Finelyson, B.L. and McMohan, J.A. 1988. A global classification of river rigmes. *Applied Geography* 8. pp. 255–272.

27. Courty, 1989 *op. cit.*

28. Offner, J.A. On the inapplicability of "Oriental Despotism" and the "Asiatic Mode of Production" to the Aztecs of Texcoco, *American Antiquity* 46. pp. 43-61.

29. Mitchell, W. 1973. The hydraulic hypothesis: a reappraisal. *Current Anthropology* 14. pp. 532-534.

30. Dayal, E. 1983. Agricultural land and man–land ratio in India – an analysis of change in Bee, O.J. (ed.) *Natural Resources in Tropical Countries.* Singapore, Singapore University Press. pp. 347–67. 1986. Cultural development in eastern Punjab in Jaccobson, J. (ed.) *Studies in the Archaeology of India and Pakistan,.* New Delhi, Oxford and IBH. pp. 195-236.

31. Bhist. 1987 *op. cit.*

32. Leshnik, L.S. 1973. Land use and ecological factors in prehistoric north-west India in Hammond, N. (ed.) *South Asian Archaeology* 1, London, Duckworth, pp. 67–84. Lewis, L.E. 1984. *The American Frontier,* Orlando, Academic Press.

33. Bisht, R.S. 1989. A new model of the Harappan town planning as revealed at Dholavira in Kutch: a surface study of its plan and architecture in Chaterjee, B. (ed.) *History and Archaeology.* Delhi, Ramanand Vidya Bhawan. pp. 397–408.

34. Milne, L. and Miln, M. 1965. *Water and Life.* London. Andre Deutsch. Goudie, A. 1984. *The Nature of the Environment,* Oxford, Basil, Blackwell; and Allchin and Allchin 1982 *op. cit.*

35. Franctort, H. P.1989. The Indo–French archaeological project in Haryana and Rajasthan in Frifelt, K. and Sorensen, P. (eds.) *South Asian Archaeology* 1985. Copenhagen, Nordic Institute of Asian Studies. pp. 260–264.

36. Boserup, E. 1965. *The Conditions of Agricultural Growth,* London, George Allen and Unwin. 1981. *Population and Technology,* Oxford, Basil Blackwell.

37. Ammerman, A. J. and, Cavalli Sforza, L.L. 1973. A population model for the diffusion of early farming in Europe in Renfrew, A.C. (ed.) *The Explanation of Culture Change: Models in Prehistory,* London, Duckworth. pp. 343–57.

38. Hassan, F.A. 1981. *Demographic Archaeology,* New York. Academic Press. Broshi, M. 1979. The population of western Palestine in the in the Rome Byzantine period. *Bulletin of the American School of Oriental Research.* 236. pp. 1–11. Zubrow, E.B.W. 1975. *Prehistoric Carrying Capacity: a Model.* California, Cunnings.

39. Dunnell, R.C. 1979. Trends in current Americanist archaeology. *American Journal of Archaeology* 83. pp. 437–49.

40. Milner, G.R. 1986. Mississipian period population density in a segment of the central Mississippi river valley, *American Antiquity* 51. pp. 227-238.

41. Hammel, E.A. and Howell, N. 1987. Research in population and culture: an evolutionary framework, *Current Anthropology* 28. pp. 141–160.

42. Kuusi, P. 1985. *This World of Man,* Oxford, Pergamon Press.

43. Engelbrecht, W. 1987. Factors maintaining in low population density among the prehistoric New York Irogwois. *American Antiquity* 52. pp. 13–27.

44. Carneiro. 1970. *op. cit.*

45. Fentress, M. A.1985. Water resources and double croping in Harappan food production in Misra, V.N. and Bellwood, P. (eds.) *Recent Advances in Indo-Pacific Prehistory,* Lieden, E.J. Brill. pp. 359–368.

46. Chapman, G.P. 1977 *Human and Environmental Systems,* London, Academic Press.

47. Adams, R. McC. 1874. Anthropological perspectives on ancient trade, *Current Anthropology* 15. pp. 239–58. Rathje, W.L. 1971. The origin and development of low land Maya classic civilization, *American Antiquity* 36. pp. 275-285.

48. McGuire, R.H. 1983. Breaking down cultural complexity; inequality and heterogeneity in Schiffer, M (ed.) *Advances in Archaeological Method and Theory* 6. Orlando, Academic Press. pp. 91-142. Embree, A.T. 1985. Indian civilization and regional cultures: the two realities in Wallace, P. E. (ed.) *Region and Nation in India.* New Delhi, Oxford and IBH. pp. 19–39; Gamble, C. 1986. Hunter–gatherers and the and the origin of the states. In Hall, J.A. (ed.) *States in History,* Oxford, Basil Blackwell. pp. 22-47.

49. Rafferty, J.E. 1985. The archaeological record on sedentariness: recognition, development and implications in Schiffer, M.B. (ed.) *Advances in Archaeological Method and Theory* 8. pp. 113-156; Leonard, R.D. 1987. Elements of an inclusive evolutionary prehistoric north–west India. *Journal of Anthropological Archaeology* 6. pp. 199–219.

50. Service, E.R. 1975. The primemover of cultural evolution, In Brady, I.A. *et al.* (eds.) *A Reader in Culture Change.* New York, John Wiley and Sons. pp. 85-1000.

51. Chase, D.Z. 1986. Social and political organisation in the land of caocao and honey: correlating the archaeology and ethnohistory of the post–classical lowland Maya in Sabloff, J.A. and Andrews, E.W. (eds.) *Late Lowland Maya,* Albuquerque, University of New Mexico Press. pp. 347–377. Graham, E. 1987. Resource diversity in Belize and its implications of lowland trade, *American Antiquity* 52. pp. 753–767. Vieck, D.T. de Gonza'lez, S.G. and Kurjack, E.B. 1985. Contemporary farming and ancient Maya settlements: some disconcerting evidence in Harrison, P.D. Turner, B.L. (eds.) *Prehispanic Maya Agriculture.* Albuquerque, University of New Mexico Press, 211-233.

52. Sanders, W.T. 1973. The cultural ecology of the low land Maya: a reevaluation. In Culbert, T.P. (ed.) *The Classic Maya Collapse.* Albuquerque, University of New Mexico Press. pp. 325-365.

53. Halland, R. 1984. Continuity and discontinuity. *Norwegian Archaeological Review* 17: 39–51.

54. Fentress, M.A. 1976. Resources, Access,. Exchange Systems and Interaction in the Indus Valley: an Investigation of Archaeological Variability at Harappa and Mohenjodaro. (Ann Arbor Microfilm) unpublished thesis of the University of Pennsylvania. Graham, 1987, *op. cit;* Soundara Rajan 1982. *op. cit.* Renfrew, A.C. 1983. Divided We Stand: aspects of archaeology and information, *American Antiquity* 48. pp. 3-16. 1986. Introduction. In Renfrew, A.C. and Cherry, J.F. (eds.) *Per Polity Interaction and Socio-political Change.* Cambridge, Cambridge University Press: pp.1-18.

55. Chatterjee, P.L. 1963. *Annotated Index of Indian Mineral Occurrences.* Calcutta, Government of India. Chakrabarti, D.K. 1987. The pre–industrial mines of India, *Puratattva* 17. pp. 65–71 Habib, I. 1982. *An Atlas of the Mughal Empire.* Delhi, Oxford University press.

56. Bisht 1984 *op. cit*

57. Allchin, B. 1979. The agate and carnelian industry of western India in Lohuizen, de Leeuw, J.E. Van (ed.) *South Asian Archaeology* 1975, Leiden, E.J. Brill. pp. 91–105. Ball, V. 1881, A *Manual of the Geology of India*, London, Trubner and Company.

58. Bisht 1984 *op cit.*

59. Bisht 1987 *op. cit.* and Thapar K. 1985. *Recent Archaeological Discoveries in India*. Paris. UNESCO.

60. Green, S.W. and Perlman, S.M. 1985. *The Archaeology of Frontiers and Boundaries,* Orlando, Academic press. pp. 1–12.

61. Chitalawala, Y.M. 1977. Harappan and post-Harappan settlement patterns in Saurashtra in Agrawal, D.P. and Pande, B.M. (eds.) *Ecology and Archaeology of Western India,* Delhi, Concept Publishing Company. pp. 93–99.

62. Suraj Bhan 1974 *op. cit*

63. Yule 1985 *op cit*

64. Pollard, H.P. 1987. The political economy of prehispanic Trascan metallurgy. *Americun Antiquity* 52. pp. 741-752.

65. Fairservis, W.A. 1971. *The Roots of Ancient India,* London George Allen and Unwin also 1986. Cattle and the Harappan chiefdoms of the Indus Valley, *Expedition* 28. pp. 43–50. Wadia, D.N. 1966. *Minerals of India*, New Delhi; National Book Trust of India. Tivy, J. and O' Hara, G. 1981. *Human Impact on the Ecosystem,* Edinburgh, Oliver and Boyd.

66. Lal, M. 1984. Summary of four seasons of explorations in Kanpur District, Uttar Pradesh, *Man and Environment* 8. pp. 61:80. Mohan, V. 1989. The Harappan Civilization; a Study in Variation and Regionalization in Haryana, India. (unpublished thesis submitted to the University of Cambridge.) and Erdosy, G. 1987. Early historic cities of northern India *South Asian Studies* 3. pp. 1–24.

67. Fairservis, W.A. 1952. Preliminary report on the pre–historic archaeology of the Afghan–Baluchi areas. *Novitates* 1587. pp. 37–39.

68. Cunningham, A. 1882. *Report of a tour in the Punjab in 1878–79.* Archaeological Survey of India Reports 14. Calcutta, Government of India Press.

69. Zimmermann, F. 1987. *The Jungle and the Aroma of Meats,* Berkley, University of California press.

70. Eder, J.F. 1984. The impact of subsistence change on mobility and settlement pattern in a tropical forest foraging economy: Some implications for archaeology, *American Anthropologist* 86. pp. 837–853 and Gamble, 1986 *op. cit*

71. Fiedel, S.J. 1987. *Prehistory of the Americas.* Cambridge, Cambridge University Press and Gamble 1986 *op. cit*

72. Allchin and Allchin 1982. *op.cit*

73. Fairservis, 1971 *op.cit*

74. Malik, S.C. 1978. *Understanding Indian Civilization.*, Simla, Indian Institute of Advanced Study.

75. Flannery, K.V. 1972. The cultural evolution of civilizations. *Annual Review of Ecology and Systematics* 3. pp. 399–426 Reprinted in Possehl, G.L. (ed.) 1979 *Ancient Cities of the Indus.* New Delhi, Vikas. Webster, G.S. 1990. Labour control and emergent stratification in prehistoric Europe, *Current Anthropology* 31. pp. 337-366. Whitehouse, R. and Wilkins, J. 1986. *The Making of Civilization.* London, Collins.

Longer Chronology of the Indus–Saraswati Civilization

S.P. GUPTA*

Dating the Indus–Saraswati Civilization has always been a serious affair with archaeologists. It started as far back in time as 1924[1], just two years later than the actual discovery of the seals and sealings deep below the Stupa Mound at Mohenjodaro[2]. This, of course, not to say that the seals and sealings were not collected as surface-finds and also published earlier; Charles Masson traversed the mound of Harappa in 1826[3], and so also A. Burnes in 1831[4]. Cunnigham also explored the mound twice — first in 1853 and then in 1856[5]. Dames published the seals in 1886; Cunnigham published the seals in 1877; and Fleet published them in 1912[6]. But all these attempts failed to understand the cultural and chronological importance of these valuable objects. However, when Gadd and Sidney Smith published their article entitled, "New Links between Indian and Babylonian Civilisation" in the *Illustrated Weekly of London*[7], their real importance was firmly established. In 1931, when a detailed report of these seals and sealings were published by John Marshall in *Mohenjodaro and the Indus Valley Civilizaton*, the world was finally convinced that the date of the Indus–Saraswati Civilization goes back to the 4th-3rd millennium B.C. at Mohenjodaro. He allowed 1000 more years for the formative period of this civilization. Similarly, he also visualised a long period for its decay. Vats, on the other hand, suggested 3500 B.C. – 2500 B.C. for Harappa. Mackay, however, proposed 2800 – 2500 B.C. for Mohenjodaro. Thus, before Mortimer Wheeler, the beginning of the Indus–Saraswati Civilization of Harappa and Mohenjodaro was placed around 3000 B.C. ± 200 years[8]. Wheeler re-excavated Harappa in 1946 (published in 1947) and dated the Indus–Saraswati Civilization to 2500 – 1700 B.C. bracket[9]. However, these opinions, generally based upon India–Mesopotamian contacts, visualised through the evidence of the seals and sealings, got a severe set back when the radiocarbon dates started coming from a number of Indus–Saraswati sites. Thus, Agrawal shortened this bracket still further and proposed 2300–1750 B.C.[10] as the maximum time-bracket for this civilization. But very soon it was realised that there were serious discrepancies between the radiocarbon dates of a sample and the dendrochronological dates of the same sample. The same was true when the same samples were tested by other scientific methods. This realisation led to the formulation of many 'correction charts' for the use of the archaeologists. Thus, in 1973 Dales proposed 2900–1900 B.C. time-bracket for this civilization, and in 1975 Brunswig proposed 2800–2000 B.C. In 1985 Ramchandran proposed the bracket of 3200 B.C. – 2100 B.C. jointly for the Early and Mature phase, of this civilization. Possehl and Rissman also used the corrected dates and proposed 2500 B.C. as the beginning of the urban phase of the Indus-Saraswati Civilization and 2650 B.C. as the beginning of the formative or early phase of this civilization — 150 years period represents the 'transitional' phase[11].

Here we are proposing a longer chronology for the Indus – Saraswati Civilization which is based upon the latest corrected radiocarbon dates[12]. It will be seen that Marshall was not too off the point as far as the begining of this civilization is concerned although the grounds on which he had proposed the beginning of this civilization

*148 Vigyan Vihar, Delhi-110 092

at Mohenjodaro were entirely different — it was based upon the Indus-Mesopotamian contacts as visualised through the discovery of the Mohenjodaro type seals at Mesopotamian sites, dated at that point of time differently than it is done now.

Relevant corrected radiocarbon dates determinning the chronological bracket of the Indus–Saraswati civilization.

Early Indus–Saraswati Phase (3100 B.C. – 2800 B.C.)

Sites 1	Sample No. 2	Radiocarbon Dates (5730 Half-life) 3	Calibrated Dates 4
Damb Sadaat (Pd. II)	L 180 E charcoal	2550 ± 370 bc	3021, 2916, 2927 cal.B.C.
Gumla (Pd. II)		2385 ± 155 bc	2883, 2796, 2784 cal.B.C.
Hathial West (Late Kot Diji)	BM-1949R	2150 ± 145 bc	2554, 2548, 2491, cal.B.C.
Harappa	BETA-33783 Hearth, charcoal	2725 ± 90 bc 3203 cal.bc	3338, 3213,
Harappa	BETA-33874	2725 ± 185 bc	3338, 3213, 3203 cal. B.C.
Ghazi Shah (Amri/Harappan Transition)	BETA–33358 charcoal	2325 ±70 bc	2867, 2808, 2772, 2723, 2699 cal.B.C.
Gonur Depe North (Namazga V, Harappan)	BETA-33558	2540 ± 60 bc	3018, 3001, 2926 cal.B.C.
Hulas	PRL-1032 charcoal	2560 ±155 bc	3028, 2985, 2930 cal.B.C.
Islam Chowki	OKA-1005	2335 ± 105 bc	2870, 2806, 2774, 2720, 2702 cal. B.C.
Jhang	BM–2201R charcoal	2440 ± 115 bc	2903 cal. B.C.
Jhukar	P-2476 charcoal	2820 ± 310 bc	3371 cal. B.C.
Jodhpura (Ganeshwar culture)	PRL-275 charcoal	2540 ± 165 bc	3018, 3001, 2926 cal. B.C.

1	2	3	4
Kalibangan	TF–241 charcoal	2265 ± 95 bc	2853, 2882, 2655, 2644, 2615 cal.B.C.
Kalibangan	TF–155 charcoal	2370 ± 120 bc	2879, 2799, 2781, 2711, 2709 cal.B.C.
Kot Diji	P-196 charcoal	2605 ± 145 bc	3070, 3040 2781, 2711, 2709 cal. B.C.
Kot Diji	P-180 charcoal	2255 ± 140bc	2851, 2830, 2653 cal.B.C.
Kot Diji	P-179 ash and charcoal	2335 ± 155 bc	2870, 2806, 2720, 2702 cal. B.C.
Lak Largai	BM-2402 charcoal	2345 ± 50 bc	2872, 2804, 2776, 2717, 2704 cal. B.C.
Mehrgarh (Pd. IV)	LY-1528 charcoal	2365 ± 145 bc	2877, 2800, 2780, 2712, 2708 cal.B.C.
Mundigak (Period III 5)	GSY-53 charcoal	2360 ±155 bc	2876, 2801, 2779, 2714, 2707 cal. B.C.
Prabhas Patan (Period I)	PRL-90 charcoal	2415 ±115 bc	2892 cal. B.C.
Rana Ghundai (Pd. IIIA)	P-2149 burnt seeds	2790 ± 60 bc	3360 cal. B.C.
Rehman Dheri (Pd. II, Kot Diji)	WIS-1699	2355 ± 70 bc	2875, 2802, 2778, 2715, 2706 cal. B.C.
Rehman Dheri (Pd. II, Kechi Beg)	PRL-676 charcoal	2705 ± 115 bc	331, 3226, 3185, 3155, 3147 cal. B.C.
Sarai Khola (Pd. II A)	BM-1936 R charcoal	2295 ± 255 bc	2860, 2817, 2693, 2684, 2662, 2633, 2626 cal. B.C.

1	2	3	4
Sarai Khola (Pd. II A)	BM-1944 R charcoal	2450 ± 255 bc	3334, 3219, 3189, 3152, 3148 cal. B.C.
Sarai Khola (Pd. IIA)	BM-1942 R Charcoal	2305 ± 125 bc	2862, 2814, 2738, 2728, 2695, 2679, 2665, 2630, cal. B.C.
Surkotada (Pd. I. A, (Mid levels)	PRL-85	2315 ± 135 bc	2865, 2810, 2747, 2725, 2697, 2674, 2668, cal. B.C.

The overall chronological bracket of the Early Indus–Saraswati Civilization falls between 3300 B.C. and 2700 B.C. However, adequate allowance should be given to a number of factors towards which scientists engaged in radiocarbon dating methods have drawn our attention repeatedly — contamination of the samples, erratic dates, pit-falls of excavations, limited amount of the samples, etc. The overall assessment, therefore, comes to the hard fact that the beginning of the early Indus–Saraswati Civilization goes back at least to the 31st century B.C.[13] while the effective data of the end of this phase, or else, which is more logical to state, the beginning of the immediately overlapping phase, called the 'Mature Indus–Saraswati Civilization', is to be placed in the 28th century B.C. It need hardly be reiterated that the culture-change process involved in the Indus–Saraswati phenomenon is to be viewed in the Evolutionary Model of our understanding of the past; no one has shown it more forcefully and convincingly than Mughal who has spent more than half of his academic career only in establishing this fact; all others have only echoed what he proposed as far back in time as 1970[14]. This has been so in spite of the fact it has yet to be convincingly demonstrated as to whether or not the Indus–Saraswati script, seals and sealings and, weights and measures evolved out of some previously made attempts or not.[15]

Let us now look at the calibrated radiocarbon dates of the beginning of the Mature or Urban phase keeping clearly in mind that the beginning of the Mature Phase did not mark the end of the Early Phase culture-complex; here we are dealing with a typical example of 'change with continuity'. The characteristic features of the Early Phase continued to determine the everyday life of the people. This has been so inspite of fact that the everyday life of the people had by now greatly changed because of certain innovations which gave power into the hands of a select group of people who, with this superior power, effected great changes in the quality of everyday life, generally called 'urbanisation'.

Mature Indus-Saraswati Phase (2800 B.C. – 1900 B.C.)

Site	Sample No.	Radiocarbon Dates (5730 Years Half Life)	Calibrated dates
1	2	3	4
Harappa (Transition Early/ Mature)	WIS-2142 carbonised wood	2316 ± 65 bc	2863, 2812, 2742, 2776, 2696, 2677, 2666 cal. B.C.

1	2	3	4
Harappa (Mature)	WIS-2140 charcoal	2470 ± 70 bc	2913 cal. B.C.
Kalibangan (Mature)	TF-942 charcoal	2225 ± 115 bc	2586 cal. B.C. cal. B.C.
Kalibangan (Mature)	TF-152(BS) charcoal	1725 ± 130 bc	1923 cal. B.C.
Kalibangan (Mature)	TF-138 charcoal	1215 ± 105 bc	1391, 1334, 1327 cal. B.C.
Lothal (Mature)	TF-136 charcoal	2080 ± 135 bc	2461 cal. B.C.
Lothal (Mature)	TF-135 chrcoal	1555± 130 bc	1735, 1717, 1701 cal. B.C.
Mohenjodaro (Mature)	P-1177 charcoal	2155 ± 65 bc	2556, 2546, 2493 cal. B.C.
Mohenjodaro (Late Mature)	TF-75 charred grains	1760 ± 115 bc	1961 B.C.
Nausharo (Mature)	BETA-18843	2540 ± 70 bc	2598 cal. B.C.
Pirak (Pd. I)	LY-1641	2250 ± 300 bc	2250, 2245, 2652, 2647, 2617 cal. B.C.
Prabhas Patan (Mature)	TF-1286 charcoal	1755± 95 bc	1953 cal. B.C.
Rehman Dheri (Pd. III; early/mature)	BM-2062 R charcoal	2130 ± 115 bc	2470 cal. B.C.
Rojdi (Mature)	PRL-1091 charcoal	2325 ± 115 bc	2867, 2808, 2772, 2723, 2699 cal. B.C.
Rojdi (mature)	PRL-1085 charcoal	2190 ± 115 bc	2573, 2535, 2506 cal. B.C.
Rojdi (Mature)	TF-199 charcoal	1750 ± 105 bc	1947 cal. B.C.

1	2	3	4
Shortugai (Pd. I, (Mature)	NY-430 charcoal	2245 ± 100 bc	2651, 2649, 2610 cal. B.C.
Shortugai (Pd. I, Mature)	NY-425 charcoal	2210 ± 105 bc	2580 cal. B.C.

Late Indus-Saraswati Phase (1900 B.C. – 1400 B.C.)

Once the Mature or Urban phase of the Indus-Saraswati Civilization started fading out, around 1900 B.C., the Late Indus-Saraswati phase of Civilization started. During this phase two things happened: (i) The cities started disappearing and villages multiplied (their number and nature of concentration, of course, did not follow a single pattern) with strong regional bias, and (ii) certain Indus-Saraswati crafts continued but some old and new local potteries predominated.[12]

These two characteristics make a very strong case in favour of the theory that the Late Indus–Saraswati Civilization was just a change in the 'form' of the culture which was continuing from the late fourth millennium B.C., and not the emergence of a new culture under any foreign impetus, or else challenge.

It may also be noted that it was during this phase that the so-called Neolithic-Chalcolithic cultures, particularly the Banas, the Kayatha and the Malwa culture-complexes, which flourished in Rajasthan, Central India and Maharashtra, closely interacted with the last sub-phase of the Mature Indus–Saraswati Civilization. It clearly shows that in spite of strong regional bias, which the period witnessed, there was nothing like 'splendid isolation of villages marked by self-sufficiency', an assessment sometimes made for the settlements. The 'oral tradition' seems to have played a strong role in the life of the people. Hence we see, for example, mother-goddess figurines, bull figurines and the depiction of *pipal* leaf on pottery still continuing as manifestations of age-old popular beliefs. Steatite, shell, faience and carnelian objects of everyday use, such as the bangles, beads and various other ornaments go a long way to prove that the Indus-Saraswati traditions in crafts continued to be practised. It is true, however, that Harappa's 'Cemetery H' presented a far different form of material culture than the Lothal 'B' culture, and Lothal 'B' culture is different from Late Rojdi culture, and this too was different what Hulas (upper levels) presented; but it only reiterates what we observed earlier — the Late Harappan develops regional culture-complexes although certain bèliefs and crafts of the old traditions (Mature Indus–Saraswati) still continued to be practised.

Let us now look at some of the calibrated dates to fix the time-bracket of this phase of the Indus–Saraswati Civilization.

Late Indus-Saraswati Phase (1900 B.C. – 1400 B.C.)

Site 1	Sample No. Material 2	Radiocarbon Dates (5730 Yrs Half Life) 3	Calibrated Dates 4
Daimabad (post-Urban)	PRL-426 charcoal	1760 ± 155 bc	1961 cal. B.C.
Daimabad (post-Urban, Pd. II)	PRL-657 charcoal	1285 ± 105 bc	1424 cal. B.C.

1	2	3	4
Daimabad (post-Urban, Pd. III)	BS-182	1275 ± 95 bc	1420 cal. B.C.
Kalibangan	TF-138	1215 ± 105 bc	1391, 1334, 1327 cal. B.C.
Kalibangan	TF-152 charcoal	1725 ± 130 bc	1923 cal. B.C.
Katelai (Late Bronze/ Early Iron)	R-476 burnt human bones	1295 ± 155 bc	1428 cal. B.C.
Loebnar III (Pd-IV, Chalcolithic)	P-2584 charcoal	1285 ± 60 bc	1424 cal. B.C.
Mohenjodaro (Late Mature)	TF-75 charred grains	1760 ± 115 bc	1961 cal. B.C.
Prabhas Patan (Late, LRW)	PRL-19 charcoal	1245 ± 165	1406 cal. B.C.
Rojdi (Mature)	TF-199 charcoal	1750 ± 105 bc	1947 cal. B.C.
Sibri Period VIII C or later)	BETA-26	1365 ± 60 bc	1514 cal. B.C.
Shortugai (Pd. III post-Urban)	NY-424	1325 ± 345 bc	1445 cal. B.C.

Plea for a new nomenclature: The Indus–Saraswati Civilization

Once upon a time the culture-complex, revealed at Harappa and Mohenjadaro, was called the 'Indus Valley Civilization' or just the 'Indus Civilization', but then it was revised and called the 'Harappan Civilization'[16]. Still later it was called the 'Harappan Civilization of Greater Indus Valley'. Although all these terms are interchangeable, scholars have given their own reasoning while using a particular term. Those who used the terms 'Indus' or 'Indus Valley Civilization' pleaded that this was the major river on the banks of which the largest town of this civilization, Mohenjodaro, was found along with several smaller ones, hence this nomenculture.

Those who used the term 'Harappan Civilization' reasoned that since the culture was first located at Harappa, on the River Ravi, in 1826, nearly a hundred years prior to the discovery of Mohenjodaro, in 1922, we should better use a term after the name of the place where it was first discovered. And those who use the term 'Greater Indus' opined that since the civilization is no more confined to the Indus Valley — its remains have been found in Baluchistan, Afghanistan, Gujarat, Rajasthan, Haryana, etc. — it is but logical to use the term 'Greater Indus'. Since every logic has a reasoning, this too has a reasoning though it is a completely outdated practice to prefix 'Greater' with a Civilization or even human being. There may have been some justification in 1970 to use this term because at that point of time the world had not known the existence of hundreds of Early Harappan sites in the dried up bed of the Saraswati-Ghaggar-Hakra stream but now it has not even that justification. To recollect, once it was a common practice to use the term 'Greater India' to cover the whole of South–East Asia where the Hindu Civilization had travelled, but, of late, it has been completely given up on the grounds that it has political and cultural overtones where the prominence of India was sought to be established over the neighbouring countries, a feeling which was absolutely understandable. The Great Mauryas, the Great Mughals, Alexander the Great, Great Britain now find place only in the golden dust bin of historiography. It is, therefore, better if we are able to coin a term which is based upon the ground realities, that is which is based upon solid archaeological data. It is now more than clear that if we have to coin a term which uses the name of a river then we should retain the Indus because of the facts: (i) that on its banks lies perhaps the biggest, and also most extensively excavated, site of Mohenjodaro, around 400 hectares,[17] (ii) it has been used repeatedly for the last 70 years, and (iii) on its banks around three dozen sites of this civilization are located. However, and this is, to my mind, most important, there are several times more sites on the banks of the river Saraswati and its tributaries than on the banks of the Indus. Mughal has already plotted 363 sites only in Cholistan, i.e. old Bahawalpur State.[18] There are 25 sites which A. Ghosh explored on the Indian side of the Saraswati in District Ganganagar.[19] J.P. Joshi and others located 62 more sites further east in Punjab, Rajasthan and Haryana.[20] Thus, there are as many as 500 sites, if not more, on the River Saraswati and Drishadvati (old courses and new courses together, plus their tributaries). Obviously, the Saraswati played a very vital role in the formation and development of this civilization. How long and why at all should we ignore the fact that the River Saraswati was an equal partner, in fact senior and bigger (here several 'Pre-Harappan' sites exist) in the evolution and growth of this culture-complex.[21] It is, therefore, argued that the realities of the situation demand that we should adopt a nomenclature which includes the names of both the major rivers in the basins of which this unique civilization of the then contemporary bronze age world flourished.[22] Hence, the civilization has been here entitled by us as the 'Indus-Saraswati Civilization.'

NOTES & REFERENCES

1. Marshall, Sir John, *Mohanjodaro and the Indus Civilization*, (London, 1931)
2. Wheeler, R.E.M. *The Indus Civilization* (3rd Edition, Cambridge University Press, Cambridge, 1976) p.1
3. Masson, Charles, *A Narrative of Various Journeys in Baluchistan, Afghanistan and the Punjab*, 3 vols., (London, 1843)
4. Burnes, A. *Travels into Bokhara*, 3 vols. (London, 1834)
5. Cunningham A. *Archaeological Survey of India, Report for the year 1872-73, Harappa*, (Calcutta, 1875)
6. Pande, B.M. "History of Research of Harappan Culture". In G.L. Possehl (Ed) *Harappan Civilization* (Oxford & IBH Publishing Co., New Delhi, 1982) p. 396. Also Possehl, G.L. "Discovering Ancient India's Earliest Cities: The First Phase of Research", *Ibid.*, pp. 405-413.
7. Gadd and Smith, *'ILN*. Oct. 4, 1924, pp. 614-16.
8. Thapar, B.K. "Six Decades of the Indus Studies", In B.B. Lal and S.P. Gupta (Eds) *Frontiers of the Indus Civilization* (Books & Books, New Delhi, 1984) pp. 19-20.
9. Wheeler, *op.cit.*, p. 5
10. Agrawal, D.P. "Harappan Culture: New Evidence for a Shorter Chronology", *Science* 3609 (1964): 950-52. Also, D.P. Agrawal and A. Ghosh (Eds.) *Radiocarbon and Indian Archaeology* (Tata Inst. of Fundamental Research, Bombay, (1973)
10. Thapar, *op.cit.*
11. Possehl G.L. and Rissman Paul, C. "The Chronology of Prehistoric India: From Earliest Times to the Iron Age". In Robert W. Ehrich (Ed) *Chronologies in Old World Archaeology*, Vol. II, (Third Ed., Chicago, 1922) pp. 465-474. Also Jim G. Shaffer,

ibid., Vol. I, pp. 441-464 (Indus Valley, Baluchistan and the Helmand).

12. Possehl, G.L. Radiometric Dates for South Asian Archaeology (Xeroxed copy, 1993 Courtesy, Dr. Possehl.
13. Jarrige, J.F. "Excavations at Mehrgarh: their significance for understanding the background of the Harappan Civilization". In G.L. Possehl (Ed.), *Harappan Civilization*, pp. 79-84. Also Shashi Asthana, *Preharappan Cultures in India and the Borderlands* (Books & Books, New Delhi 1987). It is now absolutely clear that the birth of the Early Indus-Saraswati Civilization lies in the cross-currents of cultures which took place during the period between 3500 B.C.–3000 B.C. on the India's western borderlands which included Baluchistan, eastern Iran, Afghanistan, Turan and southern Turkmenia. Within this bracket the date of 3100 B.C. is crucial as is clear from the evidence of Mehrgarh (Pd. IV) and Nowsharo (Mature Indus–Saraswati phase) put together. See also H.P. Francfort, "The Harappan Settlement of Shortughai" in B.B. Lal and S.P. Gupta. (Eds.) *op.cit.* pp. 301-310
14. Mughal, M.R. The Early Harappan Period in the Greater Indus Valley and Baluchistan 1970) (Unpublished Ph.D. thesis, University of Pennesylvania.)
15. Asthana, *op.cit.* Possehl G.L. "The Harappan Civilization in Gujarat: The Sorath and Sindhi Harappans", *The Eastern Antrhropologist*, Vol. 45 (Nos. 1 and 2) 1992, The Indus Civilization, Special Number, pp. 117-154.
16. Wheeler, *op.cit.*, p.3
17. For this information, which is based upon recent discoveries made at several places around the older remains of the city but far away from them, including the bed of the Indus, I am extremely thankful to Dr. G.L. Possehl (Personal communication). Earlier the extent of Mohenjodaro was calculated to be only around 83 hectares. See Mughal, M.R. "The Harappan 'Twin Capitals' and Reality", *Jr. Of Central Asia*, Vol. XIII, No.1 (1990) pp. 155-161.
18. Mughal, M.R. "Recent Archaeological Research in the Cholistan Desert". In Possehl (Ed.) *Harappan Civilization* (New Delhi, 1982) pp. 85-96.
19. Ghosh A. "The Rajaputana Desert — Its Archaeological Aspect", *Bull. of the National Institute of Sciences of India*, No.1. pp. 37-42. Also K.N. Dikshit, "The Sothi Complex: Old Records and Fresh Observations". In B.B. Lal and S.P. Gupta (Eds) *Frontiers of the Indus Civilization* (New Delhi, 1984) *op. cit.* pp. 531-537.
20. Joshi, J.P., Madhu Bala and Jassu Ram, "The Indus Civilization: A Reconsideration on the basis of Distribution Maps". In B.B. Lal and S.P. Gupta (Eds) 1984 *op. cit.* pp. 511-530.
21. Mughal, 1982 *op. cit.*, clearly shows that at least two cultures, a Neolithic Culture (Jalilpur Neolithic), and after that, Hakra Culture, preceded the Early Harappa Culture in that part of the basin of the Saraswati which lies in the Cholistan Desert which, before 1947, formed part of the Bahawalpur State. This is not the case with the basin of the Indus river. Also, Mughal, M.R. "The Protohistoric Settlement Patterns in the Cholistan Desert". In M. Taddei (Ed.) *South Asian Archaeology 1987* (Naples, ISMEO, 1989)
22. I am extremely thankful to Shri K.S. Ramachandran, Dr. Dilip K. Chakrabarti and Dr. G.L. Possehl for several rounds of discussion with them on this issue. See also, K.S. Ramachandran, "Dating the Indus Civilization". In B.B. Lal and S.P. Gupta (Eds.) 1984 *op. cit.*, pp. 538-539.

The Harappan Horse was buried under the dunes of . . .

A.K. SHARMA*

On 16th of December, 1991 I was pleasantly surprised to be suddenly congratulated by a galaxy of scholars on the eve of the Indian Archaeological Society meet at Bhopal. From the podium of the inauguration hall, it was declared by one of the scholars, who matters in Indian archaeology, in the presence of political and scholar-luminaries, that my findings about the presence of skeletal remains of 'True (domesticated) horse' at Surkotada (Gujarat), a Harappan site excavated by Jagat Pati Joshi in 1971-72, have been found to be absolutely correct as they have now been confirmed in writing (13th Dec. 1991) by Prof. Sandor Kokonyi, Archaeologist and Director of the Archaeological Institute, Budapest, Hungary, who has spent more than 40 years of his life in the study of horse and horse alone, in Asia and Europe.

The credit for publishing this epoch-making findings goes to *Puratattva* which published this article in its Number No. 7, 1974. Everyone in the hall applauded clapping for two minutes. This was the saddest day for me as the thought flashed in my mind that my findings had to wait for two decades for recognition, until a man from another continent came, examined the material and declared that 'Sharma was right'. When will we imbibe intellectual courage not look across the borders for approval. The historians are still worse, they feel it is an attempt on the part of 'rightists' to prove that the Aryans did not come to India from outside her boundaries. But truth must prevail, science is science, it is neither 'left' nor 'right'.

The immediate impact of Prof. Sandor Bokonyi's seal of approval was that many other excavators of Harappan sites started searching for the bones of *Equus caballus* Linn. in their collection. I now learn from R.S. Bisht, the excavator of the Harappan site of Dholavira in Kutch that bones of "True Horse" have been identified from his collection also. When K.R. Alur, the renowned veterinary surgeon, who later turned an archaeo-zoologist, examined the faunal remains from a large number of sites, declared the presence of bones of *Equus caballus* Linn. from the Neolithic site of Hallur, District Dharwad, Karnataka, there were scores of searching enquiries from archaeologists and historians; some even going to the extent of doubting some mix-up somewhere. This led Alur and the excavator to re-excavate Hallur and collect fresh samples of animal bones wherein also the presence of horse bones were decisively established. Dr. Alur identified the following bones of Horse from Hallur.

S.No. 212 small metacarpal (splint bone)
S. No. 467 proximal extremity of small metacarpal
S.No. 497 Molar (from middle series)
S.No. 517 Second phalanx

In his paper on "Aryans and Indian History: An Archaeo-zoological Approach", Dr. Alur wrote that "Archaeological remains of Animals, whatever may be the opinion expressed by archaeologists, it cannot either deny or alter the finds of a scientific fact that the horse was present at Hallur before the (presumed) period of 'Aryan invasion"....[1]

Dr. Alur wrote about the erroneous findings of

* Indira Gandhi National Centre for the Arts New Delhi

earlier archaeo-zoologists like S. Swell[2] and B. Prasad[3] who, not acting strictly on the basis of scientific findings but biased by the opinion of their British masters, declared 'that there is no evidence of the presence of the horse in the Indus Valley', though they declared that they had recovered a few metacarpals of the domestic ass".

After critically examining the data of Swell and Prasad J. C. George of M. S. University of Baroda stated that the "the study of the above table of comparative measurements shows beyond doubt that the metacarples recorded by Prasad are definitely not of domestic ass and it is, therefore, possible to conclude that the smaller size of horse did exist in Harappa. It is rather incredible that in a great civilization like India, the horse alone should be conspicuous by its absence, while allied species like that of the ass have been identified. It is equally unbelievable that the domestication of the prehistoric horse has been established in all the neighbouring countries such as Turkestan and Palestine but not so in India".

After S.R. Rao[4] discovered a terracotta figurine that resembled true horse, B.Nath[5], after examining the animal skeletal remains from Lothal, identified the bones of rhinoceros, elephant and true horse (*Equus caballus* Linn.). Though the rhinoceros has so far not been found on the Lothal seals, terracotta figurines and bones of the animal were found from the site. Rao suggests that the horse bones at Lothal came from the Mature Harrappan levels, as at Surkotada. He noted[6] that the horse was known in the 4th phase of Lothal A (Mature Harappan) as well as in Lothal B (Late Harappan).

As early as in 1963, B. Nath[7] identified the remains of the horse (*Equus caballus* Linn.) and the Indian elephant (*Elephas maximus* Linn.) from the unworked collection from Harappa, lying with the Zoological Survey of India. The skeletal remains of the horse were recovered from Area G of the site. Nath claimed that this was the first record of the true horse and the Indian elephant from the region. Bhola Nath had also reported the bones of true horse from Ropar, another Mature Harappan site in Punjab.

It is really strange that no notice was taken by archaeologists, of these vital findings and the oft-repeated theory that true domesticated horse was not known to the Harappans' continued to be harped upon, coolly ignoring these findings to help our so-called veteran historians and archaeologists of Wheeler's generation to formulate and propagate their theory of 'Aryan invasion of India on horse-back', even though the term *aśvārohi* never occurs in the *Rigveda* and there is absolutely no proof that horse-driven chariots were used by very many other hordes of people who entered India in the early period as is known from very many historical and archaeological sources.

As far back as 1964-65, when I was participating in the excavations conducted at Kalibangan, I had the opportunity that year to work in the pottery-yard where everyday's collection of the animal skeletal remains from different trenches used to be stored and sorted out. While going through the collection, I could notice the bones of *Equus caballus* Linn. from the following trenches.

1. KLB -1, F.12, Qd. 3, date 8.1.65-Upper molar.
2. KLB-2, XA II, street 3, date 30.12.64 - Fragment of shaft of distal end of femur.
3. KLB.2, XA II, stratum 3, date 30.12.64 -Distal end of left humerus.

Later, on enquiry from the Zoological Survey of India (vide their letter dated 30th November, 1992) I was supplied with the identification report on Kalibangan animal skeletal remains and I reproduce it below. This list very clearly contains *Equus Caballus* Linnaeus (the true horse).

Animal species (faunal remains) reported from Kalibangan, Ganganagar, Rajasthan.

1. *Lamellidens marginalis* (Lamarck)–The Fresh water mussel
2. *Parreysia corrugata* (Muller)–The Pond snail
3. *Teleostei fish*–The bony fish
4. *Kachuqa toctum* (Gray)–The roofed turtle
5. *Bataqur baska* (Gray)–The River terrapin
6. *Chitra indica* Gray–The Narrow heads Soft shell turtle
7. *Lissemys punctata Gray* The Indo-Gangatic flop shell turtle
8. *Gallus sp.*–The domestic or Jungle fowl.
9. *Columba livia* Gmelin–The Rock pigeon

10. *Canis familiaris* Linnaeus–The Indian pariah dog
11. *Canis lupus* Linnaeus–The Indian wolf
12. *Folis chaus* Guldenstaedt–The Jungle Cat
13. *Elephus maximus* Linnaeus–The Elephant (Indian)
14. *Rhinoceros unicornis* Linnaeus–The Great One-horned rhino
15. *Equus asinus* Linnaeus–The domestic ass
16. *Equus hemious* Pallas–Wild ass
17. *Equus caballus* Linnaeus–The horse
18. *Cervus duvauceli* Cuvier–The Swamp deer
19. *Cervus unicolor* Kerr–The Sambar deer
20. *Axis axis* Erexleben–The Chital deer
21. *Muntiacus muntjak*–Zimmermann-The barking deer
22. *Sus scrofa* Linnaeuss–The Indian pig wild or domesticated
23. *Bos indicus* Linnaeus–The Zebu or humped cattle
24. *Bos gaurus* H. Smith–The Indian Bison or Gaur
25. *Bubalus bubalis* Linnaeus–The water buffalo
26. *Ovis orientalis vignei* Blyth–The Wild sheep
27. *Capra hircus* Linnaeus–The goat
28. *Boselaphus traqcamelus* Pallas–The Nilgai
29. *Camelus dromedarius* Linnaeus–The one humped camel
30. *Camelus* sp.–The camel

As already reported in brief[8] in Puratattva No. 7 and in detail in the report on Surkotada excavations[9], bones of true horse (*Equus caballus* Linn.) were clearly identified as far back as 1974 by the author. When shown to Dr. Alur at Dharwad, he confirmed the findings and was happy to know that his findings from Hallur are not isolated findings. During the same period when I was co-authoring the report on animal skeletal remains from Malvan (Gujarat), a Late Harappan site, jointly excavated by Jagat Pati Joshi and F. R. Allchin, we had identified the presence of the bones of *Equus caballus* Linn. from Period I, i.e., Late Harappan. Unfortunately, this detailed and important report, written in 1972-73 and submitted immediately to the excavators, has not been published so far. Specimen No. 63 and 25 are the bodies of the lumbar vertebra of horse. Their transverse processes are cut off at the base. The point of identification is the thickness of this base which is present in case of cattle. "The medial part of the 6th process is thick, the lateral part thinner, narrow and curved forward. The medial part of the 5th is also somewhat thickened - Horse" "their borders are thin and irregular and bear projection of variable size and form-Cattle. The character present is a diagnostic point[10]. At Surkotada the bones of true horse (*Equus caballus* Linn.) identified are from Period IA, IB & IC. These periods have been dated on the basis of Radiocarbon determination as under.

Period IA

PRL 85-4365±135 BP 2315 BC
TF 1305 – 3890 ± 95 (4005 ± 100) BP 2055 B.C.
TF 1310 – 2810 ± 95 (3920 ± 100) BP 1970 B.C.
TF 1304 & 109 – 3645 ± 90 (375 ± 90) BP 1805 B.C

Period IB

TF 1295 – 3635 ± 95 (3770 ± 95) BP 1940 B.C.

Period IC

TF 1297 – 3635 ± 95 (3740 ± 95) BP 1790 B.C.
TF 1311 – 3625 ± 90 (3730 ± 90) BP 1780 B.C.
TF 1294 – 3620 ± 95 (3730 ± 100) BP 1780 B.C.
TF 1307 - 3510 ± 105 (3610± 100) BP 1660 B.C.

With the correction factors, the dates fall between 2400B.C. and 1700 B.C.[10a]

In Period IA *Equus caballus* Linn. was 1.2%, in Period IB 2.2% and in Period IC 1.49%. This shows that horse meat formed part of the diet only marginally because cattle bones predominate.

The bones recovered were very distinctive, first, second and third phalanges and few vertebral fragments.

Incissors	: 2, one 1st and the other 3rd incissor. Both from the middle levels of Period IB.
Molar	: 4,Two from early levels of Period IC and two from early levels of Period IA.
Canon bones	: 2, one from the late levels of Period IA and the other from the middle levels of Period IC
First phalanx	: 1, from the middle levels of Period IC
Second phalanx:	2, One from early levels of Period IA and the other from the late levels of Period IC.

From the above it could be seen that bones of *Equus caballus* Linn. occur from Period IA to IC at Surkotada. The presence of a few fragments of charred bones of the true horse is significant.

The discovery of bones of *Equus caballus* Linn. from so many Harappan sites and that too right from the lowest levels clearly establishes that the true domesticated horse was very much in usely the Harappans though this animal did not find any pictorial, or three dimensional depiction in clay, except one each at Lothal and Mohenjodaro. In 1938 Mackay[11] had remarked on the discovery of a clay model of horse from Mohenjodaro. "I personally take it to represent horse. I do not think we need be particularly surprised if it should be proved that the horse existed thus early at Mohenjo-daro". About this terracotta figurine Wheleler[12] wrote, "One terracotta from a late level of Mohenjodaro seems to represent a horse, reminding us that the jaw bone of a horse is also recorded from the same time, and that the horse was known at considerably early period in northern Baluchistan". He notes, "There is no evidence of any kind for the use of the ass or mule. On the other hand the bones of horse occur at a higher level at Mohenjodaro and from the earlier (doubtless pre-Harappan) layer at Rana Ghundai in northern Baluchistan both horse and ass are recorded. It is likely enough that camel, horse and ass were in fact all familiar feature of the Indus caravans."[13]

The above discoveries, of which no proper account was taken by 'anti-horse archaeologists' (deliberately, or due to their technical ignorance, or else under undue influence of Marshall, Piggott and others whose theory of Aryan migration/invasion of India was based upon the absence of horse and iron at Harappan sites), demolish the arguments of Parpola and others. To Parpola's oft-repeated argument that the horse is conspicuously missing among the many realistically depicted animals Sethna[14] pertinently asked, "As there are no depiction of the cow, in contrast to the pictures of the bull, which are abundant, should we conclude that Harappa and Mohenjodaro had only bulls? What about that mythical animal, the unicorn, which is the most common pictorial motif on the seals? Was the unicorn a common animal of the protohistoric Indus Valley? Surely, the presence or absence of depictions cannot point unequivocally to the animals known...." Further, "The depicted male animals do not cover all the fauna known to the Harappan Culture." In support of Sethna's observations it could be easily pointed out that though the skeletal remains of camel (*Cameus dromedarius* Linneaus) have been duly reported from Kalibangan, Harappa[15] and Mohenjodaro[16], this animal does not find depicted on any Harappan seal. Similar is the case of domestic ass (*Equus asinus*). After the discovery of bones of *Equus caballus* Linn. from Sukortada Lal[17], though unwilling to believe, was not so dogmatic. He reluctantly refers to an area outside the Punjab as being "known for having had its own indigenous variety of the horse." But after Prof. Sandor Bokonyi's categorical assertion on the findings of the author from Surkotada, his reluctance is perhaps no more there. How long can any one justifiably ignore the claims of scientific studies? Surprisingly Romila Thapar and R.S. Sharma chose not accept this evidence in an international conference held at ICHR in 1989.

It would be worthwhile to refer to the latest MASCA corrected dates[18] of Harappan sites in relation to remarks of Parpola who holds that the evidence of horse bones at Harappa and Surkotada does not go earlier than *circa* 2000 B.C.

Dates based on Radiocarbon and relative Dates

Mohenjodaro 2500-1800 BC
Kalibangan 2350-1700 BC
Surkotada 2400-1800 BC
Lothal 2450-1600 BC
MASCA Corrected Dates
Mohenjo-daro 3100-1900 B.C.
Lothal A 3000-1900 B.C.
Kalibangan II 2900-1900 B.C.

If however, we forget the evidence of horse from Harappan sites, then how would we account for the appearance of true horse from the neolithic sites of Koldihwa and Mahagara in Uttar Pradesh? G.R. Sharma[19] observs, "The fossils obtained from the Gravels I and II of Belan belong to *Bos namadicus, Bos bubalis, gravialiss, sus, elephus,* antelope, *Bos, elephas*, stag deer, *equus, chelonia* (tortoise)...." Further, "The domesticated animals include cattle, sheep, goat and horse. Evidence of wild sheep/goat and *Equus* have also been found from cemented gravels II & IV in the Belan valley". And with G.R. Sharma Desmond Clark and others were also associated in the excavations of these sites.

That the horse is an indigenous animal and was domesticated during the times of the Harappans is now proved beyond doubt. The only need now is for our young archaeologists, in India at least, who unfortunately are not well trained to handle animal skeletal remains coming out from the excavations, need to be very cautious. They need not attempt any 'weeding out' the 'unwanted fragments and other parts', according to their personal judgment and choice, to lessen the volume of the finds, for fear of cost and labour involved in transporting them to the headquarters. The entire bone collection, including small fragments, should be carefully preserved and labelled at the site. They should not be packed and transported like pottery and dumped for years or in some packing case for decades, to be examined by experts. It will be rewarding to examine them, first in the field itself by an expert zoologist.

Under no circumstances the bones should be washed in the manner pottery is washed in the sites generally with hard brushes because that may destroy the vital clues and also hasten the process of decay.

Regarding the occurance of only few bones of horse in excavations, it should be noted that the horse, whether in rural or urban set up, is not a prolific animal like cattle, sheep, goat, dogs, etc. the bones of which are found in larger quantity in all the habitational sites. The proportion of horse population to that of cattle is very much less, except of course, if by chance, we come across a stable or a breeding centre. In a village only a few horses could be found in India even in the medieval period. There are many villages presently, which do not boast of even a single horse though the horse is well in use everywhere. Fortunately, the Harappan horse, that lay buried under the dunes of ignorance, suspicion and prejudice of historians and archaeologists, alike, has new come out, unharmed, and now stands erect in full view of all.

REFERENCES

1. Alur, K.R. *Skeletal remains (vertebrate), Proto-historical Cultures of the Tungbhadra Valley* (Dharwad, 1971) p. 107.
2. Swell, R.B.S. and Guha, 1931, Zoological remains in Sir J. Marshall *Mohenjodaro and the Indus Civilisation*, Vol. II, London 1931 pp. 649-73.
3. Prasad, B. 1936 *Animal Remains from Harappa* in Mem. Archaeological Survey of India, No. 51 Delhi, 1936.
4. Rao, S.R., 1979, *Lothal a Harappan Port-town* (1954-62) Vol. I in Mem. Archaeological Survey of India, No. 78.
5. Nath, B., "Advance in the study of prehistoric and ancient animal remains in India - A Review" in *Rec. Zoological Survey of India*, Vol. 61 Calcutta, 1968 pp. 1-13.
6. Rao, S.R. "Excavations at Rangpur, and other explorations in Gujarat" in *Ancient India* Nos. 18-19 pp. 5-27.
7. Nath, B. "Animals of prehistoric India and their affinities with those of the western Asiatic countries" in *Rec. of the Indian Museum*, Vol. 59, pp. 335 = 367.
8. Sharma, A.K. "Evidence of Horse from the Harappan settlement at Surkotada"; *Puratattva*, No. 7, 1974, pp. 75-76.
9. Sharma A.K., "Animal bone Remains" in Jagat Pati Joshi, *Excavation at Surkotada 1971-72 and Explorations in Kutch*, A.S.I., New Delhi, 1990.
10. Sisson and Grossman, *The Anatomy of the Domestic Animals* (London, 1967), pp. 34-35, and 128-129.

10a. Schaffer, J.G. Indus Valley Baluchistan and Helmand" in Ehrich, R.W (ed) *Chronologies in Old World Archaeology*, Vol. I, (London and Chicago 1992),p. 435.

11. Mackay E.J.H., *'Further Excavations at Mohenjo-daro*, Vol. I (New Delhi, 1938), p. 289.
12. Wheeler, Mortimer, *The Indus Civilization*, Cambridge, 1968, p.92.
13. *ibid.* p. 82.
14. Sethna, K.D. *The Problem of Aryan Origins*, (New Delhi, 1980).
15. Prasad, B. "Animal Remains from Harappa" in Mem. of Archaeological Survey of India.
16. Wheeler, Martimer, 1968, *op. cit.*, p. 82.
17. Lal, B.B. "The Indus Civilization" in A.L. Basham (ed.) *A Cultural History of India* (Oxford 1975).
18. Rao S.R. *Dawn and Devolution of the Indus Civilization*, (New Delhi, 1991).
19. Sharma, G.R. *History to Prehistory: Archaeology of the Vindhyas and the Ganga Valley*, Allahabad.

Ayodhyā and God Rāma

Ajay Mitra Shastri*

According to the age-old Indian tradition Rāma flourished in the second aeon (*yuga*) known as *Tretā*, thousands of years before Christ and considerably prior to Kṛishṇa who is supposed to have lived at the close of the third *yuga* (*Dvāpara*). These dates have been doubted, perhaps not without reason, by many a historian as divergent traditions prevailed in ancient India in this matter.[1] Irrespective of what one might think regarding the exact dates, the fact remains that the entire Indian tradition is at one in placing Kṛishṇa posterior to Rāma and correspondingly the *Mahābhārata* episode later than the *Rāmāyaṇa*. This is also supported by the occurrence of the Rāmāyaṇa story called there Rāmopākhyānaparvan in the Vanaparvan of the *Mahābhārata* and the casual manner in which the *Mahābhārata* refers to the Rāmāyaṇa episodes should leave absolutely no doubt about the priority of the *Rāmāyaṇa* to the *Mahābhārata*, both as episodes and texts.[2] The doubts expressed by a few modern scholars have no real basis to stand upon.[3]

The two epics as they are now available represent only the final form and their compilation was actually a gradual process. According to M. Winternitz, whose opinion is commonly accepted by historians of Indian literature, the original *Vālmīkīya Rāmāyana*, portraying Rāma only as a human being and bereft of a major portion of the first (*Bāla*) and the whole of the last (*Uttara*) *kāṇḍa* and a few other portions deifying Rāma and were added later, was composed in the fourth or third century B.C. and with all the later interpolations, viz. *Bāla* and *Uttara kāṇḍas* as well all the later accretions deifying Rāma and identifying him with god Vishṇu, it had come into existence by the close of the second century A.D.[4] And the *Mahābhārata*, according to the same authority, cannot have received its present form earlier than the fourth century B.C. and later than the fourth century A.D.[5] These latest dates are highly crucial for our purpose as they show that by the second century A.D. at the latest Rāma had already come to be recognised as an incarnation of god Vishṇu.

The same is indicated by the rich epigraphic and numismatic data. Leaving aside evidence of a general nature which may be interpreted as referring to Rāma as an ideal human being,[5] we may refer here to an important inscription on a stone-slab from the well-known antiquarian site of Kauśāmbī (modern Kosam, Allahabad district, Uttar Pradesh) which has been discovered recently. It provides the most important evidence on Rāma's supreme divinity. The inscription is very fragmentary, and much of its important portion is lost due to the damage to the stone. It purports to record some pious act performed by a *gṛihapati* along with his son named Indraghosha in connection with *Bhagavat* (God) Rāma-Nārāyana. The adjective *bhagavat* being in genitive singular, it is apparent that the intention was probably to record the erection of a shrine of the god or installation of his image or some emblem.[7] The inscription was dated, but a major portion is lost so that we have missed the year, and only the day (*divasa*) remains. It is 10 + 2 = 12. The month may have been *Karttika* as the eleventh day of of the bright half of this month and is/was regarded as very sacred by the Vaishṇavas because of their belief that god Vishṇu wakes up from his four-month-long slumber that day. Following that day, viz. *Kārttika śukla dvādaśī*, is the

*Deptt. of Ancient History and Archaeology, Nagpur University, Nagpur

pāranā or breaking the fast when the *gṛihapati,* whose name is lost, must have performed this pious act. Although the date is lost irretrievably, the paleographic features, the mode of dating and the employment of Prakrit clearly show that the inscription belongs to about the middle of the second century A.D. This record is of inestimable value despite its highly damaged condition for the history of the Rāma cult. For it conclusively establishes that by about mid-second century A.D. Rāma's identity with god Vishṇu-Nārāyaṇa had become deep-rooted in public mind and his independent cult had not only come into existence but had become quite popular. This is very significant as veterans like R.G. Bhandarkar[8] and H.C. Raychaudhuri[9] held that the worship of Rāma, not to speak of a cult in his honour, had not become quite popular even as late as the Gupta age. This notion has now to be substantially modified in the light of this and other evidences to be citeo presently.

Some coins from Mathurā prove the existence of a king named Rāmadatta of the Mathurā region in the second century A.D. at latest.[10] Meaning 'given by Rīma' or 'devoted to Rāma', it is comparable to names like Vishṇudatta and Kṛishṇadatta of Vaishṇavite affiliation current even now. Of equally great significance is the name of the Gupta emperor Rāmagupta, elder brother of Chandragupta II Vikramāditya, which means 'protected by Rāma'. And as the name is normally given by parents, it may be reasonably assumed that at least one of his parents was a devotee of Rāma.

Another evidence of perhaps the greatest importance in this context comes form an unexpected source. It is from a Bāgh (Dhār district, Madhya Pradesh) copper-plate of Mahārāja Bhuluṇḍa, dated in the year 47 published recently[11] but whose value from our viewpoint is being highlighted for the first time here. The record registers the grant of five villages for the performance of the rites called *bali, charu* and *sattra* of the god Vishṇu, who is described as the lord of gods, the demons, the mortals and the serpents, the *bhāgavatā,* sleeping in the ocean, who is put to sleep by the music of the bees inhabiting the lotus blooming out of his navel, who is endowed with eight arms carrying conch shell, arrow, spear, wheel, the sword called Nandaka, a radiate mace, a lance (in seven hands, the eighth arm supporting his head in the Śesha-śayana form), who had broken the pride of Bali, Naraka, Namuchi, the Keśi horse, the Kāliya snake, Daśavadana (Rāvaṇa), Kaṁsa, Chāṇūra, Arishṭā and Siśupāla, who as Varāha (Boar incarnation) retrieved the lost earth, and who is without beginning, middle and end.[12] This is, in fact, the earliest known datable description of the eight-armed Śesha-śāyin (reclining on the primeval snake Śesha or Ananta). What is, however, most interesting from our point of view here is the reference to the demons killed by him. It is interesting to find the 'Ten-headed', viz. Rāvaṇa is included in this list along with Kaṁsa, Śiśupāla etc. It leaves absolutely no doubt that the allusion here is to god Vishnu's incarnations such as Rāma, Kṛishṇa, Varaha, etc. And most interesting for our present purpose is that the eight-armed reclining Vishṇu is credited with all these achievements, showing that Rāma and Kṛishṇa were regarded not just as Vishṇu's incarnations but were identified with Vishṇu. They were verily Vishṇu himself. As regards the date of this epigraph, it was issued in the forty-seventh year of an unspecified reckoning which has been identified variously by different scholars. But the identification with the Gupta era of A.D. 319-20 appears more likely[12]. The inscription, therefore, belongs to about A.D. 366[13] It may thus be concluded that by the third quarter of the fourth century A.D. Rāma had been completely indentified with Vishṇu.

Further, Bhāsa, the well-known Sanskrit dramatist, and Kālidāsa take Rāma's divinity for granted. Kālidāsa is now generally believed to have lived in the Gupta age, though the view placing him in the first century B.C. is also not impossible. And Bhāsa is cited with reverence by Kālidāsa.

As such the available evidence clearly shows that Rāma had come to be treated as divine by the beginning of the Christian era at the latest and the process must have begun much earlier.[14]

Vālmīki, it need hardly be added, associates not only Rāma, son of Daśaratha, but also his predecessors of the Aikshvāku dynasty with Ayodhyā which was their capital. And so does the poet-laureate Kālidāsa in his famed poem *Raghuvaṁśa*. It need hardly be stressed that both as well as the entire Hindu tradition regard Ayodhyā as the place of birth of the hero-turned-god Rāma. As per the accepted date of Vālmikki, this tradition dates from the fourth century B.C. at the latest. It has been a matter of faith with the Hindus just as the birth of Jesus Christ at the site of Church of Nativity at Bethlehem and the association of Prophet Muhammad with Kaba.

Archaeologically it is already well-established that Ayodhyā was well settled in about 800 B.C. And as NBP and ordinary grey ware sherds dating from an earlier period have been found from the surface as well as in the course of levelling in July 1992, an excavation at the lofty mound adjoining the disputed Bābrī Masjid site is likely to yield evidence of a considerably earlier settlement.

Although Ayodhyā had been a seat of several Indian religions like Jainism, Buddhism and various Brāhmanical cults, including Śaivism and Śāktism,[15] it was especially sacred to Vaishṇavas, including those of the Rāma cult. While the excavations have revealed the existence of a huge structure, possibly of a Hindu temple, at the locality where once there stood the disputed structure by revealing the bases of columns in the eleventh-twelfth centuries A.D. levels, we have also definite epigraphic evidence from the Gāhadavāla period.

The Chandrāvatī plates of the Gāhaḍavāla king Chandradeva, dated V.S. 1150 (A.D. 1092-93), inform us that the king visited Ayodhyā and performed various rites, including the worship of god Vāsudeva, i.e. Vishṇu.[16] The Ayodhyāmāhātmya of the *Skanda-purāṇa* (Vrindvana manuscript), dating from about the thirteenth century A.D., refers to an idol called 'Chandrahari' in the Vāsudeva temple at the Svargadvāra *ghāt* at Ayodhyā which was believed to have been installed by Chandra who had come on a pilgrimage to worship Vishṇu.[17] As pointed out by Hans Bakker, who has made a detailed study of Ayodhyā from various angles, here we have a veiled allusion to the construction of the temple or the installation of the image therein by Chandradeva.[18]

Another inscription of Jayachchandradeva, dated A.D. 1184 from Ayodhyā which, *inter alia*, records the construction of a Vaishṇava temple, remains unpublished.[19] As we have seen above, at least from the second century A.D. Rāma had come to be identified with god Vishṇu. Hence we are inclined to believe that the god worshipped by the Gāhaḍavāla kings must have been none else than Rāma himself, at least in so far as Ayodhyā is concerned.

And as if this were not enough, a large rectangular stone-slab (measuring about 5×2 ft.) bearing a twenty-line inscription was recovered on December 6, 1992, from the walls of the so-called Bābrī Masjid which finally established this fact. The inscription is composed in high-flown Sanskrit verse, except for a very small portion in prose, and is engraved in the chaste and classical Nāgari script of the eleventh-twelfth century A.D. It has yet to be fully deciphered, but the portion which have been fully deciphered and read are of great historical significance and value for our purpose here. It was evidently put up on the wall of the temple, the construction of which is recorded in the text inscribed on it. Line 15 of this inscription, for example clearly tells us that a beautiful temple of Vishṇu-Hari, built with heaps of stone (*śilā-saṁhati-grahais)*, and beautified with a golden spire (*hiraṇya-kalaśa-śri-sundaram*) unparallelled by any other temple built by earlier kings (*pūrvvair-apy-akṛitaṁ kṛitaṁ nṛipatibhir)* was constructed. This wonderful temple (*aty-adbhutaṁ)* was built in the temple-city (*vibudh-ālayanī)* of Ayodhyā situated in the Sāketamaṇḍala (district-line 17) showing that Ayodhyā and Sāketa were closely connected, Sāketa being the district of which Ayodhyā was a part. Line 19 describes god Vishṇu as destroying king Bali (apparently in the Vāmana manifestation) and the ten-headed personage (Daśānana, i.e. Rāvaṇa).

Line 20 contains an allusion to the serious threat from the west (*pāśchātya-bhīti)*, apparently posed by Sultan Ibrahim and his son Mahmud of Gazni, and its destruction by the king.

The inscription was composed by the poet Āyushyachandra, son of Alhaṇa. Perhaps he was also the king and as royal poet he is said to have excelled even Sāhasāṅka and Śūdraka (line 16) and is credited with the excavation of tanks and laying wells as well as stepped wells (line 17). In lines 7 and 11 we get a reference to a powerful king named Sallakshaṇa, who, in view of palaeographic considerations and in keeping with the extant information of the history of this period, was perhaps the Chandella king Sallakshaṇavarman who ruled at the end of the eleventh and the beginning of the twelfth century A.D. It is also not impossible that there was another king of this name belonging to some other dynasty.[20] But the inscription certainly proves the building of a magnificent temple of Hari-Vishṅu, the killer of Rāvaṇa, i.e. Rāma.[21]

In the debris of the disputed structure were also found some intact and broken stone images. The former included a very important 3 ft. figure of standing Rāma in the pose called Kodaṇḍa-Rāma iconographically. This image, dating from late 19th century A.D. fashioned of Jaipur marble and painted black and yellow depicts Rāma as holding bow-and-arrow by posture and clearly establishes the fact that Rāma worship continued at this place even after the demolition of the original Hindu temple.

In the so-called Bābrī Masjid itself there has been a very important evidence to indicate that prior to its construction there stood a Hindu temple, apparently the one referred to in the epigraph just mentioned, and that material of the demolished temple had been used in the disputed structure. We have noticed the letter *si* which, palaeographically speaking, belongs to the Nāgarī alphabet of the eleventh-twelfth century A.D.[22] inscribed on a black stone pillar then found fixed at the main gate located below the central dome. And during the levelling work for the building of the Rāma temple in June 1992 was noticed a huge pit which we observed in October 1992, also yielding a lot of evidence for the prior existence of the temple which was demolished to make room for the mosque in the sixteenth century A.D. apparently by Bābar's general Mīr Baqī at his master's orders. This consisted of a number of architectural members and and sculptural fragments found at a depth of some 10 to 12 ft. from the ground level. These included, *inter alia*, several half *āmalakas*, evidently of side spires, stencil-decoration, a pillar capital, a cornice, a floral frieze, a door-jamb, relief sculptures of Vishṇu's incarnations, terracotta figures etc.[23] Then, there are various recessions of the Ayodhyāmāhātmya of the *Skanda-purāṇa,* the oldest of which as noted earlier, goes back to about the thirteenth century A.D.[24] These should suffice to show that Ayodhyā was quite an important holy centre of the Hindus, especially the Vaishṇavas, long before the disputed Bābrī Masjid was erected over the remains of a Vaishnava Hindu shrine.

And even after Bābar built a mosque over the remains of a Hindu temple, the Hindus not only could not and did not forget this humiliation but continued to lay claims to it with their unflinching zeal to regain it,as indicated by the rich Muslim and European references.[24]

NOTES & REFERENCES

1. For divergent traditions on this point, see Ajay Mitra Shastri, *India as seen in the Bṛihatsaṁhitā of Varāhmihira*, Delhi, 1969, pp. 7-11.
2. It has been shown by several scholars that the Rāmopākhyāna of the *Mahābhārata* as well as other allusions (there are as many as eighty-two parallelisms) to the Rāmāyaṇa episodes contained in it at different places are drawn from the *Vālmīkīya Rāmāyaṇa*. Vide V.S. Sukthankar in *Kane Commemoration Volume*, pp. 482-87, quoted by A.D. Pusalkar in his chapter on "The Rāmāyaṇa: Its History and Characters" in *The Cultural Heritage of India*, II, Calcutta, 1962, p. 31. The manner they are cited would show that they had already become proverbial by the time of the composition of the *Mahābhārata*.
3. It is true, of course, that B.B. Lal in his excavations at Ayodhyā could not find any evidence of its existence prior to 800 B.C. See his "Keynote Address" in Sinha B.P. (ed) *Śrīrāma in Art, Archaeology and Literature,* Patna, 1989, pp. 1-11. The Deptt. of Ancient Indian History, Culture and Archaeology, Banaras Hindu University, also in its limited excavations at Ayodhyā had also come across Northern Polished Ware in the lowest layers at Ayodhyā. B.P. Sinha concedes the archaeological position and points out certain contradictions between the literary and archaeological evidences and rightly pleads for more digging at Ayodhyā and other Rāmāyaṇa sites. See *ibid*., pp. 12ff. As we shall see below, there is scope for further work which should take back the antiquity of Ayodhyā much earlier, at least by a few centuries, though that is not of any great value in the present context since the cut-off date is A.D. 1528 when the disputed mosque was built.
4. *History of Indian Literature*, Engl. tr. by Ms. S. Ketkar, Calcutta, 1927, pp. 500-517, where all the evidences in support of this position are discussed at length.
5. *Ibid*., p. 465.
6. For these evidences, see Ajay Mitra Shastri, "Rāma : His Divinity in Literature, Numismatics and Epigraphy", in Nayak BU. *et al* (eds) *New trends in Indian Art and Archaeology*.
7. Shukla B.C., "the Earliest Inscription of Rāma Worship", in Choudhury R.D. and Shri Bhagwan Singh, (Eds) *Studies in Indian History and Culture (Kanklal Barua Commemoration Volume),* Ramanand Vidya Bhavan, Delhi, 1990, pp. 207-12. The text of the inscription runs as under:

   ... *divase 10 2 gahapati* ....

   .... *saha dārakena Īddaghosena* ....

   ..... *bhagavato Rāma-Nārāyaṇa* ....

   We don't agree with B.C. Shulka on certain points relating to interpretation and here we have given our own interpretation.

8. Collected Works of Sir R. G. Bhandarkar, IV, Pune, 1929, p. 67.
9. *Materials for the Study of the Early History of Vaishṇava Sect.*. 2nd ed., Calcutta, 1936, p. 174.
10. For his coins, see J. Allan, *Catalogue of Indian Coins in the British Museum: Coins of Ancient India*, London, 1936, pp. cx, 179-81, pl. XXIV, 5-14.
11. Ramesh K.V. and Tewari S.P., *A Copper-plate Hoard of the Gupta Period from Bagh, Madhya Pradesh*, New Delhi- Mysore, 1990, p. 1, text-lines, 1-5:

    Bhagavataḥ sur-āsura-nar-oraga-guroḥ amara-vara-ripu-rudhira-sṛita-śara-prasarasy-aikārṇṇava-vipula-vimala-paryyaṅka-tala-śāyinaḥ nābhi-sambhav-āravinda-shaṭpad-opagīyamāna-nidrasya śaṅkha-bāṇa-śakti-chakra-nandaka-jvalāṅgad-āgra-śūla-bhāsvar-āshṭa-bāhu-śālinaḥ Bali-Naraka-Namuchi-vara-turaga-bhujaga-Daśavadana-Kaṁs-Chāṇuūr-Ārishṭa-Śiśupāla-darppa-mathanasya sura-gaṇ-ālaṅkarishṇos-trailokya prabhavishṇor-asura-gaṇa-jishṇor-Vvishṇoḥ.
12. *Ibid.*, Introduction, pp. vii-viii.
13. However, according to Mirashi, the records of the Mahārāja Valkhā are to be dated in the Kalachuri-Chedi era commencing A.D. 249-50 his *Inscriptions of the Kalachuri-Chedi Era*, CII, IV, Ootacamund, 1955, pp. 6, 9, 11. If this view were to be accepted, the record would date from A.D. 297-98.
14. Some scholars are inclined to date Bhāsa as early as fifth-fourth century B.C. See A.D. Pusalkar, *Bhāsa - A Study*, 2nd ed., Delhi, 1968, pp. 63ff. For other evidences of an early belief in the divinity of Rāma, see our paper "Rāma: His Divinity: in Literature, Numismatics and Epigraphy", in Nayak B.U. *et al.* (ed). *New Trends in Indian Art and Archaeology*, S.R. Rao 70th Year Festschrift.
15. For this evidence, see Hans Bakker, *Ayodhyā*, Egbert Fosten, Groningen, 1986, Ch. II.
16. *EI*, XIV, pp. 193ff.; also Hans Bakker, *op. cit.*, p. 51.
17. *Ibid.*, p. 52.
18. *Ibid.*, This plate is now in the possession of the State Museum, Lucknow.
19. This was observed for the first time by a team of renowned archaeologists during its visit to Ayodhyā in October 1992. The credit of inviting attention to this important evidence is due to Shri R.C. Agrawal, formerly Director, Archaeology and Museums, Rajasthan. The letter might stand for the auspicious word *siddham* or might be a mason's mark. Ths letter also occurs on a black stone pillar still standing in a small triangular park located near the Military Hospital, in the Cantt. area of the township of Faizabad. It was apparently shifted here from Rama Janmabhumi area in the late 19th century.
20. The credit of deciphering and interpreting this inscription goes to Dr. T.P. Verma, Dr. A.K. Singh and myself.
21. Hans Bakker, *op. cit.*
22. The inscription may substantially contribute to our knowledge of the dynastic history of early medieval India.
23. This information is based on some extracts of the record made available to us by Dr. Sudha Malaiya of Bhopal. There may be some minor changes when the record is fully deciphered, but the fact of the construction of a magnificent Vaishṇava temple during the eleventh-twelfth century is indisputably established.
24. We are thankful to our colleague Dr. Chandrashekhar Gupta for collecting some of the data on this issue and providing them to me.

Taj Mahal –Some Issues of Conservation

O. P. Agrawal*

The preservation of Taj Mahal has been a matter of great concern to the whole world, particularly after the setting up of the Oil Refinery at Mathura, because it was feared that the emission of pollution from the Mathura Refinery may have a serious adverse effect of the marble on the Taj Mahal. It is true that, in course of time, the white marble of the Taj Mahal acquired somewhat yellowish appearance. Several scientists ascribed yellowing of the white marble to the pollutants emitted by the Oil Refinery. It was also observed that there were cracks at various places in the marble slabs fitted on the walls of the great monument. These cracks were also seen by many as a result of the effect of pollution from the Refinery. Reports appeared in newspapers that the Taj Mahal was threatened by the Mathura Oil Refinery and it should be closed down. Some scientists described the black spots on Taj as 'cancer' and probably in a bid for sensational news, opined that the Taj Mahal was suffering from 'stone cancer', although what does the term 'stone-cancer' means was not explained.

These statements unfortunately, were not based on any in-depth scientific studies on the nature of the deterioration, on the behaviour of the materials and the role of pollution and other factors in such a deterioration. These days 'pollution' seems to have become a catchword which attracts immediate world-wide attention and the situation at Taj Mahal is no exception.

2. *Varadarajan Expert Committee*

On account of the apprehensions that were expressed about the possible ill-effect of the effluents from the Oil refinery on the monuments in the Agra-Mathura Region, particularly on the Taj Mahal, the Government of India constituted in 1974 an Experts' Committee under the chairmanship of Dr. S. Varadarajan, at that time Chairman of the India Petrochemicals Ltd.[1] The Committee was formed to advise the project authorities of the Mathura Refinery on the measures to be taken by it for keeping the pollution effect to the absolute minimum. The Committee was not only to guide the Mathura Refinery project in planning and implementing effective pollution control measures, but also to advise the Government of India on the pollution aspects of other units in the area. Initially, representatives of the Ministrý of Petroleum and Chemicals, National Environmental Engineering Research Institute, Nagpur; National Committee on Environmental Planning and Coordination; Indian Institute of Petroleum, Dehra Dun, Meteorological Department and representative of the Government of Uttar Pradesh were nominated as members of the Expert Committee. Managing Director, Indian Oil Refinery, was its Member Secretary. Later, from December 1975, a representative of the Archaeological Survey of India was also nominated as a member. Afterwards, Dr. B. B. Lal, retired Chief Chemist, Archaeological Survey of India, at the instance of the Committee, was appointed as its Consultant.

The Committee instituted a number of studies considered essential for its recommendations. These studies which were in several spheres, have mainly been the following:

a. Existing levels of pollution in the Agra region.

These studies were conducted by NEERI for a period from 19th Nov. 1975 to March 1977. It was

*The Indian National Trust for Art and Cultural Heritage, A-1/11, Sector B, Aliganj Scheme, Lucknow - 226 020.

found that the sulphur dioxide content in the atmosphere was negligible.

b. Studies on the effluents from the Refinery

These studies were conducted by specialists of Tecnco, Italy[2] and the results are briefly mentioned in Section 3 below.

c. Present status of the monuments at Agra

These studies were also conducted by Tecneco of Italy.

3. *Scientific Studies by Tecneco*

The most significant part of the Varadarajan Committee's work was the scientific study by Tecneco.[3] Tecneco Experts collected samples from different places in various monuments of Agra. Pieces of old marble and other stones which were removed from the monument for previous conservation work were also used by them for scientific studies. They also collected samples of marble and sandstone from the original quarries at Makarana in Jaipur. They conducted petrographic, chemical and physical analysis on the samples. Superficial layers of marble were analysed by X-ray diffraction, chemically and microscopically. They came to the conclusion that *the major cause of alteration at Taj was biological. Presence of soluble salts was found to be extremely low. Sulphate, a sign of the effect of pollution, was not found to be present.*

Among the soluble salts, the percentage of chloride was larger.

Biological investigations indicated that both marble and sandstone were similarly altered by black spots. This type of alteration is attributed to multiplication of microscopic algae which are also accompanied by decomposing organisms or atleast using their organic and inorganic remains. Algae responsible for black spots was generally found to be blue-green algae, i.e. cynophiceae. Since this type of algae has pigments they can survive even in low light conditions. The major portion of the algae that was determined by Tecneco specialists is of covering and corrosive type, because of action of their constituents, like Oxalic and Muramic acids. These forms can cause disintegration and splitting of the stone. Other forms are able to fix atmospheric nitrogen components which are used by nitrobacteria, causing further corrosion attack. This type of attack, however, was not noticed in the Taj at that time.

The Tecneco specialists also monitored the air quality and also measured meteorological parameters like air temperature, inside and outside monuments, and their surface temperature. Their finding was also that pollution in the atmosphere was not every high.

On the basis of their experiments and analysis of data of a large variety it was stated that the state of conservation of the marble was 'good' but on the other hand, the sandstone did not appear to be in good condition, mainly because of the natural causes of deterioration. Alterations both in the marble and the sandstone were assigned to algae. It may be mentioned that the main thrust of Tecneco studies was towards the likely effect of pollution and so other types of deteriorations were not dealt with by them in any great detail.

4. *Varadarajan committee Recomendations*

The Varadarajan Committee considered all the reports submitted to it and gave some far-reaching recommendations.[4] The important ones were :

a. Effort should be made to minimize the existing pollution from sources close to the monuments in the Agra Zone by various means like replacement of present locomotives with diesel-based ones, and removal of thermal power station.
b. Steps should be taken to ensure that no new industry which can cause pollution be located north-west of the Taj Mahal. Also the existing small industries, particularly the foundries, may be relocated in the area south-east of Agra beyond Taj Mahal. No large industry in the Agra region and its neighborhood be established without conducting detailed studies.
c. An appropriate authority be created which should monitor emissions by industries as well as air quality at Agra on a continuous basis.
d. Periodic scientific studies be conducted to ensure that the monuments at Agra are not affected further from the pollution or from any other cause.
e. Studies should be undertaken to explore the possibility of protecting the monuments by measures such as provision of a green belt in and around the Agra region between Mathura and Agra.
f. Use of coal by the Refinery power-plant should be deferred till such time as suitable technologies have been found to be satisfactorily in use elsewhere. There should be a minimum of 3 monitoring sta-

tions beyond ten kilometres from the Refinery in the direction of Agra at suitable intervals.

The report of the Varadarajan Committee was extremely important as it went into detailed examination of the effort of pollution on the Taj Mahal. Most of these recommendations have already been carried out. But the question remains whether it will solve the problem in its totality.

5. *Other studies*

The Department of Environment appointed a Committee under the Chairmanship of Prof. J. M. Dave, Head of the Department of Environmental Sciences at the Jawaharlal Nehru University, to prepare a report on the effect of atmospheric pollution on the Agra monuments. The main aim of the Committee was to find out the threshold values of various pollutants in the atmosphere that could be said to be the tolerance-limits of marble against their effects.[5]

The National Environmental Engineering Research Institute, Nagpur and the Science Branch of the Archaeological Survey of India have been engaged in the monitoring of pollution levels in Agra.

The Department of Environment also supported some projects for the study of air pollution on the Taj Mahal. Out of these projects, we are aware of two, namely programme being done at the Shriram Institute for Industrial Research, Delhi and the other at the Birla Archaeological and Cultural Research Institute, Hyderabad. The work at the Shriram Institute was concerned with the laboratory studies on weathering of marble, attack of mineral acids on marble, damage by sulphur dioxide on marble. The project also intended to study the effect of polymeric coatings on marble.[6]

The project being pursued at the Birla Institute, Hyderabad concerned itself with the development of an Infrared Spectrophotometer for monitoring of the effect of sulphur dioxide on marble. In fact it did not have a direct bearing on the Taj Mahal.[7]

The report entitled 'Taj Mahal : Some Problems of Environmental Monitoring and Weathering Studies' presented by Dr. B.B. Lal at the Seminar on Environmental Pollution held at Rome in 1984 is also a significant contribution.[8]

B.N. Tandon, Director (Science), Archaeological Survey of India, had conducted analysis of marble, plaster, mortar, etc. of the Taj Mahal[9]. However, his reports have not been published yet.

M. Aslam of the Central Building Research Institute, Roorkee has studied the characteristics of mortar and plaster of Taj Mahal.[10]

Aslam[11] conducted detailed physico-chemical, petrographic, infrared and SEM studies on the deteriorated lime plaster of the Taj, but he did not find any evidence of degradation due to sulphur dioxide.

6. *Experts Committee of the Archaeological Survey of India*

It will thus be seen that the terms of reference of the Varadarajan Committee were limited and so it looked at the question of the conservation of the Taj Mahal only from the point of view, and that was: the effect of pollution either from the Oil Refinery or from other sources; it did not look at the totality of the problem which is influenced by other factors as well. Most other studies were also largely limited to the potential effect of pollution on Taj Mahal. It was, therefore, a most welcome step when the Government of India appointed a Task Force under the chairmanship of the Secretary (Culture) to overview the situation at the Taj. This Task Force was appointed as a result of an alarming Report by Dr. Rohtagi, Director of the Regional Research Laboratory, Bhopal, submitted to the Government of India on the effect of pollution on the Taj.[12] This report went to the extent of suggesting to coat the Taj with a resin, imported from the U.S.A., to make it water-proof. On the instructions of the high-powered Task Force, the Archaeological Survey of India appointed an Experts Committee to look into all aspects of deterioration and preservation of the Taj Mahal. The Experts Committee was divided into three Working Groups, of which one was to study the deterioration of the material of the Taj Mahal in order to determine the causes of its alteration and the author of this paper was nominated to be its coordinator. The Working Group immediately took up the task and started to collect data on Taj Mahal. We thought that if we look at the problem only from the point of view of the effect of pollution, we start with a predetermined premise and may therefore, reach a wrong conclusion. We, therefore, wanted to keep an open mind and look at the problem afresh from all points of view and not from the angle of pollution.

7. *Studies conducted by the national research laboratory for conservation of cultural property*

7.1 TYPES OF DETERIORATION

Our approach was that in order to understand the phenomenon of deterioration of Taj Mahal, we should first of all overview the different types of deterioration which are observed in the monument. We visited Taj Mahal several times for visual examination, analysis of deterioration and documentation of the observed deterioration. During these visits, the following main types of changes were noticed:

1. Discolouration of the surface – either uniformly or in spots.
2. Breaking of marble slab edges.
3. Formation of cracks in the marble slabs.
4. Bulging of marble slabs.
5. Pitting or erosion of marble surface in some areas.

These different types of alterations were studied by us singly, and in each case an attempt was made to ascertain its root cause so that it can be eliminated at that level. These studies were carried out in the main marble structure and did not include the case of sandstone.

7.2 TYPES OF STUDIES AND THEIR AIMS

The studies undertaken by us included:

1. Chemical analysis to identify the elements present in the marble samples by emission spectrograph, atomic absorption spectrophotometer and microchemical techniques.
2. Mineralogical studies by X-ray diffraction.
3. Analysis of surface accretions by microchemical methods, X-ray diffraction and infrared spectrophotometer.
4. Porosity by mercury porosimeter.
5. Climatic measurements, on a limited scale, for relative humidity and temperature values – inside and outside the monument.
6. Evaluation of methods for cleaning the surface of the marble.
7. Testing to record the adverse effect of atmospheric pollution on marble.
8. Study of the crack-formation patterns, if any, and their types.
9. Determination of soluble salts present in marble.
10. Analysis of the dust accumulated at various places on the surface and on the floors of the Taj.

The goal that we set for ourselves was more practical-oriented than theoretical. Thus, we wanted to find answers to some of the problems of major concern, namely:

i. Nature of various types of discolouration on the marble surface.

ii. Why discolouration is taking place? Was it due to pollution or due to some other cause or causes?

iii. Development of techniques for cleaning the surface of the marble without using hard brushes which are commonly employed for this purpose.

iv. Determine causes of formation of cracks in the marble slabs.

v. Ascertain the effect of atmospheric pollution on the Taj Mahal marble

7.3 DISCOLOURATION

The marble used for Taj Mahal is white, but some slabs have spots or streaks of different natural colours on account of the presence of mineral impurities. It was being observed for some time that the white marble of Taj Mahal was getting discoloured. A matter of great concern was the appearance of a yellowish layer over the white marble, particularly in the niches and arches. This type of yellowing and discolouration of the marble surface were taking several forms, like :

i. Uniform yellowing of the surface, particularly inside the niches and the arches.

ii. Blackish accretions on the cenotaph and on the walls of the gallery inside the monument.

iii. Yellow-grey deposits on the brackets used on *minars*.

iv. Brown rust like stains.

v. Brown spots.

vi. Green-black deposits in small dots.

vii. Black patches due to algal growth.

We tried to ascertain the causes of each of these alterations. The results are discussed below:

7.3.1 *General yellowing of the marble surface*

It was generally observed that the walls of the large niches have acquired somewhat yellowish appearance, particularly on their upper portions, while those parts which receive rain appear cleaned. Micro-samples from these yellow deposits were collected by us and analyzed. Their X-ray diffraction did not show anything except calcium carbonate (which is from marble), silica and clay. In none of the samples any sulphate could be detected. One of the reasons for the yellow appearance seems to be a deposit of dirt which does not get washed by rain water.

We also wanted to ascertain whether the yellowing could be on account of any type of coatings that might have been applied for preservation in the past. Ten samples from different places were collected on cotton swabs soaked in organic solvents. Identification of resins was done by infrared spectrophotometer. Specular-reflectance technique was used for identification. Simultaneously, Infrared spectra of several known resins were also prepared. It was seen that spectra of the samples from the Taj Mahal matched with the spectrum of polymethyl methacrylate, or "Perspex" sheet, which is also an acrylic resin. All the collected samples gave similar results. Polymethyl methacrylate and polyvinyl acetate are the two resins most popular as preservative coatings for monuments.[13] Solution of polymethyl methacrylate is transparent when applied, but it acquires a yellowish colour after sometime. We, therefore, surmised that the general yellowing was either on account of the deposit of dirt or due to the alteration of the resin, which seemed to have been applied on the marble surface as a preservative.

7.3.2 *Blackish greasy spots on marble*

We discovered that at various places, there was a black oily looking layer on the marble, mainly on the lower portions of the walls inside the building, on the cenotaph and on some other areas which are constantly touched by visitors. In order to determine the nature of these marks we tried several analytical techniques. We found that these accretions were insoluble in water, but with organic solvents it is completely dispersed, leaving a slightly blackish residue, resembling soil. On ignition, it burns easily, leaving small amounts of similar powdery residue. It can, thus, be safely said that this type of black accretion is due to hand grease.

7.3.3 *Yellowing/Blackening of Brackets in the Minarets*

The brackets used for supporting the balcony of minarets have also yellowed in general and have blackened in some areas. Some places were having a uniform blackish deposit and the rest were yellowish. Small samples were collected by us and analysed for elements present, for minerals by X-ray diffraction analysis and ignition test. The sample did not burn off on ignition but turned reddish in colour. The qualitative analysis by emission spectrography confirmed the presence of aluminium, silica and iron. This indicated that the surface dirt was a deposit of soil. Black colour was possibly on account of algae.

7.3.4 *Brown Stains*

There are brown stains at various places on the surface of the Taj. According to our experiments these brown stains are on account of two main causes:

a. Rusting of the iron dowels or clamps used for fixing the marble slabs in position. These iron clamps when exposed get rusted and this rust flows down with rain water and gets deposited on the marble.

b. Iron minerals present in the marble

There always are some mineral impurities present in the stone which also undergo chemical changes due to the contact with moisture. Thus, the iron minerals present in marble are converted into iron salts producing brown stains on atmospheric oxidation.

7.3.5 *Small black spots on marble*

Some black dot-like spots were also noticed on the surface of the marble, particularly on the north side towrds the Yamuna river. Presence of these spots was perplexing and in the beginning we were at a loss to understand how they have been formed. Later, we discovered an unexpected cause of the formation of such black spots and that was a dense deposit of mosquito excreta on the marble surface. (Fig. 1) The cool northern side of the monuments is apparently a very good resting place for mosquitoes, particularly during the summer. It seems that the stagnating water on the bank of the river forms a good breeding ground for mosquitoes and during summer, swarms of mosquitoes rest on the lower portions of the monument. These form a greenish accretion which later turns black.

7.3.6 *Blackish patches due to algal Growth*

In some areas of the monument, there are black spots which can be attributed to the growth of algae. This type of deterioration, however, is limited to some areas, particularly these which remain wet for long periods.

7.4 BREAKING OF THE EDGES OF THE MARBLE SLABS

In several places, it was noticed that the edges of several marble slabs have chipped off and in some places marble pieces have broken near the joints of the slabs. These types of deterioration can never be on account of pollution. According to our observation, this phenomenon may be attributed to the combined effect of chemical and physical weathering, the main agent responsible for chemical weathering being water which dissolves or dissociates the stone constituents.

Some types of chipping, particularly in the lower portions of the marble samples, we feel, have been produced, due to the weight of one slab over the other. The weight of each slab is very high and when several of them rest one over the other, the total weight is tremendous. We also observed that the lower portions of some of the lowermost slabs resting on the platform of the outside niches have chipped off extensively. At these points, rain water accumulates and the bottom edge of the slabs resting there, remains wet for considerably long periods of time. Prolonged action of water weakens these portions and chipping takes place. In these areas algae is also present.

Another cause for breaking of the marble is on account of the rusting of dowels used for joining marble slabs and consequent increase in their size.

7.5 FORMATION OF CRACKS IN MARBLE SLABS

7.5.1 *Causes of Cracks*

Cracks of varying types and magnitude are seen on the Taj marble veneer. Though most of them appear to be superficial, some of them are quite deep, and in some cases they are extending beyond one slab. However, it is observed that cracks on minarets are fewer than on the mausoleum. Also there are fewer cracks on the upper part of the dome than on the lower side.

Formation of the cracks could be attributed to the following possible factors:

a. Inherent defects in the stone developed due to residual stress at the time of quarrying, trimming, etc.
b. Effect of the weight of the marble slabs placed above.
c. Shift in the foundation level.
d. Chemical weathering due to water.
e. Insolation weathering.

There are different types of cracks present in the Taj marble. The main ones are described below:

7.5.2 *Vertical Cracks*

There are some 'line cracks' present all over the monument. Most of the cracks have developed on the marble veneer along vertical plain and they appear to be superfical. First, we thought that the difference of temperature between day and night might be causing a stress on this stone and thus producing stress, resulting in the formation of cracks.[14] However, if that was so, stone cracks would have appeared in the horizontal, vertical and other directions equally. But that is not happening. We know that when a rock is under compressive stress, it may fail by induced brittle fracture and cracks will develop parallel to the direction of stress.[16] We, therefore, postulated that these vertical cracks in the Taj mable could be due to the downward pressure exerted by the slabs placed above. We also observed that these cracks are present not only on the outside but also in the inner part of the building. Our other observation was that there are more cracks on the lower side of the walls than on the upper side. We also perceived that in most examples, the marble slabs fitted on the floors, that is the ones which are horizontal and do not carry any weight on them, are not showing cracks. These observations indicate that the weight of the heavy slabs is mainly contributing to the formation of cracks in the slabs.

7.5.3 *Cracks due to mineral veins*

In marble, mineral impurities are quite often present as veins, as can be seen on many slabs in the Taj. At several places these mineral impurities have got preferentially leached by rain water leading to the formation of cracks.

7.5.4 *Cracks due to iron dowels*

Dowels and clamps that were used on the Taj Mahal to support the marble veneer, when exposed, get rusted due to oxidation and thus exert pressure on the marble, resulting in crack formation.

7.5.5 *Cracks near replaced portions*

Sometimes it becomes necessary to replace highly

deteriorated portions of marble slabs. When the replaced portion fits too tightly, it may exert pressure on the surrounding areas poducing cracks in the surface. This type of crack formation is also seen in the Taj at several places.

7.6 BULGING OF SLABS

7.6.1 *Causes of bulging*

It was observed in the Taj Mahal that at some points marble slabs have bulged and it is likely to cause extensive damage. According to our analysis this may be on account of two factors:

a) Plastic deformation:

In stone slabs, plastic deformation is caused due to intergranular movement on glide planes or gliding along twining planes.[17] Deformation due to stress relief also produces similar effects. Water which seeps behind the slabs hastens the process. In such places where the slab is distorted, a gap develops between the brick wall and the middle portions of the slab which allows continuous entry of water inside.

b) Bulging due to iron dowels:

If iron dowel corrodes and swells the portion of the slab over the dowel bulges and it finally breaks off (Fig. 2) This phenomnon has particularly been noted on a number of points on the walls of the central hall.

7.7 EROSION OF MARBLE SURFACE

On some slabs, formation of pits or erosion of the surface is noticed. However, this type of deterioration is located only at a very few areas. In some slabs, pitting in the form of a long continuous band, running from top to bottom, has been formed (Fig. 3). Our observation was that this type of erosion-formation is more prominent in the areas which are directly under water spouts from which rain water falls on the slabs (Fig. 4). Rain water carried through the spouts, falls on the marble, flows over it and causes physical and chemical erosion. In this process, some part of the marble is leached out. The physical impact of the rain water also is a cause for this type of erosion. It was also observed that algae was growing more in the area below the drains. It is also well known that the area of the stone once eroded, becomes more vulnerable to weathering than the other areas.

8 *Report of UNESCOexperts*

It will not be out of place to mention that two Unesco Experts, Dr. Marissa Tabasso and Dr. Maurizio Marabelli[18] were invited by the Government of India in January 1987 to visit the Taj Mahal and provide advice on measures to be taken for its conservation. These experts reached the same conclusion, as were reached by us at NRLC.[19]

9 *Conclusion*

From the above studies it will be seen that apart from the atmospheric pollution, which at present plays a very minimal role, there are so many other factors for the alterations and deterioration of the monumental structure of the Taj Mahal. Control of atmospheric pollution, either from the Mathura Oil Refinery, or from locomotives, or from the local factories and foundries, although extremly important and desirable, is not going to solve the entire problem. Pollution is only one aspect and one factor of deterioration and it should not be thought that by shifting the factories from the Agra area, while fully justified, the battle against other agencies of deterioration has also been won. All the processes of deterioration have to be tackled in order to be able to save this unique marvel of world heritage. In order to reach to some final conclusion, many more studies are required, not only pertaining to the environmental pollution, but also to all other factors which are causing damage to the Taj.

10 *Acknowledgements*

The studies described above were done by me when I was the Director of the NRLC. Dr. Tej Singh and Dr. K. K. Jain, carried out experiments on stone behaviour, and Mr. B.V. Kharbade and Joshi analyzed the yellow accretions on marble. I am grateful to all of them. I also like to thank Dr. M.V. Nair, Director, NRLC for allowing the use of photogaphs from NRLC Photo Division. All the photographs were done by Anil Risal Singh, Sr. Photographer, NRLC, to whom also I express my thanks.

REFERENCES

1. *Report of the Export Committee on Environmental Impact of Mathura Refinery, Dec. 1977.*
2. *Studies for the Preservation of monuments in Agra from Mathura Refinery air pollution.* Third Report, TECNECO. Italy (1976)
3. *Ibid.*
4. *Report of the Expert Committee on Environmental Impact of Mathura Refinery, (Dec 1977),* pp. 27-30.
5. Dave J.M., Key note address. National Seminar on Effect of Atmospheric Pollutants on Monuments, Lucknow, 1986.
6. Report on 'Air Pollutants Effect on Historical Monuments' submitted to the Department of Environment by Shriram Institute for Industrial Research, Delhi (1985)
7. Ganorkar, M.C. and Reddy, M.B., *Studies on pollution profile of Taj Mahal,* National Seminar on Effect of Atmospheric Pollutants on Monuments, Lucknow, 1986.
8. Lal, B.B., "Taj Mahal - Some problems of environmental monitoring and Weathering Studies." Rome Conference (1984)
9. Tandon, B.N., "Comprehensive researches on the effect of weathering, pollutants e.g. SO_2 and particulates on the marble of Taj at Agra," A Report submitted to the Archaeological Survey of India.
10. Aslam, M., "Characterisation of ancient mortar and plaster - A Report" submitted to ICCROM, Rome (1986)
11. Aslam, M. "Studies on Taj Mahal Plasters", *Studies in Conservation,* 35 (1990) pp. 102-106.
12. Rohtagi, P.K., Raju, C.B., Ray A.K., Modi, O.P. and Rao, U.M., "Materials damage and research imperatives at Taj Mahal, A Report" submitted to the Government of India (1984).
13. Agrawal, O.P., Singh, Tej Singh, Jain, Kamal K., Kharbade, B.V., Joshi, G.P. "Studies on Materials of Taj Mahal" (A report submitted to the Archaeological Survey of India, Nov 1986).
14. Tandon, B.N., "Stone in Indian monuments and other art objects - Problems in its conservation," *Conservation of Cultural Property in India,* 13, 17 (1980)
15. Winkler, E.M., *Stone: Properties, durability in Man's Environment,* Springer-Verlag, Vienna (1975), p. 172.
16. Ollier, C., *Weathering,* (Longman, London, 1984), p. 11.
17. *Ibid.* 15, p. 57
18. Tabasso, M, and Marabelli, Maurizo, Report on Conservation of Taj Mahal, (Submitted to the Archaeological Survey of India, 1987)
19. Agrawal, O.P. "Further Studies on Materials of Taj Mahal, (Part II)". Report submitted to the Archaeological Survey of India, January 1988.

NOTES AND NEWS

Excavations at Golbai Sasan, Dist. Puri, Orissa

In 1961 B.K. Thapar undertook excavations at Kuchai and Baidipur, both in Mayurbhanj District. At Kuchai 4 trenches, each measuring 6′ × 12′, were dug upto a depth of 1.2 m. Deposits belonging to the Mesolithic and the Neolithic, were encountered. The upper one measuring 40 to 45 cm and composed of clayey deposit yielded neolithic artefacts, such as polished stone axes in association with a coarse grit tempered red ware, sometimes also slipped and showing incised or finger-tip decorations. No clear date is available from Kuchai but a Thermoluminiscence date of *circa* 1000 B.C. is reported. According to this the neolithic culture in this region appears to be late. Baidipur has also produced a similar evidence, alongwith the significant evidence of domesticated rice.

Shankar-junga, in Dhenkanal District, excavated by the Department of Archaeology, Government of Orissa, produced polished stone celts in association with hand-made pottery. Some of the celts are quite narrow but large in size, and have thus been described by the excavator as bar-celts. However, nothing is known about the related material or dates, if any obtained.

At Manamunda in Sambalpur District, excavated by the Sambalpur University, evidence of chalcolithic period has been noticed, which is succeeded by a period in which megalithic pottery and iron are present.

These attempts have contributed significantly in narrowing down the "dark age"; still two things remain clear: (a) southern Orissa largely remains unexplored, as all the previous work was confined to the northern region, and (b) no evidence of copper or bronze age settlements has been recorded from Orissa.

Surface explorations at village Golbai Sasan in Puri District of Orissa conducted in 1987 yielded polished stone tools and pottery akin to the Neolithtic Chalcholithic cultures of the northern region. Some bone pieces picked up during explorations showed secondary working on their edges. A trial trench taken at the site, in 1991, besides confirming the evidence of the presence of neolithic and 'chalcolithic'pottery, showed the presence of a full-fledged bone tool industry consisting of points, burins, scrapers, digging tools, and one single harpoon carved on an antler. No metal was found but the composition of deposits and pottery clearly indicated two distinct horizons of occupation.

Golbai Sasan, Lat 20° 01'N and Long 83° 33′0°E, is located in the laterite zone and is situated on the left bank of river Mandakini, a tributary of River Daya which flows into the Chilikha lake. The mound, locally known as Mabi Dhipa, is of considerable size and has been cut into two parts by a cart-track, going south across the river.

During the excavations conducted in 1991–92, seven trenches, were laid on the northern slopes of the mound and were dug upto different depths, depending upon the level of the natural soil as well as structural remains needed to be preserved. Excavations revealed that the total deposit at the site was around 8 m and was practically undisturbed.

On the basis of the materials obtained from the excavations , the sequence of cultures has been worked out as under:

Period I	Neolithic
Period II A	Chalcolithic
Period II B	Iron Age

Seven carbon samples collected from various levels have been sent to PRL, Ahmedabad, for Radiocarbon dating and the results are awaited.

Period I- Neolithic

A very small area, belonging to this period, in Trench B could be exposed. Consisting of 4 layers, sitting over the natural soil, the total depth of this deposit, was a little more than one metre. It appears that a filling of clay, sloping from north to south, separated the neolithic deposit from the chalcolithic deposit of the succeeding period. The layers were generally composed of compact clay of blackish, dull red and bluish colours and traces of several post-holes and floor levels were noticed.

No stone or bone tools were met with but one or two pieces of bone with working marks on them were found alongwith some partially mineralized bones and antlers. The pottery was hand-made, showing cord and reed impressions, although some sherds indicated that slow-wheel or turn-table techniques were also used. The pots were mostly vases in dull red and grey wares. In the eastern part of the trench, a structure of unshaped stones on a bed of rammed clay was noticed. Traces of this structure were also noticed in the rain gullies, further south.

Period IIA-Çhalcholithic

The excavated area, belonging to this period, and covering seven trenches, was 175 sq. m. The total deposit was about 5 m divisible in 14 layers. A large number of stone tools and implements of bone and copper were recovered alongwith other antiquities of terracotta and faience. In the upper levels, floors of laterite *murrum* and reddish clay with post-holes were met with; hand-made pots, possibly for storage purposes, were found placed on these floors.

In the lower levels, remains of circular huts with post-holes and hearths were noticed. A total of 13 huts were found. The diameter of these huts varied from 3.90 m to 7.90 m. The biggest hut, possibly served as a community hut; alternately could be the hut of the head of the settlement. In majority of the examples, the central area of the hut had a floor of dull reddish clay and boundary of yellowish clay; in two examples, however, greyish clay formed the boundry.

In the upper layer of this period an extended burial was found; the head and the portion of legs below the ankles were missing. On the wrist of the skeleton, a copper bangle was found. Other copper antiquities consisted of a chisel, a few rings, and a fishhook.

Polished stone tools consisted of celts, adzes, chisels, and one tool-edge polisher. Some querns were also found. A beautiful shouldered celt was found embeded in a compact clay floor of yellow colour. A thin film of yellowish clay was found firmly deposited all over the shouldered celt, which clearly indicated that the celt belonged to an earlier level, the mid-level, of the Chalcolithic. Two microlithic tools, one blade and one backed knife-blade, were the only other stone tools.

Bone tools were recovered in quite good numbers. These were both polished and unpolished, crude and developed types. The tools were made on antlers, semi-mineralised bones of humped cattle, sheep and goat. In most of the cases bones were charred in order to give strength to the tools. Tool-types include points, burins, chisels, digging tools, adze, needles, long points (about 27 cm in length) blades, denticulated blades, arrow-heads and one harpoon with a single row of barbs.

It may be added here that three long points or spears, measuring abbout 27 cm in length and made on antler, were found embeded, in pieces, in a lump, in a floor of red *murrum* belonging to upper level of Period II A. It, therefore, appears that those points may have, in reality, belonged to an earlier phase.

Amongst other antiquities of bone were pendants and ear-studs. Some small beads of faience were amongst the other ornaments found.

The terracottas included sling balls, some spindle-whorls and one crude human figurine. One spindle whorl showed the remains of a wooden shaft.

The pottery was hand-made, although some wheel-made specimens were also found and appeared to be well developed. Pottery produced by slow -wheel or on turn-table technique were also noticed. Black-and-red ware, mostly hand-made, unpainted and with some unusual shapes, was noticed throughout the period. Other wares met with were red ware, dull red ware, burnished black ware, burnished chocolate coloured ware. Post-firing paintings in red ochre were seen on several examples; the paintings were confined to necks and lips. These decorations consisted of vertical and oblique strokes and hatched triangles. The shapes commonly met with were vases, bowls, pots with carination at the waist, dishes, lids, jars and dishes-on-stand. The uncommon shape met with was a tumbler with slightly out-curved sides and featureless rim and a cut disc base, i.e. there was a recess between the base and the body. The shape was found only in black-and-red ware, and the pot was hand-made. Besides these shapes, miniature pots, about 5 cm in height, with featureless rim and curved base, were found from all levels of the period. These miniature pots were found in fairly good number and possibly were used as crucibles for smelting copper. Charred grains collected from the deposits of this period showed the presence of rice and *kulthi*, a coarse cereal. A detailed report on botanical studies is awaited.

Period II B – Iron Age

The deposit, a little over 1 m, belonging to this period , was confined to three top layers. The material recovered from this level was hardly different from the material found in the preceding level. The only difference lies in the fact that now iron also appears on the scene. One iron tool, resembling a polished celt in shape, was, however, the only discovery of its kind. It is possible that there were other examples too but so far we have not found them. Or else, it was imported here from some neighbouring iron-using site.

An examination of the iron celt shows that the knowledge of iron working was very primitive; some crude method of extraction of iron from the ore was employed. The object shows layers, and it appears that the ingot was beaten into the shape of a celt. As said earlier, all the cultural traits of Period IIA continue.

Animal remains found from different levels show on primary examination the evidence of humped cattle, deer, *Elephas maximus,* and *Capra hireus*. The material from the last deposits of the last period does not bear any affinity either with the megalithic material in the neighbouring states or with that found in the earlier levels at Sisupalgarh which was dated by Lal to *cirea* 300 B.C.

In the absence of radiocarbon dates, we can only propose some tentative chronology.

It is well established that the metallurgy of iron in India was known around 1000 B.C. Thus, the Iron Age level may be placed in the time-bracket of 1000 B.C. – 800 B.C.

Period II A at Golbai Sasan with a deposit of over 5 m can be dated to *circa* 1400 B.C. to 900 B.C. Period I, i.e. the Neolithic period, which is separated by a filling from period II A, may be dated to *circa*1600 B.C.

B. K. Sinha

Dy. Supt. Archaeologist,
Archaeological Survey of India
Bhubaneshwar

Ancient Ports of Orissa: Probable causes of their decline

The *Brahmāṇda Purāna*, a text probably of 10th century A.D. mentions that Chilika in Orissa was a big harbour providing shelter to the seagoing vessels. Ships from Chilika plied to Java, Malaya, Sumatra, Bali, Burma, China, Thailand, Ceylon and other places and they could carry thousands of passengers[1]. Palur, was an international port which flourished from 600 B.C. to the 16th century. *The* Jaina *Uttaradhyāyana Sūtra* and the Hathigumpha inscription mention that the deserted Pithunda port was renovated by King Kharavela and had a direct contact with Champa[2]. Che-li-ta-lo, which Hiuen Tsang placed in the south-east region of Orissa, has been identified with modern Puri[3]. Tamralipti carried out the flourishing trans-ocean trade with Burma, Ceylon and the islands of the Far East. The literary and inscriptional sources of Java and China frequently mention about the people of Orissa. The Jaha inscription of Java of A.D. 840 mentions that the Kling (Kalinga) people had some contact with Java. Two thousand families migrated to Java along with the prince of Orissa, and later-period contact have been reflected in the art history of Orissa[4]. Apart from trade and cultural contacts, Orissa had matrimonial alliances with Sri Lanka[5].

The excavations at Sisupalgarh[6], Khalkatapatna[7] and Manikapatna confirm that Orissa had overseas trade contacts with Rome, China, Africa and the Arab countries. Apart from direct voyages, the merchants of Orissa used to sail with the Tamil and Kerala sailors to South-east Asian countries, Rome, and Arabia[8]. Orissa had her colonies in Burma, Thailand, Malayan peninsula, Champa, Java, Sumatra and beyound South-east Asia. The ancient time voyages from Orissa to Malayan peninsula were through the straits of Malacca to Sumatra, Java, Bali, Celebes, Borneo and the Sunda straits to Champa and Kambuja[9]. How these ports could have gone to into disuse? Possibly both man-made and natural causes would have played their crucial role for the non-functioning of the ports.

Man-made Causes

The historical studies reveal that weak dynasties of Orissa could not protect the maritime trade interest due to internal disturbances. Economy was under the control of feudatories and producers as well as manufacturers had lost their interest in trade. The Imperial Cholas captured the islands of South-east Asian countries. The naval battle between the Sailendras and Cholas continued upto 11th century A.D. The interference of the Arabs in the Indian Ocean again disturbed the maritime trade and China became an important maritime power in the Bay of Bengal. The Muslims collected commercial taxes from the rulers of Orissa.

In ancient period, navigation was based on the skilled manual manoeuvere depending on the sun and stars. Moreover, vessels were sailing with the aid of favourable wind and in fair weather. Unskilled navigation and lack of communication facility at times caused the loss of lives and vessels. The sailors of Orissa lost their interest in marine trade due to above reasons. The absence of peace and order cut slowly at the roots of the seaborne trade of Orissa. The trade enterprises disappeared leaving only the memory of the overseas trade and was limited to rituals and festivals.

Natural Factors

Coastal Orissa played a major role in seatrade, fishing and human settlement since ancient times. The geomorphological features and network of rivers are important for marine archaeological search. The Orissa coast is characterised by long sand-beaches with high and wide backshore. Natural factors like tectonic movement, coastal sedimentation, development of sand dunes in the navigational channels, change of river courses, floods, cyclones, sea level fluctuations etc. perhaps played a crucial role in the destruction of the port-cities of Orissa. A general description as to how these factors could have played their role is given below based on available scientific data.

Tectonic History

Tectonic activity can bring about major changes on the coastline. Evidences for this are present on the Orissan coast. For example, Balasore, the ancient sea port, is only 15 km away from the present seashore. The Konark temple was on the seashore once upon a time but presently the temple is situated about 4.8 km away from the shore. Ahmed[10] feels that this is due to upliftment of the land. Ptolemy, the geographer of A.D. 100 stated that Konarkanagar (Konark) was a port. Perhaps he referred to the same Konark which was subsequently disused due to tectonic movement. Khalkatapatna[11] served as a port nearby Konark in early medieval period.

Coast and Coastal Processes

The coastline is constantly affected by the physical processes which are the net results of prevailing coastal currents, causing sedimentation in a particular pattern. The important factors for coastal processes are the long shore sediment transport which is mainly due to the wave characteristics and near shore topography. The beach sediment transport is having a regional variation due to the geological and physiographic factors. The studies on sediment transportation carried out along the coast-line of Orissa show that the direction of annual net transport is towards north-east and during south-west monsoon due to strong wind activity the transport is much higher[12]. It is probably possible that these processes might have swallowed some of the port-cities like Palur in course of time. Based on 10 years' data of sedimentological studies at Konark and Puri, Chauhan concludes that the amount of sediment input is higher at Konark coastal region than at Puri coast[13]. On the basis of the above studies it seems that Khalkatapatna might have also got silted up due to sedimentation.

During monsoon the tropical rivers of Orissa transport huge quantity of sediments to the Bay of Bengal. River Mahanadi discharges several tons of sediment load into the sea. According to Pascoe the Chilika lake was an inlet of the sea that was first swallowed by the debris delivered by one of the tributaries of Mahanadi, later isolated by the formation of the spit. The formation of spit at the mouth caused due to the south-west monsoon and it is responsible for brackish water in the lake[14]. Chilika lake was a busy port in the early historical times and ships plied to South-east Asian countries. The sedimentation probably caused the disuse of the port and some objects might have been, buried in it waiting archaeologists' spade.

Natural Hazards

The Bay of Bengal is prone to cyclones. Depressions in Bay of Bengal sometimes lead to cyclonic storms and cause havoc to the coastal settlements. Statistical studies show that between 1891 and 1970, as many as 1,036 depressions have occurred in the Bay of Bengal, out of which 360 intensified into storms[15]. The wave height rises to 6 to 7m which bring deluge by inundating lowlying coastal areas. The timely monsoon sometimes brings heavy rainfall and rivers swell up with flood which damage the coastal and agricultural land. It is worthwhile to mention that some storms, cyclones and floods might have washed out some of the coastal structures and port installations like warehouse, wharf and buildings.

Shifting and Diversion of River Courses

The coastal zone of Orissa is marked by sand dunes. These dunes have also been blown inland by the force of wind. The inner limit of the coastal dunes may be set by some topographic obstruction and prevent the rivers falling directly into the sea. The diversion of river course made the port inoperational and this would have been the case perhaps with Palur port also. Recent explorations at Palur revealed pottery and other antiquities which are extensively scattered in the sand dunes[16] and it deserves a systematic excavation. The studies carried out on Mahanadi delta provide that five million cubic metres of coarse sediment is deposited at the mouth of the Mahanadi river. Hence the reworking of the sediment by waves elongated spits and barriers at the northern side of the Mahanadi river mouth encloses a large body called Hakitola Bay[17]. Hakitola Bay near Paradip served as a berthing place of ships but due to barriers and spits, it is non-functional now.

Sea level Fluctuations

The sea level fluctuation and changes in the climatic phenomenon are partly responsible for the decline of ports and coastal cities. On the basis of recent studies conclusion has been drawn that the rise of sea level is 60 to 90 m in the last 11,000 years on the west coast of India[18]. It is obvious that the coastal Orissa might have also been affected due to similar transgression on east coast. The systematic study of sea level on east coast is required to ascertain it.

The recent explorations on coastal Andhra have brought to notice the evidences of palaeolithic cultures at places like Barua, Bhimunipatnum, Rishikonda and similar evidences also have been found in Tamilnadu[19]. This may be attributed to the sea level changes. Since no exploration is known to have carried out on coastal Orissa, it can be inferred from the above that being in the same coastal belt, the possibilities that the palaeolithic culture may have existed along the Orissa coast, cannot be ruled out.

Based on the above facts,the history of the ports of Orissa and the causes of their decline is to be reconstructed. Generally after the decline of a particular port a new port is built in the same vicinity for marine trade. Man-made causes for decline of ports cannot be ignored. Whether natural causes collectively contributed to the decline of individual ports, or a particular fact is responsible for the decline of a port is yet to be found out. The natural cuases of decline and the present state of preservation of the submerged and buried structures as well as artifacts can be ascertained by marine archaeological studies.

Acknowledgements

The author is grateful to Dr. B.N. Desai, Director, National Institute of Oceanography for permitting to publish this paper. He is also grateful to Dr. S.R. Rao for his valuable guidance. The author is also thankful to Shri J.H. Vora for critical study of the paper. Thanks are also due to Sri M.C. Pathak and Dr. M.V. Ramana for reviewing the paper.

Marine Archaeology Centre
National Institute of Oceanography
Dona Paula, GOA, 403 004.

SILA TRIPATHI

REFERENCES

1. Das, A.C. 1975. Kalinga, the Ancient Maritime Power, *Orissa Historical Research Journal*, Vol XVI–4 to Vol. XXII–1, Bhubaneswar, pp. 6–15.
2. Das, D.N. 1977. *The Early History of Kalinga*. Calcutta, p. 303
3. Cunningham, A. 1963. *The Ancient Geography of India* (Reprint) Varanasi, p: 473.
4. Misra, P.P. 1981. The Contact between Orissa and South–East Asia in Ancient Times, *Jr. of Orissa History*, Vol. I No. 2, Bhubaneswar, pp. 10–17.
5. Das, M.N. 1977 Kalinga and Sinhala in *Side lights on History and Culture of Orissa*. Cuttack, pp. 122–130.
6. Lal, B.B. 1984. Excavations at Sisupalgarh, *Ancient India*, Bulletin of Archaeological Survey of India. (Reprint) No.5, New Delhi, pp. 62–105.
7. *Indian Archaeology– A Review* 1984–85, New Delhi, pp. 56–61.
8. Mookerjee, R.K. 1912. *Indian Shipping*, Bombay, p. 256.
9. Kanchan, R.K. 1990. *Hindu Kingdoms of South-East Asia*, Delhi, p. 301.
10. Ahmed, E. 1972. *Coastal Geomorphology of India*, New Delhi, p. 222.
11. *IAR* 1984-85 *op. cit.*
12. Chandramohan, P. 1989. *Sediment Transport along the Indian Coast*, Technical Report, NIO. Goa, p. 34.
13. Chauhan, O.S. 1990. Sedimentological Parameters of Beach Sediments on the East Coast of India in *Jr. of Coastal Research*, Vol 6, No 3, Florida, pp. 573–585.
14. Ahmed 1972. *op. cit.*
15. Mohanti, M. 1990 Sealevel rise: Background, Global concern and implication for Orissa Coast, India in G.V. Rajamanickan (Ed) *Sealevel variation and its impact on coastal Environment* Thanjavur, pp. 197–232.
16. *IAR* 1984-85. *op. cit.*
17. Rao, K.N. 1988. Development of Spits and Barriers at the Delta, *Monograph on short course on Modern Deltas*, Andhra Univ. Visakhapatnam, pp. 35–38.
18. Nair, R.R. 1974. Holocene sea-levels on western continental shelf of India in *Proc. Indian Acad. Sci.* Vol. 79 No. 5, Bangalore pp. 197–203.
19. Subrahmanyam, B.R. and Sireesha, E.J. 1990. Fossil Beaches and Palaeolithic evidences in Coastal Andhra, *Jr. of Marine Archaeology*, Vol. 1, NIO, Goa, pp. 24–38.

On the Identification of Bhakti-Deities in Rock Pictures

A rock-painting accomapnied by an Ashokan-Brahmi inscription which was found almost 35 years back at a site near the village Tikula (1), some 56 km south of Gwalior[1], could be identified as an early icon of the Bhakti cult.

The painting is on the vertical back-section of a well protected rock-shelter, inside which a two metre high rubble packed platform was constructed to form a level ground. On account of the accompanying Brahmi-inscription this rock- painting has always been considered as very important, since pictures with obviously related inscriptions in early Brahmi are extremely rare.

The picture (Figs.: 1-2) shows three persons, the heads and bodies strictly en face with arms stretched sideways, only the legs and feet drawn as seen from the side. The central and largest figure is of approximately 20 cm height, after the artist in an afterthought lengthened the height of the legs, probably to adapt the figure to an accepted hierarchic order. The right and smallest person is an adjutant umbrella-bearer, the stake of the umbrella is slanting in such a way as to position the parasol over the central person, which I take as a further indication of its first position in the hierarchic order. The left person holds a plough-shaped instrument in his right hand and a stick with oval protuberances in his left. His head is quite circular with a vertical line for nose, a horizontal for a mouth and simple dots for the eyes. On top of the head is some headgear(?) indicated by concentric arched lines. Two filled-in circles, left and right, at the crown of the head might belong to the coiffure or indicate some ornament, or it may show the then current convention of depicting the ears. Ear-ornaments assembled of interlinked rings of a rather large proportion are indicated on all the three person's ears. .

The schematic depiction of the bodies of all three figures does not allow the identification of the clothes; but it seems that they are without shoes, since toes are shown clearly on the two persons at the left. The central person is holding in his right hand a similar staff to the one with the former person except for a horn-like protuberance at the top, and its length extending below the hand downwards. The features of the central person are quite similarly formed as the first person's, except that he is sporting a moustache, if not a full beard. As the figures are rather small, delicate details are not easy to distinguish from unintentional ones. This person sports a diadem on the forehead in contrast to the adornment of the two flanking persons. The fingers of the left are stretched out almost to touch -or actually touch- a disc or wheel, in which rudiments of at least four spokes radiating from the centre can be distinguished.

As already mentioned, the initially drawn shorter legs can be seen at knee-level; the cloth of this person seems similar to the former, but since the picture does not elaborate on the droppings, it is difficult to really understand the nature of the clothes. At the centre of the body the person is displaying a T-shaped sign which might be a pendant or a symbol related to this particular deity.

The third and smallest person holds the staff of an umbrella in his right hand. Since the fingers are not indicated clearly, it is impossible to speculate on the relation between the umbrella-bearer and the disc. The left hand is free from any paraphernalia. Facial features, headgear and adornments are similar to the ones on person to the left . The right ear-ornament seems to be denoted. This person also wears a neck-ornament shaped like a torque.

The gender of the umbrella-bearer is difficult to guess. The upper body seems to be filled in with colour, which might indicate a blouse or shirt of some sort. As the positioning of this persons is unique in rock-art, we have no good grounds to speculate on the gender of this adjutant.

The umbrella itself is a rather schematic, nonetheless it is important in the iconographic reasoning as we shall see later on.

The strict frontality of this picture is a rather rare example in rock-paintings, although not altogether unknown. Depictions of personalities en face are common in the chalcolithic rock-pictures of the Chambal Region, particularly at sites in the vicinity of Bhanpura in the Mandasor District of Madhya Pradesh[2]. The en face position is chosen particularly for the depiction of prominently drawn personalities, whose paraphernalia or weapons suggest, that we are actually viewing images of gods or deified men. But since we know very little about the iconography of gods or heroes during the protohistoric period, we can only speculate. Anyway, it seems that the en face depiction was chosen for iconic representations of personalities which form the centre in the linear-narrative-progress of pictorial action. These figures do not interact any more with the pictorial environment, but rather communicate towards the viewer, very much like an image, which most probably they are.

In absence of any further explanation from the artists, or from persons enculturated into the cognitive systems during the times of origin of the pictures, we as well could only speculate about the identity of the three figures.

The votive inscription — besides giving us a chronological frame for the picture — does not help us to identify the personalities or deities depicted. The inscription only tells, that a person named Dambuka has made it *(Dambukena karitam)*[3].

For further identification we only could rlie on the paraphernalia in the hands of the icons. But for this identification it has to be remembered, that the lines of rock- pictures are not always as clear and smooth as one would wish them to be. For this reason the identification of rock-pictures can never be without ambivalence, particularly in so small figures as we are dealing with here

The paintings are often obscured by a more or less transparent patina or silica skin. The applied pigment is not always in sharp contrast with the natural tint of the rock. In most of the cases only the most permanent pigment of originally polychrome pictures has remained. In the case of the picture dealt with here it was done in a dark reddish-violet iron-oxide.The capillary spread of the liquid colour-pigment away from the applied lines — rather like in an ink-drawing over a fibrous paper — leaves us with ambivalent lines and blobs, which in a small picture can play havoc on the fantasy and imagination of the modern viewer. Still a close and careful scrutiny of the paraphernalia during my first visit at the site in 1975 allowed me to interpret the tool in the left person's right hand as a plough, and a corn-stalk in the other; the later identification of course was influenced by the recognition of the plough, with which it would from a symbiotic pair.

The plough as agricultural implement is depicted rarely in the huge body of prehistoric and historic rock-pictures in India. As far as I can remember by 1975 not a single of these was known to me. Still now I know of only one chalcolithic and one historic picture showing a ploughing person and I don't know of even a single other picture of a person carrying a plough. So one had to be extremely careful with the identification of an implement which otherwise is not depicted at all in rock-pictures.

The paraphernalia of the central figure — a corn-stalk like staff in the right hand and the left hand reaching towards or actually touching a disc — are quite indicative in the Indian context. The umbrella held by the right person surely forms an hierarchic emblem over the central figure. Incidentally this picture is one of the earliest rock-pictures to show an umbrella of honour held over a person.

Umbrellas are known otherwise from pictures of *stupas* (Fig.: 6), and from a few pictures showing horse-riders or elephant-riders which are accompanied by an adjutant holding an umbrella aloft. These "chieftain" depictions are generally thought to belong to the Gupta period at the earliest[4].

The diadem on the forehead of the central person as well is a unique feature in rock-paintings. In this particular picture group, it definitely gives the person adorned with a flair of elevation in comparison with both flanking persons.

With the paraphernalia identified as a plough in the right hand of the left person and a disc in the hand of the neighbouring personality it was more than probable that we are looking at icons of Balarama – who is also known under the epithet of *halablırt*, the wielder of the plough-share — and the second personality – wielding a disc – as Krishna-Vasudeva. Balarama and Vasudeva-Krishna form an inseparable divine pair at the centre of the Bahagavata religion.

For some reasons rock-pictures are understood to be iconographically rather ambiguous, and as I have explained earlier, the identification of the figures' paraphernalia was not obvious enough for other scholars to comment upon, so that this unique and important painting did not draw much further comment.

Within the last few years some more rock-pictures of Krishna and Balärama were noticed in the large body of bruising and engravings along the Indus River near the city of Chilas.

The rather inauspicious looking icons, whose importance easily could have been overlooked on account of their unpretentious size and finish, have the great advantage of being accompanied by an inscription giving the name of the deities. Although the iconographic form of the deities is not very detailed, but the gods' paraphernalia are quite revealing. Again we see the plough carried rather like a standard, by one of the gods, and disc with arrow-shaped protuberances by the other. Both gods carry a club or pestle *(musala)* in the other hands (Fig.: 5). The accompanying Kharoshti-Inscription reads *"Rama-Krishna Dhamaputrasa"*, which Dani translates as "of (Bala)rama and Krishna, erection of Dhamaputra"[5].

In a further depiction Balarama is shown with a spear-like standard having a plough-share affixed to it

(Fig.:4). The accompanying Khoroshti-inscription saying *"Balodebo"* leaves no doubt about the identification as Balarama.

An other revealing discovery was made during the excavations of Ai-Khanoum. Within a hoard of silver coins, six square coins, struck during the reign of Agathocles and showing detailed pictures of Vasudeva and Balarama respectively on the reverse and obverse of the coins, too were found (Fig.:3). Since these six coins are subject of a detailed and well informed monograph by Audouin and Bernard[6], I shall limit my observations here only to a few points relevant for comparing the rock-pictures. The six coins from Ai-Khanoum are struck on strip-shaped silver ingots, from which the individual-square shaped- coins were detached by denting the strip with a chisel, and finally breaking them away by hand. This corresponds to the Indian square punch-marked coins.

The Greek legend on the obverse giving the title and name of the king reds *"Basileos Agathokleous"*, on the reverse the Ashokan Brahmi inscription translates this into *"Rajine Agthuklayesa"*. The obverse shows Balarama between the two lines of the Greek legend. He is seen standing en face with both feet pointing sideways. A plough is placed in his left and a club in his right hand. A scabbard is shown extending at the left from his middle. The reverse shows in a similarly en face position Vasudeva, holding his right arm akimbo, holding an oval attribute — a vase or a conch — below his chest. His left hand is obscured by an eight-spoked wheel possessing more or less T-shaped protuberances at the periphery, which are placed alternating between the spacings of the spokes.

Both deities seem to wear a helmet (?), from which the stem of an umbrella issues forth. From the underside of the baldachin branches some flourish, which may be tassels or strips of wavy cloths. Audouin and Bernard[7] took this arch-like crest over the head of the deities as the crest of Greek military helmets shown in a twisted perspective.

The painting at Tikula shows clearly an umbrella held over the figure of Vasudeva. There are several examples of flourishes under umbrellas of the very kind as shown in the coin's impressions in the rock-painting of Central India.

Most of the umbrellas are related to depiction of *stupas* (Fig.:6). These umbrella-depictions also show frequently flag-like flourishes issuing from the underside of the baldachins (Fig.:6). The identification of the arc over the heads of Balarama and Krishna on the coins as crest of a military helmet of Greek origin can be securely discarded.

The knee-length skirt seems to be assembled from rigid strips of material. Interpretation is of course difficult, but it seems both heroes are wearing a military costume, a leather skirt and shoes with curled-back toes. Over the shoulders both are wearing the drape of scarf with two loose ends showing.

The identification of the skirt-like garment as military costume would be in accordance with the evidences from one of the earliest sculptures of a vaishnava image from Malhar in Madhya Pradesh, which shows a military leather scale-skirt, and a soft flowing dhoti beneath[8].

In the general area where the paintings at Tikula were found several other rock-painting sites were found. A very important site close to Shivpuri houses several early Brahmi-inscriptions, the longest of which refers to one Sivarakhi who as a devotee of Krishna, got a rock-shelter(?) and a tank to be constructed[9]. This inscription is thought to have been painted during the 2nd cent. B.C., which of course would tally vary well with the dates of other early inscriptions belonging to the Bhakti religion or mentioning it *en passant.* One of the most well known inscriptions of this kind is the one which Heliodorus caused to be inscribed on a pillar erected or positioned in the vicinity of an early Vishnu temple near the ancient city of Vidisha. This shows that already during the 2nd cent. B.C. the Bhagavata religion was well established in the urban setting.

The iconographical features of the rock-pictures from Tikula are difficult to bring into a chronological frame as no adequate painted material exists, with which one could compare particular features. As already mentioned, the style and positioning of the painting is unusual and if we would have to look for stylistic analogies, the closest examples would come from chalcolithic paintings in the Chambal region. The iconographic features of the figures are not detailed enough to allow much further interpretation or speculation without getting painfully superficial. The rosette diadem, ear-rings and other adornments can be compared to early Kushana sculptures, the rather schematic-indicated garments might refer to military costume. But all these details are to be found in the iconography of India at least from the Sunga period onwards.

Still the paintings clearly prove that Krishna and Balarama had a considerable vertical distribution in the society of the early historic period, and that the iconic representation of the Bhakti heroes was homogenous within a large territory of northern India by the 2nd cent. B.C.

Notes

1. The Tikula rock-paintings are distributed over four rock- shelters in the small hillock west of the village. Traces of rock-paintings of the Mesolithic period are available. The majority of the paintings belong to the chalcolithic period. The pictures described here are surrounded by a multitude of early historic pictures, which are not very well visible, but in most cases obviously older than the Bhakta icons.

7060, Vienna
Gumpendorferstr 114/21
Austria

Description of Figures

Fig.:1 Tikula; Paintings in different shades of red; Free eye copy.

Fig.:2 Tikula; The Bhakta Deities; Drawing from a colour slide.

Fig.:3 ab Ai-Khanoum (Afghanistan); Agathocles coin;

a): obverse: Samkarsana/Balarama, b) reverse: Vasudeva-Krishna; After a photograph, (courtesy: Delegation Archaeologique Francaise en Afghanistan).

Fig.:4 Chilas II; Rock-engraving; Balarama accompanied by a Khoroshti-inscription giving the name of the deity as *Bahladebo*; After a photograph, (courtesy: Jettmar).

Fig.:5 Chilas II; Rock-engraving ; Balarama and Krishna; After a photograph, (courtesy: Dani).

Fig.:6 Ghambipura, Painting, contour lines in red, in filling in white, flags in white.

Fig.:7 Gupha Masir-Engraving.

Erwin Neumayer

REFERENCES

1. *IAR* 1956/57 "Rock Shelters in Madhya Pradesh," p. 79; Neumayer E., 1983 Prehistoric Indian Rock Paintings, New Delhi.
2. Neumayer 1983, *op. cit.*
3. Wakanakr, V.S., and Brooks, R..R.R., 1976 *Stone Age Painting in India*. Bombay
4. Neumayer, 1983, *op. cit.* photo 13.
5. Dani, A.H., 1983 *Chials - The City of the Nanga Parvat*, Islamabad and Jettmar, K., 1982 *Rock-carvings and Inscriptions in the Northern Areas of Pakistan* Institute of Folk Heritage, Islamabad.
6. Audouin,R., and Bernard,P., 1974 Tresor de monnaies indiennes et indo-greques d'Ai Khanoum (Afghanistan), *Revue Numismatique* 1974, pp. 7-41; (Engish Translation from the French by Olivie Guiluaume, Manuscript, forthcoming).
8. Srinivasan, D.M., 1989 Vaishnava Art and Iconography at Mathura, in: Srinivasan, D.M., (ed.) 1989 *op. cit.* pp. 383-92.
9. Jain, J.P., 1984 Rock-paintings of Shivpuri, in: Chakravarty, K.K (ed.) 1984 *Rock Art of India*, New Delhi, p. 241, PI.LXXVI; and Dubey, A.K., 1988 Inscribed painted rock shelters from Shivpuri, in: Indian History Congress, Proceedings of the forty-eight session, Panjim 1987, pp. 750-75.

Fig. 1. *Tikula: Eye copy*

Fig. 2. *Tikula: Copy from a slide*

Fig. 3. *Coin of Agathocles (Court. Delegation Archaeologique Francaise en Afghanistan)Left. obverse Balarama Right: reverse Vasudeva*

Fig. 4. *Chilas II: After a photograph from: Jettmar, K., 1984 Rock Engravings and Inscriptions in the northern areas of Pakistan; Institute of Folk Heritage, Islamabad. Engraving of Baladebo*

Fig. 5. *Chilas II: After a photograph from Dani, A.H., 1983 Chilas, The City of Nanga Parvat; Dyanar, Islamabad. Engraving of Balarama and Krishna*

Fig. 6. *Ghambipura: Contour lines in red, flags in white*

Fig. 7. *Gupha Masir: Engraving*

Ships and Shipping in Orissan Art

In Orissa the material for the study of shipping in art is not much. There are only a few representations of boats and ships in sculptural art and in manuscript painting. The earliest representation of boat can be noticed on a punch-marked coin now preserved in British Museum, London[1]. The *Periplus*, mentions ancient ports of Orissa and the pirates of Orissan coasts.

One of the earliest representations of ship in sculptural art is noticed in a stone panel in the Orissa State Museum, Bhubaneswar[2]. It was found on a mound near Brahmeswar temple, Bhubneshwar. The panel depicts two ships, one fully represented and only the frontal part of the second one. In the first ship there are standing elephants in the front end. In the middle of the ship, two persons are represented seated, and two sailors are shown steering the ship with oars in the rear end. K.C. Panigrahi believes that the long ear lobes of the two seated personages show Buddhistic affinity and the persons are a prince and princess holding something in their hand, probably the relics of Buddha, and are transporting to other countries[3]. The second ship depicts a standing elephant on its frontal portion. Below the ships, graphic depiction of waves with aquatic and amphibious animals can be observed. However, it may be also be suggested that probably the sculptural panel depicts the transportation of elephants from ancient Kalinga by ship to other countries. The panel may be dated to early medieval period.

In the Lingaraj temple, Bhubaneshwar (11th century A.D.) one representation of a boat can be noticed. The scene presents a female, steering a boat with an oar. In another medieval example at Deokund (Dist. Mayurbhanj Orissa), goddess Ambika is shown seated over the boat which is significant because of Ambika's association with boat[4]. The Bhairava images on the Beki of the *jagamohan* of Sun Temple, Konark (13th cent. A.D.) are depicted dancing on boats[5]. There is an interesting eight-armed Mahisamardani image near the Brahmeswara temple at Bhubaneshwar. The goddess is engaged in a fierce sea-battle with demon issuing out of the trunk of a buffalo. She holds discus, shield, snake, and arrow-head in four of her hands whereas; her other four hands are severely damaged. Scenes of such naval fight between the goddess and the demon extremely rare[6]. The image is datable to the 9th century A.D.

An interesting stone sculpture of a complete boat from Orissa is preserved in Indian Museum, Calcutta. This stone medallion was also from the Sun Temple, Konark. At the front end of the boat is a figure of an attendant holding a parasol while next to him are seen one standing and one squatting figure; the latter is without his head. At the rear end of the boat is the helmsman holding the rudder. Four men are shown rowing the boat. There is a representation of a cabin with an upraised platform, inside which a man is sitting with a bow and arrow, probably a royal figure which Kalpana Desai[7] has identified the scene as Rama in the middle holding bow and arrow; he is crossing the river with king Guhaa. However, the scene seems to be the *Nava Keli Utsava* scene or rowing festival, where the king is in the cabin. This type of boat is a *'Madhya Mandir'* type of royal pleasure boat as described and classified in *Yukti Kalpataru* of king Bhoja[8]. The panel may be dated to 12th century A.D. if it is really from Konark.

Another scene of boat representation of *Nava Keli Utsava* is preserved in the *Bhoga Mandapa* of the Jagannath temple at Puri (12th cent. A.D.) Here the king and his attendants are shown preparing for rowing festival[9]. The middle portion of the boat is having a cabin and in its entrance, representation of attendants on either side can be marked. Four women are shown seated with their oars. In the rear end, a lady is standing with a *chhatra*. Besides her, another lady is shown holding something in her hand, probably associating with a sort of worship to be performed before the rowing festival begins. This boat may also be of *Madhya Mandir* type .

Some fine representations of boats and ships are preserved in the paintings is manuscripts now in State Museum, Orissa.[10] There are four manuscripts of 18th century showing five drawings. Among them, four deal with a story from *Usha-Vilas*. Once Siva was engaged in water sports with Parvati in a boat. At that time, Usha, royal princess, was looking from her palace garden. She saw the happy couple and became very much embarrassed. Siva could know it and blessed her that she should be married on *Jyestha Sukla Treyodashi* (thirteenth day of bright fortnight of *Jyestha* month). In four manuscripts, Siva is shown with Parvati with his vehicle bull near him. In all the examples, ladies are rowing the boats; other details like flags, birds (probably water bird, swan, sea gulls(?) etc.), masts and other details can be seen. Out of the four representations, two of the boats are of general type and the other two have bird and elephant faced bows, respectively. The first two boats are beautifully designed and well-carved. Below the boats can be noticed fish, tortoise and other animals.

The last one is a representation of a beautiful ship. It is fully covered ('Sar*va mandira'* type as referred to by Bhoja). Three masts can be noticed. The middle mast is fastened with ropes and its top is decorated with a temple like design in which representation of a god or a symbolical representation can be seen. Above it, a flag is noticed. On the top of the ship, a flying bird is artistically shown. Below the ship, representation of waves, aquatic animals like crocodile, fish, etc. are depicted is an artistic manner. On both sides of the ship, can be noticed two sailors. The ship is realistically depicted with essential details as cabins, masts, flag, birds, etc.

Besides these the boat is also represented in the folk-art and folk-lore of Orissa. On the full-moon day in the month of *Kartika* (October-November) men, women and children take holy bath in river and tanks, and float toy boats. This sailing of toy boats is supposed to be done in the memory of past maritime activities of the forefathers who sailed for distant lands with the on set of favourable wind during this time of the year.

Another indigeneous folk-art is produced by the aged ladies and widows in the month of *Kartika*. Those who observed this month as sacred take a dip early in the morning after giving a cow-dung wash around the pedestal of a *Tulasi* plant which becomes their place of worship. Then they start decorating the place with dust colours, *"Muruja"*, as it is called. There they draw the figures of the Trinity, enclosing them inside the drawing of a Rekha temple. On either side of the temple, they draw lion figures, Aruna Pillar at a distance, *sankha* (conch), *chakra* (discus), *gada*(mace) and *padma* (lotus), cow, elephant, Garuda, *navagunjara*, ladder (that would help them to reach heaven), boat and many other motifs.

In one particular type of *Vrata* (observance), known as *Somanathi vrata*, pictorial representations of boat are also drawn in *Muruja*. During the *Gamha-Purnima* or *Sravana Purnima* (full moon day of July-August), on the walls of houses in the villages of Orissa are painted a figures like a *"Boita"*, (boat) in the form of crocodile face. In the middle of it, a room is shown full with cereals and wealth. Besides, even now as a memory of the past, housewives draw the pictures of ships loaded with wealth in their courtyard on *Dipavali* night (October-November) and worship them in the morning.

The folk-paintings of Orissa, i.e., *Paṭṭa* and wooden painting, also include themes based on local subjects such as *Biota Bandapana* (welcome ceremony of vessel), story of Ta'poi, the lone sister of seven *Saudagars* (merchants) who in the absence of her brothers was tortured by her six sisters-in-law. *Khudrukoni Osha*, *Navakeli Utsava* and other subjects relating to the maritime trade and commerce of the Orissa people in the past find adequate coverage in these paintings.[11]

One of the most interesting traditions in Orissa was the association of God Purushottam (Jagannath) and Lord Lingaraj with boat rowing. There is one festival called *Chandan Jatra* in Oriya. It is observed at Puri and Bhubaneshwar. It starts from *Akshya Tritiya* (the third day of bright fornight) in the month of *Baisakh* (April-May) and continues for 21 days. The images of Madan Mohana (representative deity of Jagannath) Goddess Lakshmi and Sarasvati are taken in palanquins by the *sevakas* (priests) to the Narendra Sarovar at Puri. These images are accompanied by different deities from different shrines in Puri. After reaching the Narendra tank, the images are placed in different decorated boats and they are rowed for a long time by the *sevakas*. During this rowing ceremony, *devadasis* dance and sing in the boat. Generally, Madan Mohan, with Lakshmi and Sarasvati, ride on the white coloured boat while Rama, Krishna, with Pancha Siva, ride in the red boat. All the deities on the boat take trips to the tank for several times. The boat is decorated in the form of a swan.[12]

In Bhubaneshwar, the representative deity of Lingaraj and other deities of nearby shrines are taken and boating ceremony (*chapa*, as called locally) are solemnized in the nearby Bindusarovar tank.

The tradition of boat rituals is also associated with social customs and rituals connected with sea. The importance and the function of sea gods and goddess in Orissa is valid only in the social and geographical context of these divinities. On the eastern coast, the goddess Chandi and Manasa are associated with the searoute. Besides, the image of Varaha who was personified as the Cosmic sea-God, rescuing the mother Earth from the ocean, come to be worshipped, hence depicted in art. The local folk-gods and goddesses, came to be worshipped in association with sea in Orissa. It is noticed that at a every dangerous confluence of rivers and along the sea-coast of Orissa, images of goddess, adorned with vermillion are believed to protect the sailing ships in their dangerous voyages. It was believed that this female deity in the form of Śakti could subdue the storm and protect the ships from the dangers of the voyage. It was this belief that led to the establishment of Mangala temples on the ancient seaports and sea-routes in Orissa. Among the Mangala temples of Orissa, the noticeable are of Mangala at Kakatpur, Ramachandi at Konark, Sarala at Jhankad, Bhagavati at Banpur, Charchika at Banki, Harchandi near Asureswar, Samalei at Sambalpur, Hingla at Talcher.

Besides, Goodess Minakali in Balasore was worshipped by the sailors and ship merchants before making offerings and setting out for sea trade. At Balaramgarhi, a medieval port of Orissa, temple dedicated to goddess Gadanayikani, one of the eight Nayikas or attendants of Chandi, is worshipped.

Assistant Supdt. Archaeologist, A.S.I., Bhubaneshwar

Research Scholar, PG Deptt. of History, Utkal University Bhrubaneshwar

At Dharma and Chandbali (two medieval ports of Orissa), Goddess Dhamrai and Dakeswari were worshipped by the marine sailors. This amply shows the importance of the folk goddesses of Orissa being associated with marine activities.

In addition, of late, the Govt. of Orissa had organised a sea-voyage from Orissa to Indonesia (Bali island) to recall the glorious maritime activity of ancient Kalinga. This famous *Bāli Dvīpa Yātrā* (Voyage) started on November 10, 1992.

The above study reveals that maritime activities of ancient Kalinga inspired artists to depict boats in sculpture and painting. The folk-art traditions of Orissa is also indicative of the maritime pride of ancient Orissa. However, the maritime art of Orissa never gained an important place as a theme, perhaps being part of normal life style of the Kalinga people. But taken into consideration the data available in marine context in the form of literary and archaeological evidences, it can be surmised that Kalinga was one of the great maritime powers in ancient India.

The authors are grateful to Dr. G.C. Chauley, Superintending Archaeologist, Smt. S. Bose, Deputy Superintending Archaeologist and Prof. K.S. Behera, Deptt. of History, Utkal University, Bhubaneshwar, Orissa for their valued suggestions and information in the preparation of this paper.

J.K. PATNAIK
B.K. TRIPATHY

NOTES AND RERFERENCES

1.Information kindly supplied by Prof. K.S. Behera, Utkal University.

2.Panigrahi K.C. "New Light on the Early History of Bhubaneswar" *J.O.A.S.*, Vol. XVII, No. 2, Calcutta, 1950, p. 114.

3.*Ibid.*

4.Parida, S.C. The Actual site of Matsyadesa, in Orissa History Congress, *Proceedings of the 11th session*, Puri, 1983, p. 124.

5.Bahera, K.S. Maritime Trade in Orissa in *Sidelights of Orissan History and Culture*, p. 115. See, also, B. Das, "Saktism in Ancient Orissa", p. 13 in *The Proceedings of Orissa History Congress*, 1978.

6.T.E. Donaldson, *Hindu art of Orissa*, Vol. III.

7.*Ibid.*

8. Rao, Nalini, "Maritime Art of India", Presd. Add. First Maritime Conference at Jamnagar, Gujarat, 1987.

9. Mishra, K.C. *The Cult of Jagannath*, p. 136, Calcutta, 1984.

10.We are thankful to the Curator, Palm-leaf Manuscripts section, Orissa State Museum, Bhubaneshwar Orissa for providing valuable information.

11.All these activities, festivals and *vratas* (observance) have traditions regarding the ancient voyages of Kalinga people.

12. Mishra, K.C. *op. cit.*, p. 136.

Human Settlements in Goa Till 16th Century : An overview

Goa, like many other regions in India, has yielded evidence of settlements from stone age through the present.

Places like Shigaum near Colem, at the foot of the Doodhsagar falls; the slopes of the present rail-line Zambolim and Quepem, on the banks of the Kushavati; Viliena rock-shelters, Fatorpa and Arali, close to the source of the Zuari river; Betul on sea shore; Pernem across the Chapora river; Masordem, Velguem and Corqua near Volpoi; the course of the Mandovi river, upto the plateau of Mapusa, Porvorim and Pilarne, Colva Betalim-Betim; Verna to Hagoa to Dabolim, Chicalim of rock-cut dwellings, are indicative of all the three stone age cultures.

Goa has so far yielded neolithic and megalithic settlements only in a small measure in places like Betul, Curdi, Chikkelim, Verna, etc. A.K., Sharma. Dr. S.A. Sali, Dr. K.V. Ramesh, and Mr. K.V.Rao have explored the area.

Traditional Accounts

The Vedic *rishi* 'Mandavya' and his daughter 'Mandavi' are associated with the river Mandōvi. It takes Goa back to the Vedic times, and perhaps giving scope for the early settlement of '*Gurukulas*' and '*Rishyāshramas*'. 'Gōmat', 'Gōpakapaṭṭana', 'Gōpakapura', 'Govapuri' are the nomenclatures going back to Mahabharata's Bhishmaparva. 'Jambudvipa', the island of bear king Jambuvant and contemporary of Lord Krishna, is another island of early human settlement. The suffixing words - *pura*, *paṭṭana*, etc. - indicate the urban settlements of that time.

In the dawn of history of this part of the country, human settlements must have been with the Konkan Mouryas (upto the 6th century A.D) and the Kadambas.

Geographic Setting

Geography plays a dominant role in the life of man. The land, the rivers, the rains, the hills and the dales, the flora and fauna influence his way of life and thus his history. In Goa, the long stretch of coastal belt, the Sahyadri slopes on the east, and further east the tablelands on hill tops have encouraged three distinct types of settlements.

1) Small hutments and scattered hamlets for lower working class, like fisher-folk, Kunbis, Kharvis, Betais, etc.
2) A more evolved type settlements for traders, craftsmen, agriculturists, etc., and
3) Towns, citadels, forts etc. for the rich.

Historical Period

All through the period of royal dynasties, like the Kadambas, the Silaharas, the later Chalukyas, the Yadavas of Deogiri, the Rayas of Vijayanagar, and upto A.D. 1510, the age-old Hindu society in this part of the country had more or less the four tier ancient *'Varnashrama'* system. The settlements for Brahmins, Kshatriyas, Vaisyas and Sudras were restricted and rigid, and also more or less exclusive. And the norms of *silpa* texts for such settlements were adopted as elsewhere in the country. *Kharvata, Kubjaka, Drona* type town-plans appear to have been adopted at Govapuri, Chandrapur and Brahmapuri in Goa.

During the period from 5th to 15th century A.D., rural life in Goa with small hutments and hamlets, remained almost unchanged, while the conspicuous change with the growing settlements leading to urban class is tangibly noticed. The capital place Chandrapur; Govapuri another port city on Zueri; Brahmapuri, an educational centre; Salcet, a commercial centre; Sangham (Sangem) as community centre; Verna settlement of Agrahara; Naroa and Saptakuteswar as religious centres; Ella port of sea gods; Mahapurusha (Mapusa) of religious greatness, Mamgirish (Mangesh) of Saivaite faith; Madugrama (Madugaon) a place of lakes; Ponda *(Honda)* of water tanks; Dodamarga (Highway) of trade route; Raibandar, a port of the Rayas of Vijayanagar; Velha Goi (Old Goa); Agasim, a gateway, etc., may be cited with reference to different objectives of the settlements with different functional aspects.

A few settlements had *agrahara* — Gopaka paṭṭana, Chandrapur, Verna, Brahmapuri, Norva, Saptakuteswara, etc., and these apparantly adorned by scholars, pupils, the other assistants, together with wells, tanks, living apartments, congregational halls, link roads to other neighbouring important locations.

Settlements in relation to Population

Undoubtedly, population and the settlements are interdependant. With reference to the population of each hamlet, town or capital of Goa, it can be explained this way. If the total population during different centuries is not warrented by any written texts, then it may be surmised with population statistics on historical context. As per 1991 census Goa has a population of 12 lakhs, (250 villages and 12 towns), and supposing that each century in the past lost 2 lakhs, then, approximately,

19th Century had 10 lakhs; 18th Century had 8 lakhs; 17th Century had 6 lakhs; 16th Century had 4 lakhs; and 15th Century had 2 lakhs.

And, therefore, the settlement numbers also get proportionately reduced and also become thinner and smaller. The towns had a small market, a few built-up houses, one or two mansions for heads of the town, places of worship, tanks, lakes and a defence wall around the settlement and may be carrying 4-5 thousand population in each, while the hamlets may have had a few haundred souls with a few huts, paddy fields, mango groves, coconut trees, wells, etc.

And, therefore, with such a thin population in the settlements of those times it was easy for the invaders with a few hundred armed and trained soldiers, to conquer and lay their hands on any such settlement, unless there was an organised and strong defence system, equal in strength and capability. That is how the such small Indian settlements became prey to the invaders in the history, and Goa was no exception to it.

Impact of Islam

This pattern of Indian society that grew gradually through ages, began to recede to hazy and dilute form when the Muslims took over the reigns.

Goa also felt the impact. In the province of Ellas, Govapaṭṭana, Ponda, etc., muslim structures came up. The domed mosques, palaces, minars, minarets, water cisterns, dockyards, chaurah-gardens, fountains, in black Deccan trap had come up. Gradually, Konkan was in Muslim hands. But in A.D. 1472 the Hindu cities of Govaspuri, Brahmapuri etc. were the ghost cities of razed temples and devastated houses.

Ella became an important centre of the Muslims, docks and ship-repair yards sprang up. It became a place of departure for Haj pilgrimage and commercial port for horses from Arabia, Petra, Ormuz, Persia, etc. Muslim Goa is what Yususf Adil Shah had made it.

During Yusuf Adil Shah's time a Portuguese historian, Duarte Barbosa, visited the city of Goa in A.D. 1500 and he figures Muslim Goa in detail: "The city of Goa was inhabited by moors, respectable men, and rich merchants and other gentlemen, by cultivators, by military men. It is a great port of trade to which flock many ships from Mecca, Aden, Ormuz, Cambay, and Malbar country. He·(Yusuf) lived much in this place. Nobody was allowed to go out or to come in without permission of Shah. Everybody should register his identity. The town was very large with tall edifices and had some streets and squares surrounded by walls and towers. There is a big fortress in it, and in the environs are many gardens and orchards of fine trees of fruits and many pools of good water. There are many mosques, gentile temples. The country all round was very beautiful and well cultivated and enjoyed much produce from both sea and land." This was the blue print of the Muslim Goa that Yusuf had conceived and created. Yusuf mapped a Muslim Goa to become an Indian Shiraz, with mosques, minarets and domes. A great place in the world between Constantinople and Chinese Cathay. And from this Muslim Goa, Christian Goa sprang up in A.D. 1510 The Persian passion now began to fade.

The Portuguese period of Goa

For a long time, almost a cenutry, after the conquest of Goa by Albuqurque in A.D.1510, the Muslim Goa almost remained the same as far as layouts of roads, dock yards, water cisterns, shopping centres, palace complexes are concerned. It is common knowledge that it was Adil Shah's shipyard which had allured the Portuguese to Goa and the rich trade the Muslims had paved the Rua-Direita (Straight road), which led into Golden Goa.

From 1510 onwards (16th, 17th century) Christian architecture started coming up: St. Catherine Chapel; the Church of Our Lady of Mount; Cathedral; Bom Jesus Church; St. Augustine Church, and convents; St. Monica Convent; St. Paul's College, all in Old Goa, were built on the razed ground of Islamic structures. Adil Shah's palace became the place of the most dreaded Inquisition, shipyard turned partially into arsenal and royal hospital, mint, market of jewellery, liquor, horses, and raw show of human flesh of slave girls; it became a place of fidalgo (of nobles and rich). Antwerp and London were probably the only European cities which could compare with Goa of the time for population and commercial prestige and a Christian land haunted by the cross everywhere. Further, during the period the city-forts like Aguada, Reis Magos, Old Goa, Chapora, Betul, Vasco, Panaji, Terekol, with Western defence-system, came up. And in the rural settlements, turned into modernity, windows and doors of the houses were always kept open due to social orderliness that arose during this period.

Architecturally and culturally, therefore, Goa became a playground of east-west encounter with happy settlements.

S.K. Joshi

Assistant Archaeologist, Archaeological Survey of India, Mini Circle, Panaji, GOA.

Stupas: A Rare Depiction in Rock Paintings of Gujarat, India

A cursory glance at the panorama of rock-art is enough to reveal its diversity in time and space. It is mostly conditioned by geographical and ecological factors and explains the role of human response to its changing environment. Most of these aesthetic works are the reflections of the effects of local geography and cultural contexts in their creation. From time immemorial such creative works of human origin have been controlled by his feelings of visual space reflecting how man perceived the world. More often, it is the reflection of cultural context which engendered it and integrated the aesthetic sensibility with elements of local environment. It also denotes human interaction with the religious or cultural ideas prevailing in the then society. This article attempts to discuss how socio-religious elements of a particular cultural period of a region are responsible for the selection of a focal theme for rock-art as a primary evidence of human experience with space.

Religion, as an integral part of the Indian society, has played a vital role in shaping socio–cultural traits prevailing among the contemporary massès. Rock-paintings of *stupas* found around Idar in Gujarat offer an excellent evidence for such an integrated study. Roots of Buddhism were well established in Gujarat right from the beginning of the Christian era and survived upto about 11th/12th cent. A.D. However, apart from the structural remains of the Buddhist *stupas* and monasteries, the literary, inscriptional and other archaeological evidences clearly reveal that Buddhism reached to its peak of glory in this part of the country from the 2nd to 7th cent. A.D. Buddhism during this period exercised tremendous influence on the life of people in Gujarat. *Stupa* as a monument commemorating the memory of Buddha and other spiritual teachers of the Buddhist faith became the vital centre of many social activities not only of the Buddhist community but also of the general populace. It is, therefore, interesting to examine the available archaeological and literary data with a view to understand the *stupa*-paintings in their proper integrated cultural and historical background.

Location of the Site

Rock-paintings in Gujarat are so far confined to the granite outcrops of the north-eastern rocky ridges. These rocky ridges are in fact the southward extension of the Aravalli system that flanks the eastern margin of the floodplains of Gujarat. Though not much work has been carried out in this region, it has yielded much evidence of rock-paintings of the prehistoric and historic periods[1]. Among the rock-paintings of historic period there is a wide diversity in the theme depicted. Of course, the paintings of *stupas* are most uncommon and found only in the Idar region.

Idar (23° 49′N. 72° 58′E.), the capital of former princely state of the same name, is situated at a distance of about 103 km to the north of Ahmedabad, in Sabarkantha district of the Gujarat State. It is a small town located in a relatively rich environmental setting. The complex landform immediately adjacent to its north and east is marked by lofty granite hills of the Aravalli system. These granite outcrops give an appearance of rocks perching one above the other at various angles and have developed cavities at places. Out of these numerous caverns, particularly which have projected ceiling hoods or hollows were generally chosen as ideal shelters for depicting rock-paintings.

Here I shall restrict myself only to those rock-shelters

wherein *stupa*-paintings have been executed. In all nine *stupa*-paintings are found in two distinct localities in a close proximity of Idar town. Of course, the first group of three shelters containing six *stupa*-paintings were found near the Gambhirpura village, situated about two kilometres to the east of Idar town, just behind the hills running north–south between Idar and Gambhirpura. The other group of three *stupa*-paintings were found in one of the small shelters located on the hill known as Idario Dungar (Hill of Idar) extending east-west facing the Idar town.

Description of Stupa Paintings

First Group: Gambhirapura Stupas

To the west of Gambhirpura village, near a step-well, there are three rock-shelters situated half way to its top at a height about 100 to 125 m above the ground level on a hill front facing north–east. The *stupa* figures executed here are quite prominent and can be seen clearly from a distance of about 200 metres. These *stupa*-paintings were reported first by R.G. Hajarnis of the Gujarat State Archaeology Department.[2]

Shelter I:

This lowermost shelter contains a single *stupa* figure flanked by *chhatra yashtis*. The central main figure of the *stupa* consists of a low hemispherical dome placed on a low platform known as *pithika* or plinth, and surmounted by a square box known as *harmika*. The *harmika* is further crowned by three superimposed parasols or umbrellas (*chhatravali*) with its shaft (*yashti*) set in the centre of the *harmika*. The most striking feature of this *stupa*-painting is the depiction of flying banners or flags (*pataka*) tied on the *chhatra yashti* between *harmika* and *chhatravali*. The depiction of *chhatra yashtis*, one on either side of the *stupa*, adorned with triple umbrellas and a banner is another noteworthy aspect of this painting. Except the banners and the side *chhatra yashtis*, which are completely filled in red, the rest of the component parts of the *stupa* and *chhatra yashtis* are marked by bold outlines in red while the inner space is filled with white colour. The entire composition, which is not in a good state of preservation, covers an area about 3 × 1.40 metres.

Shelter II:

The second shelter situated about 15 metres higher up from the first one contains two *stupa*-paintings. Though the *stupa* depicted on the left is bigger than the second, both of them show the same components of the structural *stupas* as seen in the earlier *stupa* described. Here, the smaller *stupa* depicted on the right hand side suggests that it is the reproduction of a developed form of the *stupa* having two platforms and slightly elongated drum of the dome. The placement of *harmika* remains as it is but the umbrella-shaft is unusually high. Originally this *chhatra yashti*-bearing banners must have been crowned by three successively diminishing umbrellas, but in the present state of preservation only one crescentic umbrella is seen in the smaller *stupa*. In both the pictures, the original configuration delineated in red has faded to such an extent that one could have missed them by oversight if it was not rendered in white. The *stupa* on the left occupies an area of about 1.85 × 1.55 metres and the right one about 1.15 × 1.25 metres.

Shelter III:

It is situated about 200 metres to the north of Shelter I at a height of 110 metres from the ground level. This shelter contains three *stupa*-paintings. The first *stupa* figure on the left lacks proportion of drawing. The *harmika*, *chhatravali* and the banners are depicted excessively large and thus it gives an effect of imbalanced picture. The other two *stupas* depicted close to each other towards right, little away from the first, are relatively symmetrical in their proportion. In all the three *stupas* the banners are tied on the upper margin of the *chhatra yashtis*. Here also the artist has preferred the same colour scheme adopted in other rock-shelters, for the effective execution of pictures. Except a little top part of the first and the third *stupas* damaged by leaching, the remaining paintings are fairly good in their state of preservation. The *stupa* on the extreme left of this shelter measures about 2 × 1.50 metres while the middle and the right one measure about 1.75 × 1.60 metres and 2 × 1.70 metres, respectively.

Second Group: Idario Dungar Stupas

The second group of *stupa*-paintings are found in one of the small rock-shelters in another granatoid hillock, locally known as Idario Dungar, about one kilometre north of Idar town. The rock-shelter is located at a height of about 500 m from the ground level.

Shelter IV:

This hooded rock-shelter facing south-west is situated

about 50 metres higher up from the Daulat Bhavan (one of the palatial buildings of the former Idar State constructed on the hill) on the right side of a stepped pathway leading to Jain temples. It contains three *stupa*-paintings. The striking feature of these paintings is that only hemispherical dome of the proper *stupa* surmounted by *harmika* and *yashti* are shown in a well proportioned manner. In all the three depictions the platform on which the superstructure of *stupa* stands, is missing together with crowning *chhatravali* and banners unlike the previously described *stupas*. Here, there is a slight variation in the depiction of *harmika*. The *harmika* in *stupa* one and three, found on either side of the central one, has been drawn in the form of an inverted stepped pyramid, whereas the central one is like those of Gambhirpura *stupas* though they are in a superior quality compared to other *stupa*-paintings of Idar area. *Stupa* one and two are of the same size measuring 0.75 × 1 m, while the third one covers an area of about 70 × 75 cm.

Observations

The *stupa*–paintings described above are quite naturalistic in their representation of the monumental structural *stupas*. The most outstanding feature of these paintings is the depiction of banners or flags in their composition. In this context, it is worth recalling that a Buddhist rock cut-cave, recently found near Siyot in Kutch district of Gujarat, has yielded a number of clay sealings showing *stupas* with banners and is datable to 7th/8th cent. A.D. A number of such votive clay plaques depicting *stupas* adorned with banners were also reported from various parts of Kashmir, Nepal, Western Tibet, Bihar etc. ranging in date from 9th to 15th cent. A.D. Two noteworthy carved stone slabs covering the relic chamber at Khanbhakun in Burma also yielded stylistically similar representations of the *stupas* ascribed to 7th/8th cent. A.D.[3] A *stupa* painting found near Narsinghgarh in the heart of rock-art treasure of Central Indian offers an excellent example of its exquisite depiction.[4] This *stupa* figure resembles with the *stupa*-paintings of Idar area under review.

Here it is interesting to note that the famous Buddhist site of Devnimori is situated about 45 km south of Idar and Vadali, identified as "O–cha–li" referred to by the Chinese pilgrim Huen-Tsang is located just 14 km north of Idar. It seems Huen--Tsang during his travel from Dasapura (Mandasor) to Brigukachchha (Broach) passed through this region of Idar. Therefore, taking into consideration the archaeological data obtained from Devnimori[5] and Vadali[6] one may conclude that the region around Idar was busy with Buddhist activities for quite some time. The *stupa*-paintings found at Idar, on the basis of their stylized structural details including dome, *harmika* and the *chhatra yashti* bearing triple umbrella can be assigned to 4th/5th A.D. The recent survey carried out in this area revealed that Idar was an active centre of various political powers right from the 3rd/4th cent. A.D. Structural remains of the Kshtrapa period were found very close to the hills bearing *stupa* paintings near Gambhirpura.

According to the tradition of the Pali *Mahaparinibana Sutta* of *Dighanikaya* 16.5.10 and its Sanskrit, Tibetan and Chinese parallel Mps 36.3–3, Lord Buddha enjoins upon Ananda (one of Buddha's favourite pupils) not only how to deal with the Tathagata's physical body but also where and how the *stupas* should be built. The Lord gives further details how the *stupas* should be adorned with umbrellas, banners and flags (*chhatra, dhvaja* and *pataka*). The banners or flgas represents glory (*yasas pataka*) and the emanicipation of the mind which is free from greed by itself (*alobhatmika–cheto–Vimukti–dhvajam*). The above account makes it very clear why the replicas of *stupas* are shown with banners or flags so prominently together with other usual structural and decorative elements of the *stupas*.

Depiction of stupas in rock-art, both petrophyphs and paintings certainly had symbolical significance. In fact they are the replicas of pre-existing momuments and also as monuments which existed in the same form as cultic structures for the Buddhists. Further these *stupa*-paintings enable us to visualise the structural monumental *stupas* of the times.

V.H. SONAWANE

Professor, Ancient History and Archaeology
Deptt.M.S. University,
VADODARA

REFERENCE

1. Sonawane, V.H. 1982. "Rock Paintings of Tarsang, Gujarat", *Journal of the Oriental Institute,* Vol. XXXI, No. 3, March, Baroda, pp. 293–299.

2. Hajamis R.G. 1987. Gambhirpura Rock Paintings, in Dhaky and Sagarmal Jain, (Eds.) *Pandit Bechardas, Doshi Commemoration Vol.* Varanasi, pp. 101–103. *Aspects of Jainology* Vol. II.

3. Soni, Sujata. 1991. *Evolution of Stupas in Burma,* Pagan Period: 11th to 13th Centuries A.D., Delhi, Fig. 3, p. 14.

4. Neumayer, Erwin, 1992. Rock Art in India, in. Michel Lorblanchet, (Ed.) *Rock Art in the Old World.* New Delhi, Fig. 14–bottom, p. 220 and 244.

5. Mehta R.N. and S.N. Chowdhary. 1966. *Excavation at Devnimori,* Baroda.

6. Shah U.B. 1960. "Sculpture from Shamalaji and Roda", *Bulletin of Museum and Picture Gallery,* Baroda, Vol. XII, p. 5.

Music and Musical Instrument in Indian Rock-Art

In the large body of chalcolithic rock-art in India I observed a few depictions of harpists.

I think that these pictures are related to mythologies known from early Indian literary sources which might reflected protohistoric customs.

To get a clear idea of thematic setting of these depictions I scanned the rock-art material collected by me for evidences of music and musical instruments.

Chronology

My chronological placing of the pictures under discussion follows an analysis of the rock-art-inherent information. This information from the pictures themselves as well as the observation of the pictures' stratigraphy led me to divide the rock-art in the pictures of the hunters and gatherers and those art of the agriculturists and animal-keepers. While the earlier will here, for convenience sake, be addressed as "mesolithic pictures" the later, the art of the agriculturists and animal-keepers will be divided in the art from periods before and after the introduction of Asokan-Brahmi. These will be addressed as "chalcolithic art" and "historic art" respectively. In this paper I will not dive into a deeper discussion on the disputed points on chronology of rock-art in India.

System

On account of the scarcity and ambivalence of the depicted musical instruments the classification has to be kept simple:

In the Indian rock-pictures we can distinguish

1. Chanting, Singing or Talking
2. Lithophones
3. Idiophones
4. String instruments
5. Wind instruments
6. Drums and (or) Gongs.

The first of these, singings, chanting/talking, is highly speculative.

The second, lithophones, are rather peripheral phenomenon to rock-art research, since lithophones are not shown in the pictures, but are at times carrying rock-pictures on them.

Ideophones are identifiable beyond doubt in historic pictures only. But it must be clear that ideophones, in their more basic forms of simple sticks and rattles are difficult to identify in rock-pictures. Still it is more than likely that these instruments formed an important group of musical instruments as indeed they still are in Indian folk-music. The fourth group, string instruments, here before all the harp, are the most prominently depicted musical instruments. These instruments are compound-artifacts of considerable complexity and a long lived entity in the music culture of India.

Wind instruments are rarely depicted and only known from historic pictures.

The last group, Drums and (or) gongs, are shown conspicuously rare in chalcholithic pictures and absent in mesolithic art. Only in historic rock-pictures drums of different shapes and sizes are shown frequently.

Chanting, Singing/Talking

We of course presume that people – within the time–limits we are dealing here – know to sing, talk or chant. The problem we face is: will we able to recognize music if people indicated it in their paintings?

However, in several of the earliest picture-groups are figures with small circles in front of their mouths. Since all these figures are scenes showing obviously dances, I presume that these small circles indicate the person's singing or chanting (Figs.: 1,2,3). On account of the green pigment used during the style period to which this depictions belong, there is an on going discussion on its possible Upper Palaeolithic origin.

Lithophone

This is a category of percussion instruments which – although not shown in rock-pictures— are sometimes decorated by rock pictures. Lithophones are natural stone–prongs whose one end are held under tremendous pressure from surrounding stone masses, while the free end stands unsupported. If these stones are beaten with a stone or a piece of wood they emit a metallic sound, whose pitch can be modulated according to the point of percussion. A stroke at the far end of the prong will create a lower pitch than one closer to the root. Most lithophones show several percussion grooves along their edges, indicating that these "instruments" were played upon.

These lithophones are often found close to neolithic/chalcolithic settlements in the granite region of the Krishna–Tungábhadra *Doab*. I observed them at the sites of Piklikhal, Korugodu, Kuppagallu and several sites in the Kishkindha Region.

A triangular, upright standing stone prong in the Kuppagallu Hill is covered by bruisings. The central figure of these bruisings is a large figure of a bull around which several other human and animal figures are found as well. Several figures obviously portray couples in sexual congress. These are the pictures which Mr. Bruce Foote did describe as "strangely obscene and quite indescribable"[1].

This stone shows well defined and smothered grooves along the edges and a singular large groove at its zenith. Several of these lithophones are situated in rock-shelters or in spacious hollows beneath granite boulders which form a resonant body, amplifying the sound which can be heard clearly over long distances. Another lithophone was found in Rajasthan's Sikar District. There at a convex rock wall a large piece of exfoliated rock shows several percussion grooves. If struck, this natural gong emits a metallic sound. Some obviously fresh battering marks indicate that this stone was used till recently as a lithophone.

Another lithophone close by consists of a cleaver–shaped piece of rock leaning precariously against the parent rock from which it got detached by natural forces. Grooves at the upper edge are patinated similarly to the natural tint of the rock, indicating a considerable time span since these grooves were battered last. In a well protected hollow above this lithophone an early historic rock picture was found showing a "vase of plenty" from which flowers emanate. Lithophone in form of musical pillars are known as architectural members in south Indian temples. The most famous of these are found in the *mandapa* of the Vitthalaswami Temple in Vijayanagar. The closeness of many of the "natural" lithophones to neolithic/chalcolithic settlements in the Krishna–Tungabhadra *Doab* as well as the bruisings belong to that period placed on their surface, suggests that these stones were played upon at least since then.

Idiophones

It has to be remembered, that figures in Indian rock-art are, generally speaking, quite small. Human figures are rarely higher than 20 to 30 centimetres. Particularly in the mesolithic paintings human pictures are not only small in size but most often reduced to mere stick figures. The minuteness of the depicted artifacts in the hands of this reduced figures makes the identification almost impossible.

One instrument held by one member in a group of dancers (Fig.: 3) might be a multi-pronged comb-like instrument, which, when struck, would give a vibrating rattling sound. Since this instrument is found only once in rock-pictures, the interpretation as musical instrument remains questionable.

The most basic idiophone would consist of no more than two sticks beaten together rhythmically. Indeed there are several Mesolithic rock-pictures showing rows of human figures, all of which are holding short staffs in their hands. In an extensive hunting group from Lakhajoar several persons are seen holding small implements in their hands which might be rattles[2]. Of Course all these identifications are very speculative.

String Instruments

Possibly a bow harp is shown in very early Mesolithic picture- group (Fig.: 4). Although this picture does not belong to the earliest Mesolithic style group available at the site of Kathotia, it is one of those rare pictures executed in green. The two patches of green paintings are the remains of an originally large picture-group which has weathered unevenly at different stretches on the shelter wall and ceiling[3] . The remaining parts of this composition are remarkably clear, although several features in this picture-group are unique in Mesolithic art.

Very clear and detailed are harps only in the pictures of the chalcolithic period. Harpists figure prominently in a number of tantalizing narrative scene-pictures. These pictures are of considerable importance, since they represent the only known material allowing us glimpses into the dramatic and mythologic culture of the chalcolithic people of Malwa. Although we have yet no means to ascertain the absolute age of these pictures, it is quite convincingly established that they were done prior to the introduction of the Asokan-Brahmi script. Indeed some of these pictures belong to the earliest pictorial style of the agriculturists and animal-keepers of Malwa. The technological inventory shown in these pictures comprises the two-wheeled chariot drawn by cattle as well as those horses[4], metal weapons like axes and spears besides the age old microlith-tipped weapons. Swords and daggers make their appearance only in the later stylistic groups of this period (Fig.: 18). Humped cattle can be considered as the "cultural centre" of these pictures. Cattle are most probably the singlemost depicted theme in chalcolithic rock-art. Bulls with lyre-shaped horns and an often exaggerated hump are the "leitfossil" of chalcolithic art.

Horses or other equids make their appearance quite early as draught animals of chariots, and are depicted ridden as well[5].

Depictions of harps are known only from two rock-art regions. The majority were found in the hill ranges south of Bhopal ((Figs., 5, 5a, 6–10, 10a–11). Other examples were found at sites close to the Chambal River or in gorges of her tributaries in the Mandasor District of Madhya Pradesh (Figs.: 14–5). Not only harps but string instruments altogether are conspicuously rare in historic rock-art, which is the more surprising, as harps and other string instruments are depicted frequently in early historic stone sculptures and reliefs. The only examples of depictions of *vina* comes from a site in Gwalior District, showing a three-eyed god with matted hair playing such an instrument (Fig. 16), and from a site close to the Chalukya temples of Pattadakkal in the Bijapur District of Karnataka (Fig.: 17).

It has to be mentioned again and again that rock-pictures are generally very ambivalent. They rarely come in the clearness rendered in a copy. Therefore, every copy has to be taken as interpretation.

The picture (Fig.: 6) of an ithyphallic harpist was recognized by me only during a slide session after I had visited this picture about twenty times over a period of more than 15 years. An earlier interpretation of the same figure can be seen in the illustration from my earlier book[6].

After recognizing the harp in the hand of the man, it was not difficult to recognize it at the original rock-picture as well when I visited the site next. After all we only can see what we know!

Most of the harpists in the chalcolithic pictures seem to be not only functionaries of dances, but an object of reverence.

The most tantalizing picture of a harpist, surrounded by rows of dancers, comes from Kathotia (Fig.: 6). It is one of these pictures of male-oriented frolics in which many of the participants are obviously ithyphallic.

The harpist here seems to be an elevated personality if one can go by his relatively large body size. The harp is rendered quite detailed. It consists of an elongated resonant body which is held close to the hip of the upright standing person so that it projects over the frame of his body backwards. The number of strings cannot really be ascertained since the rock surface is quite rough and took the pigment only at elevated particles.

I believe that the number of strings rendered in the pictures of harpist is rather conventionalized since a viewer at the time of the making of these pictures would have been familiar with the number of strings on a harp anyway. In one of the pictures even the loosely knotted ends of the strings are shown (Fig. 7, 13). The harpists are either depicted staining or squatting but facing a row of dancers, which often are shown with interlinked hands (Fig. : 6–8). Equally common are harpists leading rows of dancers (Figs. 5, 5a, 9).

In several scenes in which harpists are incorporated fantastic animal figures (Fig. 5) and persons with fantastic features (Fig. 5, 9, 10) are to be found as well. I believe these paintings are to illustrate myths.

In one of these pictures from Firengi (Fig. 9) the harpist is surrounded by gesticulating persons. Following him are two persons carrying some load extended from a pole between them. Although it is not clear what load these persons are transporting, load-carrying is a prominently depicted stereotype theme in chalcolithic procession scenes. Load carriers are frequently depicted in chariot–related compositions[7]. In one procession scene a harpist is shown walking in front of a chariot (Figs. 10, 10a). These chariot processions feature, besides pot-bellied ithyphallic gods or heroes enthroned on little seats, jesters and acrobats as well as dancers and fantastic figures.

One of these scene pictures from Firengi (Fig. 5) shows a harpist accompanied by dancers in the vicinity of a large carnivorous beast which holds a diminutive scorpion-like being between its fangs. Below this animal are several squares which I believe to be unfinished animal figures. In the same scene is a large figure of a man goading two cattle across water. The water here is indicated by two fish. Cattle being led by a man or carrying a man across water bring to ones mind similar design on the large funerary urn from the Cemetery "H" in Harappa. I have speculated about soul transportation elsewhere[8], as indeed we can not overlook the many instances in chalcolithic rock-art where a man is shown leading-or being led by- a bull.

Another very interesting scene which includes the depiction of a harp comes from a rock-art site south of Bhopal (Fig. 11). It shows an archer facing a multitude of different animals, several of which are rareiy depicted in chalcolithic rock-art, for example the snake and the crocodile.

The bowman wields two microlith-barbed arrows and his bow. A quiver and some other implements are placed close to him. Before him lays a harp with spherical resonant body. Facing him are the creatures of the forest, the rivers and the skies — the running, crawling, swimming and flying ones — representing the beasts of the three spheres. Even a bee hive is seen placed between the legs of one of the antelopes.. At the lower fringe of this picture is a man holding a club in his hands. To his back a huge tortoise is depicted. This painting belongs to the earliest style group of chalcolithic art.

Depictions of harps are absent in historic rock-pictures except for three known examples in the rock art of the Mahadeo Hills. Indeed, the most well known picture of a harpist comes from there (Fig. 13). This picture was first published by Gordon[9] and subtitled "The harpist and his family". This painting shows the instrument in most detailed manner. Its construction is slightly different from chalcolithic harps insofar as the resonant body is shaped like a basket. A further picture of a harpist appears close to the picture of a demon figure. This spatial arrangement might be incidental rather than intended (Fig. 14). What concerns us here is the detailed portrayal of the harp with its basket-like resonant body. A third harpist from the Mahadeo Hills was noticed in the pictures inside the large shelter at Kites Crag (Fig. 15). The harpist is placed in a scene centred around a honey comb.

I believe that the harp was an instrument for the cult practice, which is particularly strongly suggested from the chalcolithic pictures in Ganesh Ghati (Fig. 11), Firengi (Figs. 5–6) and Jaora (Fig. 10). This of course does not exclude the use of harps in perfectly profane music as well.

Only two depictions of other string instruments are known to me in historic rock pictures. One depiction of a three-eyed god holding a *vina* or an *ektara* comes from a site in the Gwalior District (Fig. 16), the other picture was found close to the Chalukyan temples of Pattadakkal, which similarly shows a person with a *vina* (Fig. 17). Both these figures belong to the historic period, the former most probably to the Gupta period, the latter might even be more recent.

Windinstruments

Windinstruments are a poorly represented class of musical instruments in rock-art. All examples known to me belong to the historic period, except a single picture from Firengi (Fig. 18) which is part of a fighting scene including a chariot and most probably belongs to the late chalcolithic or very early historic period[10].

Detailed depictions of trumpets are known from the pictures in the Mahadeo Hills. In the "Chieftain Shelter" at Marodeo close to Panchamarhi there are figures of persons in fighting scene blowing horn–shaped wind instruments (Figs. 19; 19a)[11]. Another picture is found in one of the Jambu Dweep Shelters (Fig. 20,) Gordon,[12]. This scene shows persons sitting at small seats, two of them holding some unknown paraphernalia before their faces. These instruments are often related to enthroned personalities and might represent a mirror[13]. A third picture found in the Upper Dorothy Deep Shelter shows a "demon" holding obviously a trumpet (Fig. 21)[14]. This figure is placed closely to a unique picture of a person lying on a cot. The only picture of a wind instrument from a rock-picture site outside the Mahadeo Hills comes from Satkunda in the Raisen District of Madhya Pradesh (Fig. 22). It shows two persons laying on a pier(?) and being carried by four persons. Some other figures obviously belonging to the same picture scene include two men locked into combat and a third person blowing a horn.

My observation is, that almost all the wind instruments are closely related to fighting scenes. This makes it more than probable that wind instruments were used for signalling during fights, or rather for noise-making during skirmishes.

Drums and Gongs

Although drums are considered a primeval musical instrument, their depiction is confined almost exclusively to historic rock-pictures.

A few depictions of implements in prehistoric pictures might be understood as cymbals, gongs or frame drums, but these interpretations are highly speculative. There is a very early Mesolithic picture-group of dancers on scaffolding (Fig. 23), in which one dancer is holding a round instrument, which might be a frame drum. In several chalcolithic procession scenes round, wheel-like, instruments in the hands of persons might be frame drums (Figs. 9, 14) and in one case larger and smaller implements are hung from a carrying-yoke carried by two persons. The interpretation of these instruments as drums or gongs has it s pros and cons. It is only in the historic pictures that drums are shown more frequently and more detailed. Most commonly depicted is the two-sided drum held vertically by an upright standing person who is striking the vertically positioned drum at either side with both his hands or with drum-sticks. This type of drum is shown already in late chalcolithic pictures from the Chambal Region (Fig. 26).

Double sided drums appear frequently in picture-groups related to large fighting scenes (Figs. 18, 19, 19a). A unique picture-scene rom Naryauli near Sagar shows a drummer holding a large drum upright, beating it with both hands on one side (Fig. 27). Two drummers flanking the image of Ganesha are shown in a historic picture from Bhimbetka (Fig. 30).

Conclusion

As we have seen, only the harp can be identified beyond doubt in the prehistoric rock-pictures. This instrument was obviously used in dramatic or mythic performance in which ithyphallic men participated or were object of reverence. It is surprising that depiction of the harp ceases in rock-pictures of the historic period, save the few examples from the historic rock-art in the Mahadeo Hills.

The cultic use of the harp is well attested from early Buddhist sculpture as well as from high demonstrative Gupta coinage showing the king himself playing the harp. The portrayal of the king as a harpist can not be taken as a profane picture of a music-loving person, but it is a heraldic portrayal of the sovereign in the act of an elevating cult-exercise[15].

We can presume, that the depiction of a harpist in the chalcolithic rock-pictures as well portray socially or mythologically elevated personalities which may fit the term hero or god.

Erwin Neumayer

7060 Vienna, Gumpendorferstr
114/21 Austria

REFERENCES

1. Foote, R.B., 1916 *Indian Prehistoric and Protohistoric Antiq uities, Notes on their Ages and Distribution* Madras p. 89.
2. Neumayer, E., 1983 *Prehistoric Indian Rock Paintings;* Ox ford University Press, New Delhi, Fig 38
3. *Ibid,* Figs 11-12.
4. Neumayer, E., 1991 Wheeled Vehicles and mounted Animals in Prehistoric Indian Rock Art; *Man and Environment,* Vol. 16/ 2 1991, pp 39–70
5. *Ibid.*
6. Neumayer, 1983. *op. cit,* Fig. 118.
7. Neumayer 1991 *op cit.*
8. Neumayer 1983 *op cit.* Fig 110.
9. Gordon, D.H. 1958 *The Prehistoric Background of Indian Culture*; Bombay
10. Neumayer 1991 *op. cit.*
11. Gordon, D.H., n.d. (1938) Warfare in Indian Cave Art. In: *Reprints from Science and Culture,* Calcutta; pp 25-7
12. *Ibid.* p. 26 pl 16.
13. Neumayer, E., 1981 *Rock Pictures in the Mahadeo Hills,* Selbstverlag, Wien
14. Gordon, M.E. & Gordon, D.H., n.d. (1939) Animals and Demons in Indian Cave Art. In R*reprint from Science and Culture,* Calcutta. pp. 27–33.
15. Stoler–Miller, B., 1992 A Dynasty of Patrons: The Representation of Gupta Royalty in Coins and Literature, In: Stoler–Miller, B.D. (ed), 1992 *The power of Art;* pp 54–64, Oxford University Press, New Delhi

Fig. 1. *Lakhajoar: Red with green contour lines; Height 40 cm*

Fig. 2. *Lakhajoar: Green: Height of the figures appx. 20 cm*

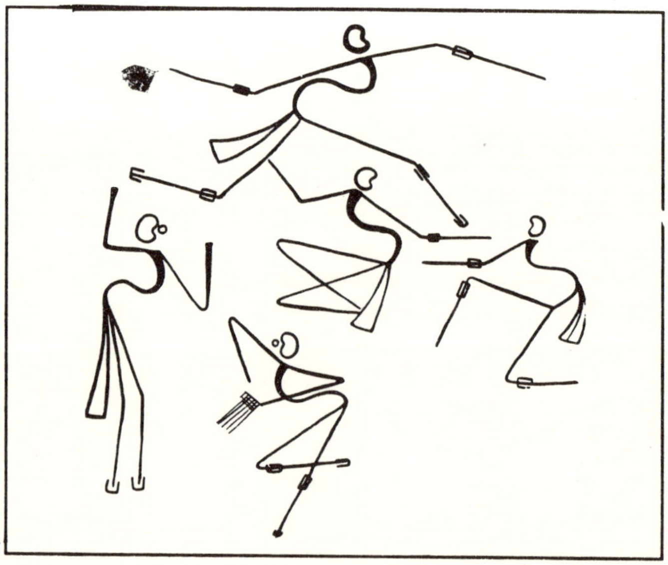

Fig. 3. *Lakhajoar: Green; Height of left standing figure 20 cm*

Fig. 4. *Kathotia: Green; Average height of the human figures 20 cm*

Fig. 5. *Ganesh Ghati: Red* Fig. 5a. *Details from Fig. 5*

Fig. 6. *Kathotia: Red*

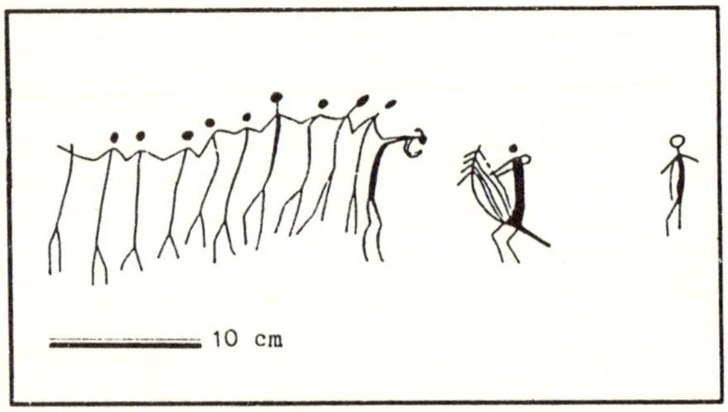

Fig. 7. *Firengi: Red*

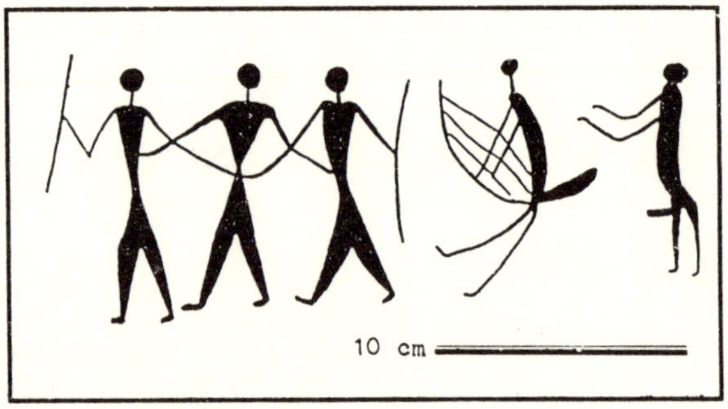

Fig. 8. *Firengi: Red*

Fig. 9. *Firengi: Red*

Fig. 10. *Jaora: Red*

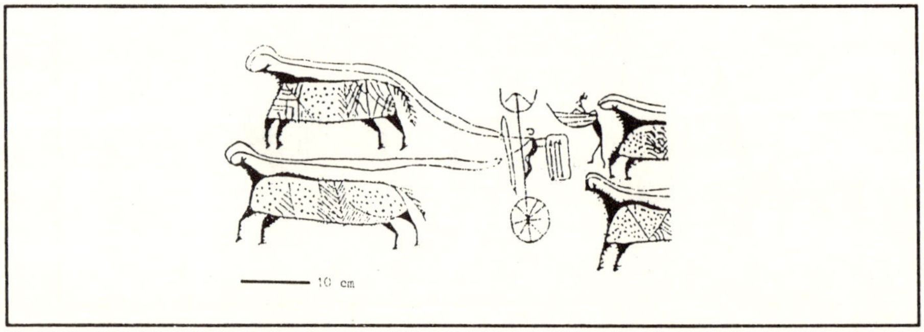

Fig. 10a. *Detail from Fig. 10*

Fig. 11. *Ganesh Ghati: Red*

Fig. 12. *Dekan-Adarshila: White*

Fig. 12a. *Detail from Fig. 12*

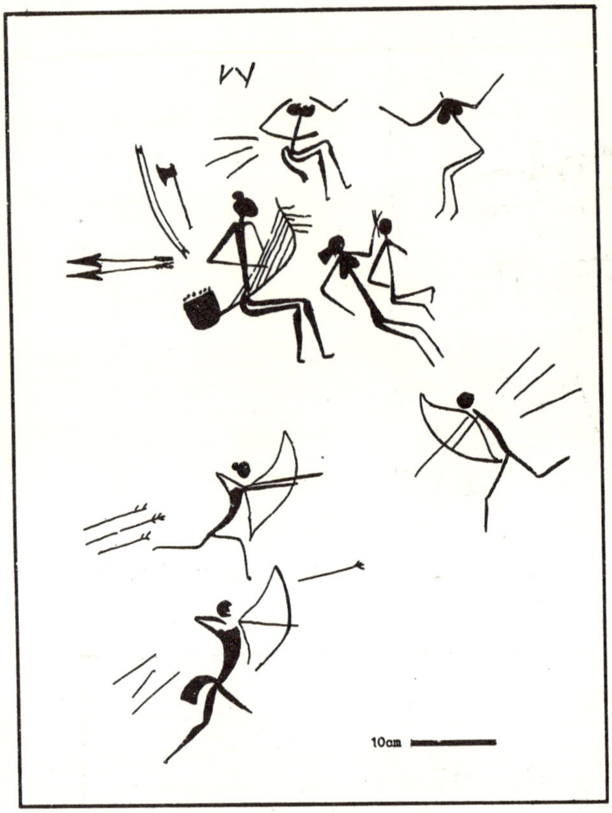

Fig. 13. *Mahadeo Hills - Jota Shanka: White*

Fig. 14. *Mahadeo Hills - Rajat Phrabat: White*

Fig. 15. *Mahadeo Hills - Kites Crag: White*

Fig. 16. *Tikula: Red*

Fig 17. *Pattadkal: Red*

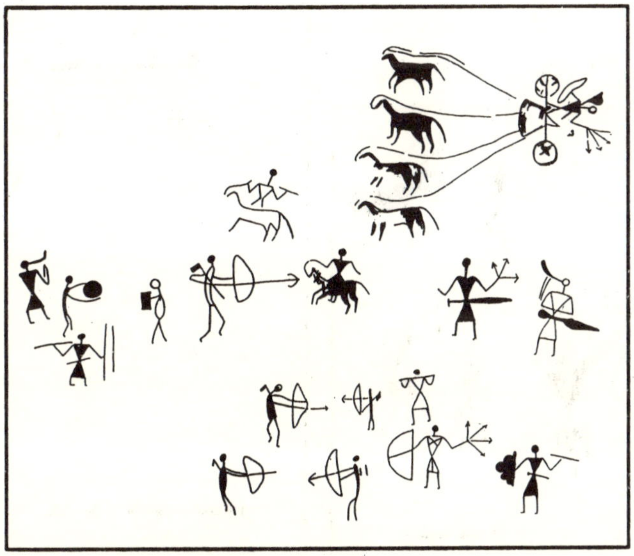

Fig. 18. *Firengi: Red*

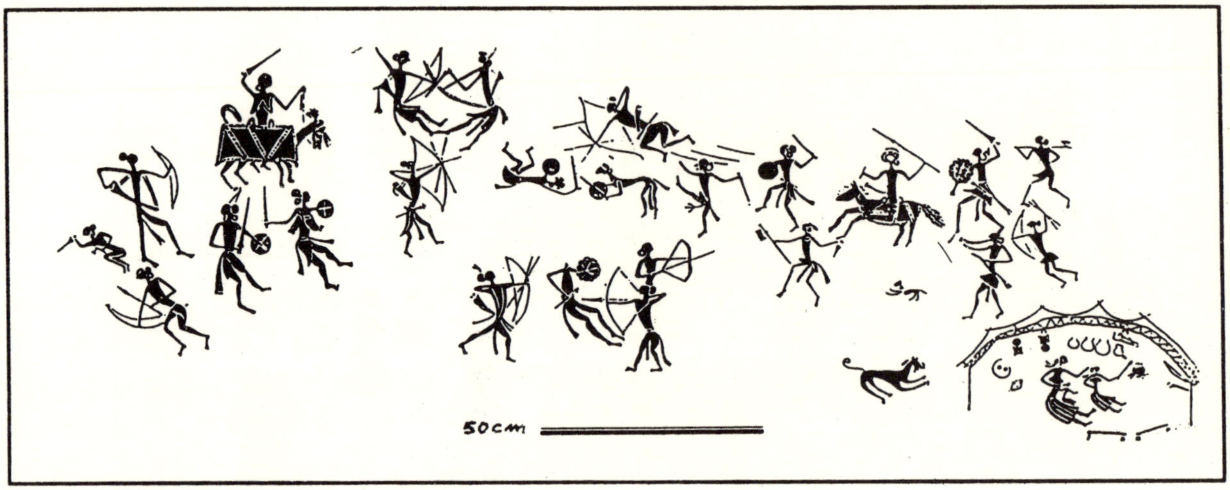

Fig. 19. *Mahadeo Hills - Marodeo White foundation; Red contour lines*

Fig. 19a. *Detail from* Fig. 19

Fig. 20. *Mahadeo Hills - Jambu Dweep: White*

Fig. 21. *Mahadeo Hills - Upper Dorothy Deep: White*

Fig. 22. *Satkunda: Red*

Fig. 23. *Lakhajoar: Red*

Fig. 24. *Urden: Red*

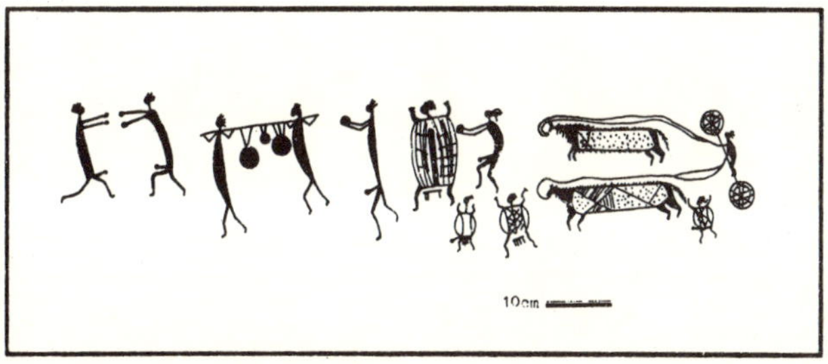

Fig. 25. *Kathotia: Red*

Fig. 26. *Chatur Bhoj Nath Nulla: Red*

Fig. 27. *Naryauli: Red*

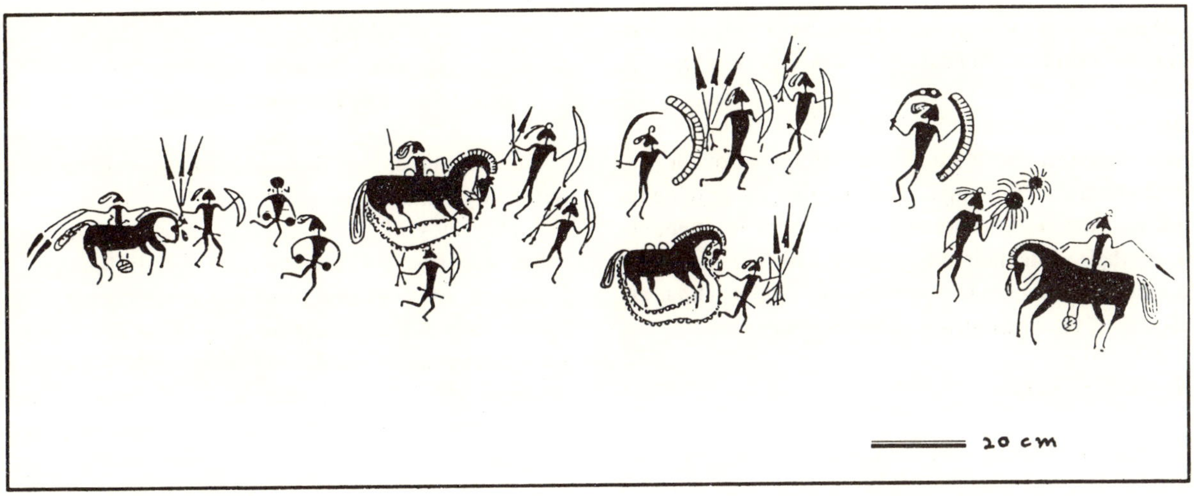

Fig. 28. *Bhimbetka: Red*

Fig. 29. *Bhimbetka: Red*

Fig. 30. *Bhimbetka: Red*

Hero Stones in Manki

Manki, a small village in the Honnavar Taluka, (11 km. from the north of Honnavar) Uttara Kannada district, Karnataka State, has artistically engraved pillars, a few hero stones, *basadis* and temples. These belong to the periods between the tenth and the beginning of the sixteenth centuries. Although a few inscriptions provide insight into the significance and antiquity of these monuments, their systematic study has yet to take place. An attempt is made here to study the inscription which apprises us of the significance of these monuments.

Pillared Inscriptions

One of the monuments worthy to be noticed is pillars. These pillars are engraved and contain inscription in Kannada language. They are now found in the compound of the S̄antinatha *basadi* at Manki. One of the inscriptions is found on a pillar at the back side of the same *basadi*. It has engraved sculptures on its three faces. Its east face is blank. *Jina's* head is carved on the top of its four. An epigraph now erased is noticed between the first and second panel (from the bottom to the top) on the south face of the pillar. The inscription is assigned to the tenth century. It seems to record a gift of money and land. It was, probably, for the basadi[1]. Further the same inscription, says that Gosugarasa Dandanayaka Komma Setti and Nadayya Senabova made provision for its protection.

The above pillar has beautiful carving of figures. The battle scene with soldiers sitting on the back of the horses and elephants, the bow, the arrow and sword, *yaksha* and *yakshini*, drum beating men and women are engraved. The study of the inscription and architectural figures allude to the existence of Jainism and organised political set up in the region.

Another artistically designed pillar[2] with four faces is situated in front of the same *basadi*. This pillar has also Kannada inscription found on its west face. The inscription is in six lines. The character of the script is assigned to the eleventh century. The inscription calls it Banasi Kallu. The Annual Report records that Honnaya, the Heggade of Boyoja and Bomma Senabova constructed and engraved it respectively[3]. However, the actual reading is

"Kannadi baliya Pattu ba
nasiya Kallu Edu Ka
ndarisi Madida
gga (da) (Ba) jara
lu .... nidu Bommar
Senabovana Likhita"

(Tr. Kannadi Bali Banasi Kallu engraved and it was written by Bommarsa Benabova.)

The study of the inscription suggests that certain communities have different names of Bali (lineage). The Senabova was entrusted to write the inscription. On all four sides in twelve panels the story of the Ramayana and early achievements of Ravana are carved. The dress and ornaments of men and women, social customs, the means of communication, vivid description of war are depicted on the pillar.

Basadis

The epigraphical sources refer to six basadis although now there is only one *basadi*, S̄antin̄atha and the latter is situated in the Kumbhar One, Manki. Its structure belongs to the early Vijayanagara period although local tradition mentions its construction in the Kadamba period[4]. One of the inscription dated Saka 1340 (A.D. 1417) from Kaikini (Bhatkala) refers to the grant of the Nagire chief, Sangiraya to the Manki *basadi* along with other *basadis* at Sirali and Kaikini. The same epigraph states that the above grant was entrusted to Sode Kiṭiyanna Nayaka[5].

The existence of other two *basadis* such as Chitrakuta and Chavvisa Tirthankara *basadis*, and their structures are known to us from a stone inscription, now found under a mango tree in the area now known as Bola basadi in Manki village. The epigraph is dated in Saka era in chronogram i.e, saka 1437 = A.D. Second April, 1514. The rule of Mahamanḍal̄esvara Saluva Immadi Devarasa with Nagire as his capital is recorded. It mentions the rule of Pratapa Deva raya (*sic* Krishnadevaraya) at Vijayanagara. Then the epigraph states[6] that Mallappa Heggade, prominent citizen, erected a *Chaityalaya* at Manki, at the instance of his *Guru* Padmaprabha deva. Heggade installed the image of Ananta Tirthankara in the same *basadi*. The *Chaityalaya*, says the inscription "was constructed in such artistic picturesque manner that the ruling king Devarasa named it *Chitrakuta"*. Further the epigraph states that the same Heggade also constructed in the same place another *basadi* and here he installed *Chavvisa* tirthankara. It is known from the same inscription that the *basadis* had storeys where different *Tirthankaras* were worshipped. The grants of Heggade and other individuals to these *basadis* and the protection of the earlier grants to the temples of Kokkesvara and Vinayaka are mentioned in the same inscription.

Hero stones

Manki has considerable number of hero stones found in front of the Santinatha *basadi* and in the compound of the *Mastamane*. These belong to the Vijayanagara period. These hero stones are known for the carvings of different styles of structures and sculptures. These hero stones have inscriptions in Kannada language. These epigraphs provide information about the heroes, their lineages, the causes of their fight, the ruling kings on whose behalf these heroes fought and the dates of the events and the names of the founders of the hero-stones. It is interesting to note that a few herostones mention their engravers. For instance, one of the herostones, found in front of the same ba*sadi*, Saka 1400 (A.D. 1478) refers to the fight between Bairavaraya, the ruler of the Nagire, and his brother, and mentions the death of Kallunayaka of Manki while encountering the enemy. Then it records that Devappa Nayaka, the brother of the deceased hero, founded the above hero stone and it was engraved by Isarachari, son of Kotiyachari of Kayakini (Kaikini)[7].

The study of a few hero stones of Manki and the area around indicates that Manki often became a battleground and that a few people of that place lost their lives while fighting the enemies[8]. The construction of different structures of the religious institutions, the social and religious beliefs reflected in the sculptures, vivid description of the battles and the strategy involved and arms and ammunitions known in the region are mirrored in these herostones.

Conclusion

The study of a few inscriptions enables us to know the antiquity of Jainism, its progress,contact with other religious institutions (local and Vedic faiths).

A few hero stones depict the battle scenes and social customs of the people and also the means of communication prevalent in the region. These hero stones mention different names of the lineages of the families and their lines of succession.

Reader in History, Vijaya College, Mulki

K.V. VASANTAMADHAVA

NOTES AND REFERENCES.

1. Annigeri A.M. and Joshi B.R. *The Descriptive Lists of Stone & Copper Plate Inscriptions* examined by Kannada Research Institute, Dharwar During the Years 1940–41, to 1942–43 (Kannada Research Institute Dharwar 1961 cited this work hereafter Discriptive List) 1940–41 No 2 to 12. The Report says that it is found near Parsvanatha Basti. But the latter is not traceable now.
2. This pillar is about 7 ft. height and carvings are found on its four faces.
3. Discriptive Lists: No. 73
* The texts of the inscription, the author of this article secured through S Ganapati Gowda Karnataka University, Dharwad.
4. Shanbbhag R.G. Maniura Endina Manki (Kannada), *Manjuvani* Ujjire September 1991. p. 23.
5. Panchmukhi R.S. *Karnataka Inscriptions* Vol. I (cited this as *K.I*) Dharwar, No 41 of 1939–40 p 99 line 56
6. *Discriptive Lists*. No. 62, p 11
7. *Ibid.*, No 51 p 9
8. *Ibid.*, Nos 52, 53, 65 pp 9, 11 *K.I* Nos 47, 56 of 1939 40 p 116, 135. Unnoticed hero stone dates saka 1384 (*sic* 1360) found at Siruru (S.K.). The author of this article expresses his thanks to Sri J. Achuta Hebbar Kergal for tracing the hero stone inscription. The author of this article also expresses his gratitude to Sri S. Ganapati Gowda, Research Scholar, Ancient Indian History and Epigraphy Department, Karnataka University, Dharwad and Mrs Ravindrakumar Jain of the Santinatha basadi.

BOOK REVIEWS

D. P. Agrawal, *Man and Environment in India Through Ages,* Books and Books, 1992, New Delhi. pp. 293, 60 illustrations, tables, Price: Rs. 1,000/-.

This book summarises the recent evidences about the environmental and climatic changes in India during the past four million years. It is interdisciplinary in perspective and the inferences are based upon a variety of latest techniques. The markers for climatic and environmental changes are based on chemical, physical, mineral, magnetic, biological and geological techniques. The chronology is based on a variety of physical, geological and pedological data. Despite the diverse data and multidisciplinary approach the book is very well integrated and presented in a very lucid style so that both scholars and layman alike can enjoy and benefit.

At the moment more definitive type of evidence comes only from Kashmir, Rajasthan, Gujarat and the Arabian Sea. Such long continental records are very rare in the world and Kashmir provides unique lake-records going back to four million years. Generally climatic changes are inferred from sea and ice cores but they give a very averaged out picture. The continental records, on the other hand provide much sharper evidence and is more important for restructuring global climatic changes. The book represents a monumental effort mounted by a number of institutions including several Universities, Physical Research Laboratory, Ahmedabad and the Geological Survey of India. The team working in Kashmir was led by the author of the book, and therefore, it incorporates the latest evidence fresh from the oven. Otherwise, it would have taken several years for the latest research to come out in book form.

The present work will be a valuable asset for archaeologists because the environmental changes have been discussed with reference to changes in the man's technology and settlements. At the moment, thanks to D.P. Agrawal and his co-workers, we have ample material on palaeoenvironmental changes, especially for Rajasthan and Kashmir. The book provides a challenge to the archaeologists to correlate the settlement pattern through time with the environmental and climatic changes in the past.

For the worker in the field, the book provides very useful description of the various techniques as also climatic reconstruction. The book serves both as a practical guide for the field worker, as also caters to the scholar with a theoretical bent of mind.

The author does not confine himself to the problems of the past alone but relates such studies to the problems faced today by human kind. The significance of such studies in this period of environmental and civilizational crises cannot be over-emphasised. The problems of global warming have been explained from the perspective of palaeoclimatic studies.

It is interesting to note that in the climatically sensitive areas of Rajasthan and Kashmir, early man inhabits the region only during the periods of climatic amelioration. During deterioration of climate, man moves to more congenial type of ecologies. For such marginal areas, therefore, environment seems to play a deterministic role.

For the archaeologists who are interested in Stone Age, this book is specially valuable, as all the techniques discussed and employed in the reconstruction of palaeoenvironment are explained in simple terms. It is necessary now that the Indian prehistory uses all such techniques and more for carrying out prehistoric reconstructions in India. This book will have an appeal to a wide spectrum of scholars belonging to archaeology, geology, pedology and those concerned about global climatic changes. The book is very well illustrated with a large number of drawings and photographs. Despite the technical nature of the discussion, the presentation has been made lucid keeping in view the layman in mind. We only wish that the author had given some more space to archaeological discussions but it seems that in such a multidisciplinary book, it is very difficult to be choosy and single out any one discipline.

K. N. Dikshit

Deo, S.B. and Kamath, Suryanath (Eds.) *The Aryan problem* published by Bharatiya Itihasa Sankalan Samiti, 528-C, Shanivar Peth, Pune, pp. 224, Price: Rs. 205/-

The Mythic Society, Bangalore, and the Bharatiya Itihasa Sankalan Samiti, Pune jointly organised at Bangalore, an All-India Seminar on the Aryan Problem in July, 1991. More than forty scholars, belonging to different disciplines such as archaeology, astronomy, anthropology, linguistics, palaeography as also Sankritists, historians and social scientists presented their papers elaborating various aspects of the Aryan Problem and also contesting various claims, refuting several theories which some scholars feel are uncontestable. The historical writings on India by the Westerners in general and the Britishers in particular, during the 19th and early 20th centuries, display clear bias and prejudice against the form and contents of the vedic culture even though they simultaneously display their admiration for Sanskrit classics.

The present volume includes papers by renowned scholars like Prof. B.N. Mukherji (Calcutta); Dr. M.A. Mehendale (Pune); Prof. S. Ritti (Dharwar); Dr. S.P. Gupta, Shri Bhagawan Singh and Shri Devendra Swarup Agrawal (Delhi); Dr. S. R. Rao (Bangalore); Dr. R. Nagaswamy (Madras); Prof. A.M. Shastri(Nagpur); Prof. S.A. Dange (Bombay); Prof. V.S. Pathak (Gorakhpur); Shri Shriram Sathe (Hyderabad); Shri L.S. Wakankar (Pune); Dr. S.R. Walimbe (Pune); Shri S.P. Annamalai (Madras); Dr. N.R. Varadpande (Nagpur) and others.

The papers are arranged in eight sections: (i) Approach to History, (ii) The Aryans - A Linguistic Approach, (iii) 'Arya' in Literature, (iv) The Aryans - Anthropological Approach, (v) Original Home of the Aryans, (vi) Archaeology of the Vedic People, (vii) Aryans and the Indus-Saraswati Civilization and (viii) Aryan Culture.

The approach has been entirely academic as these papers incorporate not only a survey and evaluation of earlier writings but also put forth quite a range of fresh evidence and new deductions which will interest every scholar of the Aryan problem. These papers provide a very balanced view of this so very important aspect of the opening chapter of the history of the Indian people. Most of the papers have questioned the very basis on which the Aryan Race, the Aryan invasion, the Aryan migration, the Aryan-Dravidian conflict etc. were built by the British and accepted by the Indian scholars. It is the first attempt of its kind since its approach is multidisciplinary.

Printed in double crown size in double column, the publication will be extremely useful to scholars, researchers and laymen who are interested to know the truth about the character of the Aryan culture and the origin of the Aryan people who have been so far very much maligned, generally painted as nomadic and tribal, primitive and warlike, invading and migrating into distant lands, including India, and destroying the settlements of the civilised people. The authors of various research papers have individually concluded that all such views are absolutely baseless and must be immediately discarded. But why? For this, read the book.

T.P. Verma

Singh A.K. *Saltanat-kala main Hindu Pratirodha* (Hindi), Published by Publications Scheme, Jaipur, pp. 612, Price: Rs. 480/-

It is a highly researched work on a very controversial issue of the early medieval history of India—why did the same Muslim invaders who had completely annihilated the ancient cultures of Iran, Iraq, Central Asia etc. within a century or so of their arrival in the new lands, completely failed to achieve the same results in India? How did the Hindus protest and fight against the Muslims for about 600 years before the Muslim rule could establish itself at Delhi? Why did the Muslims fail to wipe out Hinduism in India in spite of centuries of their ruthless rule? Not that Dr. Singh has given answers to all these questions, but he has tried to collect most of the relevant data from different historical sources— Islamic and Hindu—to show the strength and weakness of the Hindu rulers. They fought the Muslims but generally without being helped by other Hindu rulers and without proper planning and innovation. Valour alone does not win a war. Riches also do not defeat the enemy. Compassion is not a friend of the nation-in-war. The Hindu rulers had all these wrongly-placed values of life. They were thus defeated in most of the battles but fortune also smiled on them in many other battles.

The theme is not new but the attempt is fresh and noteworthy because the author knows so many languages, including Persian, Pali and Sanskrit. There are in all nine chapters dealing with Arab invasions, the earliest of which goes back to A.D. 636 i.e. within four years of Prophet Mohammad's death and within the rule of the first Khalifa, Umar. Chapter after chapter, the author narrates the stories of wars, all arranged in a neat chronological order covering the period from 7th century to 15th century. It is, thus, a story of political history. The printing is unfortunately not very good but the contents are excellent.

T.P. Verma

Singh, Chandramani and Vashishtha, Neelima (Eds.) *Pathways to Literature, Art and Archaeology* (A Felicitaion Volume in Honour of Pandit G.N. Bahura). 2 volumes, Publication Scheme, Jaipur, 1993. Price: set Rs. 2500/-

It is a publication containing 86 articles by several leading Indian and foreign Indologists on a vast variety of subjects— art, Archaeology, Sanskrit, Pali, Persian, Literature, astronomy, architecture, iconography etc. —written in Hindi, Sanskrit and English and dedicated to one of the doyens of Indian studies who spent most of his life in studying and publishing rare manuscripts in the collections of the royal house of Jaipur.

Articles such as the 'Vedas as Science' by K.C. Kulish, 'Rigvedic Seas and Deserts' by J.N. Asopa, 'Contribution of Rajasthan to Sanskrit Literature' by Kala Nath Shastri, 'Treatises on Dadupanthi Monastic Disciplines' by M.T. Horstmann; 'The Philosophy of Yoga of MM Dr. Gopinath Kaviraja' by Jaidev Singh'; 'Did Nalanda Exist During the Gupta Times' by B.N. Misra; 'Nilakantha Mahadeva Temple, Bavaka, Gujarat' by P.K. Trivedi; 'Amber's Antiquities: Text and Context' by Michael W. Meister; and several Hindi articles by such eminent scholars as Vidyanivas Mishra, Purushottam Lal Bhargava, Brijamohan Javalia are only a few of the notable papers which the reviewer read and benefitted immensely. Illustrated with more than eighty photographs and drawings, the publication is a very good reference book for Indologists.

S.P. Gupta

Yavanika, Journal of the Indian Society for Greek and Roman Studies, Vols 1 for 1991 and 2 for 1992, both eidted by Prof. U.P. Arora, Rohilkhand University and published by the ISGRS, Rohilkand University, Bareilly, UP. Price: Rs 100/- $ 25/- each.

Cultural and trade interactions between India, Greece and Rome has always been a two-way traffic in ancient times. While the North, particularly North-West subcontinent came under the influence of the Bactrian Greeks, the South had more trade relationship with the Roman World, albeit a little later. Again it was the invasion of the Macedonian, Alexander the Great, in 326 BC provided the sheet-anchor for the chronology of the historical period in India. It was not an episode in Indian history unlike the Arab conquest of Sind.

The Tamil word for rice -*arisi* - has near resemblance to the Greek *Oryza*. The 'lady with lamp' - *dipalaksmi* - is popular in Tamilnadu even today and it is certainly the lagacy of the Indo-Greeks. It is referred to as *Yavanappavai/pavai vilakku* in the Tamil Sangam literature. In the North, the Greeks seem to have impacted on art, especially the Gandharan art and coinage. They ultimately got assimilated in local population.

To further Indo-Graeco-Roman-studies in India it was decided, in an informal meeting of the assembled archaeologists and historians there in Guntur to form a Society called Indian Society for Greek and Roman Studies (ISGRS) in 1989. It held its first annual conference in 1991 and what is worth congratulating is the publication of *Yavanika* its organ, in 1991 even in the inaugural conference;all kudos to its founder editor Prof. Arora.

These two volumes of *Yavanika* carry several interesting and thought-provoking papers by distinguished savants. In the first volume Soundara Rajan appreciates the name *Yavanika* which at once means an Ionian girl and a stage curtain (Skt.) and hopes it would be a multi-coloured curtain unravelling the Indo-Graeco-Roman research in all its splendour. 'A New approach to the history of the Greeks in India' by Bopearachchi gives a new dimension to the study of Indo-Greek numismatics and thereby to the history of the Greeks in India; Arora's essay 'Roman-Age authors on ancient India' tells us in fine that the materially affluent and pleasure-seeking Romans impelled the Roman philosophers to look to India for spiritual fulfillment. 'Indians of distant east continued to remain noble'. Do we have an American parallel here?

In his 'The Warehouse Theory of Indo-Roman trade between First and Fourth century A.D.' Siddiqui concludes that the Indo-Roman trade during this period was Warehouse-oriented. B.N. Mukherjee (A Note on the Greek version of RE XII of Asoka) gives a new interpretation to the term *didabhatita* (Greek version *Besileos Sumpheronta noein*) and concludes that the term means 'firm devotion to the king, the head of the State'. Sinha's 'Carvaka and Epicurus- A study in parallels' is thought provoking.

The second volume embodies the Presidential Address by A.K. Narain who, most appropriately, was chosen to preside over the Society's first Conference in 1991. Arora's (Understanding Greek Nomenclatures in Classical Accounts of India) highlights the pitfalls in relying translations of foreign texts. 'The Image of Dawn in the Indo-Graeco-Roman Mind' subtly explains the perpetual youth of the goddess of Dawn, (though 'causing men to age') from the Vedic, Greek and Roman mythologies. Liu Yinsheng in his article, 'Indirect Graeco-Roman influence on Chinese Muslims' recaptures Graeco-Roman influence on the Chinese works of science.

Yavanika is the answer to the direly needed forum for venting the views on Graeco-Roman interactions with India and the vacuum that existed for a long time is filled up now.

K.S. Ramachandran

INDIAN ARCHAEOLOGICAL SOCIETY

LIST OF LIFE MEMBERS*

Mr. R.K. Agnihotri
58, Zone 1
Maharana Pratap Nagar
BHOPAL (MP)

Prof. D.P. Agrawal
Physical Research Laboratory
Navrangpura
AHMEDABAD – 380 009

Dr. R.C. Agrawal,
Archaeological Survey of India
Bhopal Circle, 10, Professor Colony
BHOPAL – 462 002 (MP)

Mr. Ravindra Nath Aggrawal
Department of A.I.H.C. & Archaeology
Dr. Hari Singh Gaur Vishwavidyalaya
SAGAR – 470 003 (MP)

Shri Ajay Kumar
C/o Shri Avinash Kumar Srivastava
Moha. Amber Chauraha
BIHAR SHARIF – 803 101, Bihar

Sri Jamnadas Akhtar
(address not given)

Dr. M. Shafiqul Alam
Department of Archaeology
22/1 Block B
Babar Road, Mohammadpur
DHAKA 1207, Bangladesh

Dr. F.R. Allchin,
Ancient India & Iran Trust
Brooklands House
23, Brooklands Avenue
CAMBRIDGE CB2 2BG, U.K.

Dr. Amarendra Nath
Excavations Branch
Old High Court Building
NAGPUR – 440 001 (Mah)

Dr. I.H. Ansari,
P.G. Department of History
Government Roaza P.G. College
Rampur – 244 901 (UP)

Dr. U.P. Arora
Department of History and Culture
Rohilkhand University
BAREILLY (UP)

Dr. Arun Kumar
Archaeological Survey of India
Lucknow Circle
Baolloe Gaurd Cottage
Golagang
LUNCKNOW – 226 018 (U.P.)

Dr.(Mrs.) P. Arundhati
A-101, Pandara Road,
New Delhi –110 003

Dr. S.P. Asthana
National Museum,
Janpath, NEW DELHI –110 011

Dr. Shubhangana Atre
Department of Archaeology
Deccan College,
PUNE – 411 006

Dr. Bachchan Kumar
Research Fellow
Indira Gandhi National Centre for Arts
Janpath, NEW DELHI –110 001

Prof. Shiva B. Bajpai
Deptt. of History
California State University
Northridge, Los Angeles
CALIFORNIA 91330

Dr. Arundhati Banerjee
Archaeological Survey of India,
Janpath, NEW DELHI-110 011

Dr. H.C. Bharadwaj
Department of A.I.H.C. & Archaeology
Banaras Hindu University
VARANASI- 221 005 (UP)

Mr. S.R. Bharadwaj
'Sraoj', G-62, Dhaka Colony
DELHI – 110 009

Smt. Bharati Shroti
83, Sethi Nagar
UJJAIN – (MP)

Shri Piyush Bhatt
House No. 111, Krishna Kunja
Laxmi Nagar
DELHI - 110 092

Dr. Rakesh Bhatt
Department of Archaeology
P.B. 16, Garhwal University
SRINAGAR - 246 174 (UP)

Dr. S.K. Bhatt
Academy of Indian Numismatics and Sigillography
115 Kailash Park, Manoramaganj
INDORE – 452 031 (MP)

Dr. D.K. Borah
Deputy Director Research (H)
ITANAGAR
Arunachal Pradesh

Subhash Brahmbhatt
3, Raopura Society
Opp. St. Xavier's School
Navrangpura
AHMEDABAD - 380 009(Guj.)

Prof. D.K. Chakrabarti
Faculty of Oriental Studies
Cambridge University
Sidgwick Avenue
CAMBRIDGE CB3 QDA, U.K.

Shri Umesh Chandra Chottopadhyay
Department of Ancient History, Culture and Archaeology, Allahabad University
ALLAHABAD (UP)

Dr. Subrata Chakrabarti
Sonajhori , Purva Palli
SANTINIKETAN – 731 235 (WB)

Dr. P.K. Chattopadhyaya
Training Centre, Alloy Steel Plant
DURGAPUR–(WB)

Dr. (Mrs.) Gayatri Chaturvedi
C/o Prof. V.N.P. Tripathi
New G/6 Jodhpur Colony
B.H.U., VARANASI – 221 005 (UP)

Dr. R.D. Choudhary
Director, State Museum
GUWAHATI – 781 001 Assam

Mr. Sumant Chowdhary
297, Tilak Ganj, Gala Mandi
SAGAR (MP)

Mr. B.P. Das
Sundar Villa
CHUKAN GHAT (UP)

D.K. Publishers Distributors
1, Ansari Road,
Delhi-110 002

Mr. Bijan Bihari De
Department of History
Gauhati University
GUWHATI – 781 014, Assam

Mrs. Devangana Desai,
'Shanti', 30-19, Peddar Road,
BOMBAY – 400 026 (Mah)

Mr. M.N. Deshpande
D-25, Press Enclave
Saket, NEW DELHI

Prof. M.K. Dhavalikar
'Srivatsa' 33, Navketan Society
Kothrud, PUNE – 411 029 (Mah)

Mr. K.N. Dikshit,
Archaeological Survey of India
Janpath, NEW DELHI – 110 011

Shri C. Dorjee
Archaeological Survey of India,
Janpath, NEW DELHI-110 011

Mr. Hemendra Nath Dutta
Registration Officer
Department of Archaeology
JORHAT – 785 001 Assam

Dr. D.P. S. Dwarikesh
Department of Linguistics
Michigan University
KALAMAZOO 49008
U.S.A.

Mr. I.D. Dwivedi
Archaeological Survey of India
Safdarjung Madarsa
NEW DELHI – 110 003

Dr. U.C. Dwivedi
Patna Museum, Buddha Marg
PATNA - 800 001 (Bihar)

Dr. H.P. Francfort
CNRS, URA No. 10
23, Rue du Maroc
75019 PARIS, Cedex 19
France

Ms. Shikha Ganguly
76-C, Sultan Alam Road
CALCUTTA - 700 033 (WB)

Prof. R.C. Gaur
4/16, Kelanagar
Manis Road Extension
ALIGARH – 202 001 (UP)

Ms. Geeta Dharmarajan
A/3 Sarvodaya Enclave
New Delhi -110 017

Mrs Geeta Narvare
C/o Dr. Giriraj Kumar,
Dayalbagh Educational Institute
Dayalbagh, AGRA 282 005 (UP)

Prof. A.K. Ghosh,
16B, R.K. Chatterjee Road
CALCUTTA – 700 042 (WB)

Prof. N.C. Ghosh
Department of A.I.H.C. & Archaeology
Visva Bharati
SANTINIKETAN – 731 235 (W B)

Mr. O.K. Ghosh
Flat No.4; 5, Russel Street
Calcutta -700 016 (WB)

Dr. I.C. Glover,
Institute of Archaeology
London University
Gordon Square,
London (U K)

Mr. Gopal Shesh
Killaward, Juna
BILASPUR – 495 001 (M P)

Mr. Chester P. Gorman
Curator, South Asian Section
University Museum
University of Pennsylvania
23rd and Spruce Street
PHILADELPHIA PA 19104
U.S.A.

Shri J.C. Grover
National Museum
Janpath, New Delhi – 110011

Dr. C.S. Gupta,
Department of AIHC & Archaeology
Nagpur University
NAGPUR, (Mah.)

Dr. Jagdish Gupta,
181-A/1 Nagavasuki
ALLAHABAD – 211 006 (UP)

Mr. Mahendra Kumar Gupta,
Department of A.I.H.C. & Archaeology,
Banaras Hindu University,
VARANASI – 221 005 (UP)

Dr. P.L. Gupta
Indian Institute of Research in
Nimismatic Studies
Post ANJANERI
Distt. Nasik, (Mah)

Dr. S.P. Gupta
148, Vigyan Vihar
Delhi-110 092

Mr. Shyam Sharan Gupta,
Archaeological Survey of India,
Prehistory Branch
Old High Court Building
NAGPUR-440 001 (Mah.)

Dr. Haertel
Museum of Indian Art
Berlin-33, Taku Street
Federal Republic of Germany

Mr. Syed Hussain Haider
Senior Curator
Department of History
Aligarh Muslim University
ALIGARH (UP)

Dr. Rajaram Hegde
Deptt. of History & Archaeology
Kuvempu University,
B.R. Project (Karnataka)
SHIMOGA-577 115 (Kar.)

Mr. Hemraj
Archaeological officer
Siradi Bhawan,
Khatiyari
ALMORA – 263 601 (UP)

Mr. Mohammad Mozammel Hoque
Deptt. of Archaeology, Deccan College
PUNE—411 006 (Mah.)

Dr. K. Ismail
275, Laxmi Nagar
NAGPUR - 440 022 (Mah.)

Mr. Ashok Jain
M/s Munshiram Manoharlal
Publishers (Pvt.) Ltd.
Rani Jhansi Road,
NEW DELHI-110 055

Ms. Kirti Jain
Deppti 31 E 15th Road
Santa Cruz West
BOMBAY – 400 054 (Mah.)

Mr. Ramesh Jain,
6/25, MACT Colony
BHOPAL (MP)-463007

Dr. A.P. Jamkhedkar
Director of Archaeology & Museums
Maharashtra State
Samaj Shikshan Mandir
Worli, BOMBAY (Mah.)

Mr. Michel Jansen,
Deptt. 4 Architecture, Indus Valley
Project, Aachen University, AACHEN,
Germany

Mr. Achyutanand Jha
Archaeological Survey of India
Janpth, NEW DELHI-110 011

Dr. S.K. Jha
Directorate of Archaeology
Vikas Bhawan
PATNA (Bihar)

Mr. Shalindra Mohan Jha
C/o Prof. K.M. Shrimali
155, Vaishali, Pitampura
NEW DELHI -110 034

Miss B.R. Joshi,
Department of History and Culture
Gujarat Vidyapeeth
Ashram Road
AHMEDABAD – 380 014 (Guj)

Mr. Jeetendra Nath
National Museum
Janpath, NEW DELHI –110 011

Dr. M.D. Kajale
Department of Archaeology
Deccan College,
PUNE- 411 006 (Mah.)

Dr. Mark Kenoyar
Department of Anthropology &
Archaeo-logy, Wisconsion University
Madison WINSCONSIN
U.S.A.

Dr. B.M. Khanduri
Deptt. of Archaeology
P.B. 16, Garhwal University
SRINAGAR-246 174 (UP)

Dr. Knox
Indian Art Department
British Museum
LONDON, U.K.

Dr. Ravi Korisettar
Department of History & Archaeology
Karnataka Unviersity
DHARWAD – 580 003 (Kar)

Shri Krishna Deva
C-121, DDA MIG Flats
Saket,NEW DELHI -110017

Dr. Krishna Kumari
Department of History
Andhra University
WALTAIR – 530 003 (A P)

Mr. K. Kumar,
C/o Shiva Kumar, Advocate
268, Pani Chowk, Kotwali Road
FATEHPUR, (UP)

Dr. Kumar Anand
Shivapuri, Beur Road
P.O. Anisabad
PATNA – 800 002 (Bihar)

Dr. Krishna Murari
Faculty of Social Science
21 Anugrahpuri Colony
GAYA - 823 001 (Bihar)

Prof. B.B. Lal
F-7, Hauz Khaz Enclave
Near Chor Minar
NEW DELHI -110 016

Dr. Makkhan Lal,
P.Box 112, H.P.O.
ALIGARH – 202 001 (UP)

Prof. Lallanji Gopal
9, Gurudham Colony
VARANASI - 221 005 (UP)

Mr. H. Laven
Institute of Genetik
University of Mainz
MAINZ (West Germany)

Mr. Suresh Lekhwani
Archaeological Survey of India
Prehistory Branch
Old High Court Building
NAGPUR – 440 001 (Mah.)

Dr. Lokesh Chandra
J-22, Hauz Khas Enclave
NEW DELHI-110 016

Ms. K. Madgavkar
41/42 Lucknow Road,
DELHI –110 007
Dr. Sudha Malaiya
Vijay Oil Mills
DAMOH (MP)

Dr. S.C. Malik,
5/90 Connaught Circus,
NEW DELHI –110 001

Dr. B.R. Mani,
Archaeological Survey of India
Delhi Circle,
Safdarjang Tomb,
NEW DELHI – 110 003

Dr. Man Mohan
Dept. of History
M.D. University
ROHTAK–124 001 (Har.)

Mr. Yashodhar Mathpal
Folk Culture Museum
Bhimtal, Nainital (UP)

Dr. C. Magabandhu
Archaeological Survey of India
Janpath,
NEW DELHI – 110 011

Dr. Richard Meadow
H-48 Elm Street Canton
MASS. 02021, U.S.A.

Prof. R.N. Mehta
Department of Ancient History,
Culture and Archaeology
M.S. University of Baroda
VADODARA (Guj.)

Prof. V.N. Misra
Department of Archaeology
Deccan College
PUNE – 411 006 (Mah.)

Prof. V.D. Misra
Department of Indian History and Archaeology
Allahabad University
ALLAHABAD (UP)

Dr. O.P. Mishra,
E-107, Mahadeo Apartments
Shivaji Nagar
BHOPAL - 462 016 (MP)

Dr. R.C. Misra
Department of History
Rajasthan University
JAIPUR (Raj)

R.S. Mishra
Deptt. of Ancient History
Allahabad University
ALLAHABAD (UP)

Dr. Rajni Mishra
Temple Survey Project
Archaeological Survey of India
A-3, professor Colony
BHOPAL–460 002 (MP)

Mr. S.K. Mitra,
Deputy Superintending Archaeologist,
Archaeological Survey of India,
Bibi Ka Makbara
AURANGABAD (Mah)

Mr. V.R. Mitragotri,
Directorate of Archives,
Archaeology & Museums
PANAJI, Goa

Mr. K.K. Mohammad
Archaeological Survey of India
B-2, Happy Home
St. Inez,
PANAJI, Goa-403 001

Mr. Vijneshu Mohan
508 Sector 13
Urban Estate
KURUKSHETRA-132 118 (Har)

Shri L.P.R. Mohnani
HF-3, Block-F
Saraswati Nagar
BHOPAL– 462 003 (MP)

Dr. G.G. Majumdar
Department of Archaeology
Deccan College
PUNE – 411 006 (Mah)

Dr. Chhanda Mukherjee
Indian Museum
27, Jawahar Lal Nehru Road,
CALCUTTA - 700 016 (WB)

Ms. Suchandra Mukherjee,
14, Lower Range,
Circus Avenue
CALCUTTA–700 017 (WB)

Dr. Ravi Murti
Deptt. of Archaeology
Deccan College,
PUNE - 411 006 (Mah)

M/s Munshiram Manoharlal,
54, Rani Jhansi Road,
NEW DELHI-110 055

Mr. K.S. Murthy,
Department of Anthropology
Andhra University
WALTAIR (AP)

Dr. Malti Nagar,
Department of Archaeology
Deccan College
PUNE – 411 006 (Mah)

Dr. B.L. Nagarch,
Superintending Archaeologist,
Archaeological Survey of India
Temple Survey Project
A-3 Professor Colony,
BHOPAL-462 002 (MP)

Prof. A.K. Narain,
'Usha Kiran'
Nand Nagar
Banaras Hindu University
VARANASI – 221 005 (UP)

Dr. B. Narasimhiah
Superintending Archaeologist,
Archaeological Survey of India
Fort St. George,
MADRAS – 600 009 (TN)

Mr. G.S. Narasimhan,
Archaeological Survey of India,
Patna Circle,
Judges Court Road,
PATNA – 800 004 (Bih)

Mr. W.V.S. Narasimhan
20/292, Lala Thota Street
Mulapet
NELLORE – 524 003 (AP)

Dr. Vidyadhar Negi
C/o Dr. M.P. Joshi
Malla Joshikhola
ALMORA – 263 601 (UP)

Mr. J.S. Nigam,
2, Nigam Bagh,
Kundri Rakabganj,
LUCKNOW – 2260 04 (UP)

Mr. S.B. Ota,
Archaeological Survey of India,
Prehistory Branch
Old High Court Building
NAGPUR (Mah)

Dr. K. Paddayya
Department of Archaeology
Deccan College,
PUNE – 411 006 (Mah)

Mr. K.P. Padhey,
Archaeological Survey of India
Ratnagiri Museum,
RATNAGIRI, Orissa

Dr. A.C. Pal,
Department of Archaeology
Calcutta University,
CALCUTTA (WB)

Dr. J.N. Pal,
Department of A.I.H.C. & Archaeology
Allhabad Unviersity
ALLAHABAD (UP)

Dr. J.N. Pandey
Deptt. A.I.H.C. & Archaeology
Allahabad University,
ALLAHABAD (UP)

Shri R.G. Pandey,
Birla Museum
BHOPAL (MP)

Mrs. Sandhya Pande
K.R.G. College,
GWALIOR, (M P)

Dr. P.C. Pant,
Deptt of A.I.H.C. & Archaeology
Banaras Hindu University
VARANASI – 221 009 (UP)

Dr. V.S. Parikh
Deptt. of Ancient history & Archaeology
M.S. University of Baroda
VADODARA (Guj)

Mr. Krishna Parolia,
C/o Ramji Lal Ratan Prakash
Cloth Dealer, Katra Crossing
ALLAHABAD (UP)

Dr. Asko Parpola
Untuvasetie 5. B. 64
00820 HELESINKI-82
Finland

Dr. K.H. Patel,
Department of Ancient History & Archaeology
M.S. University of Baroda,
VADODARA – 390 002 (Guj)

Ms. Anjali Pathak
Deccan College,
PUNE – 411 006 (Mah)

Mr. Sridhar Pathak
A.S.P.
LAKHIMPUR KHERI (UP)

Dr. P.V. Pathak,
203, Shanta Bhavan
Sai Nagar,Vasai Marg
Dist. THANE – 401 202 (Mah)

Shri Shashi Kant Pathak
National Museum,
Janpath, NEW DELHI – 110 011

Dr. G.L. Possehl
Deptt. of South Asian Studies
University of Pennsylvania
33rd and Spruce Street,
PHILADELPHIA PA. 19104, U.S.A.

Dr. Sadashiv Pradhan
Deptt. of History
Sambalpur University
Qr. No. C/23 Joyti Vihar
SAMBALPUR, Orissa

Dr. Pratibha Prakash
Old G/8 Jodhpur Colony,
Banaras Hindu University,
VARANASI – 221 005 (UP)

Mr. Nayakanda Prakash
Excavation Branch
Archaeological Survey of India
Old High Court Building
NAGPUR – 440 001 (Mah)

Dr. P. Vijay Prakash
Department of Anthropology
Andhra University
WALTAIR – 530 003 (AP)

Mr. Ajit Kumar Prasad
Sunder Bhavan,
Gardani Bagh, Kacchi Talab
PATNA – 800 001 (Bihar)

Dr. P.C. Prasad
B-357, Baily Road,
PATNA – 800 015

Mr. G.C. Rai,
10A/4 Shakti Nagar
DELHI – 110 007

Dr. K. Rajan
Department of Archaeology
Tamil University
THANJAVUR – 613 001 (TN)

Dr. Ravindra Kumar
B-13/78 Sonarpura
VARANASI – 221 001 (UP)

Shri Sunil Kumar
Old E/2, Jodhpur Colony
B.H.U.
VARANASI – 221 005 (UP)

Dr. David B. Raju,
Reader,
Department of History & Archaeology
Nagarjuna University
NAGARJUNA NAGAR – 522 511 (AP)

Prof. Wilhelm Rau,
3553, Reddeharser,
HONNEQ-3
Germany

Dr. M.S. Nagaraja Rao,
C/o Dept. of Archaeology and Museums
Karnataka, State Palace
MYSORE, (Karnataka)

Mr. L.S. Rao,
Archaeological Survey of India
Prehistory Branch,
Old High Court Building
NAGPUR – 440 001 (Mah)

Dr. Amita Ray
Deptt. of A.I.H.C. & Archaeology
Calcutta University,
CALCUTTA (WB)

Dr. (Mrs.) Himanshu Prabha Ray,
C-93 South Extention Part II
NEW DELHI – 110 049

Mr. S.B. Roy,
B-20, Sujan Singh Park
NEW DELHI

Smt. Veena Sachdeva
W 57 Greater Kailash II
NEW DELHI – 110 049

Dr. M.D.N. Sahi,
Department of History,
Aligarh Muslim University,
ALIGARH – 220 001 (UP)

Mr. Binoy Kumar Sahay
National Museum, Janpath
NEW DELHI – 110 011

Sri Santosh Kumar, I.P.S.
DIG, C.I.D.
Road No.8, Patel Nagar,
PATNA – 800 023 (Bihar)

Dr. K.S. Saraswat
Bibal Sahani Inst. of Palaeobotany,
University Road
LUCKNOW (UP)

Ms. G. Sarvamangala
No. 217 Parasanna
II Stage II Block
Vinoba Nagar
SHIMOGA – 577201 (Karnataka)

Shri Jinendra Sena
C/o Malwa Sugar Mills
DHURI (Distt. Sangrur)
Punjab

Ms. Aparna Sengupta
C/o Dr. P.K. Sengupta
Ratnapalli
SHANTINIKETAN – 731 235 (WB)

Mr. Vinod Kumar Seth
H-17, Maharani Bagh
NEW DELHI – 110 014

Dr. A.K. Sharma
Indira Gandhi Centre for Arts
Janpath, New Delhi – 110 001

Shri D.P. Sharma
National Museum,
Janpath
NEW DELHI – 110 011

Mr. Kamlesh Kumar Sharma
National Museum,
Janpath,
NEW DELHI – 110 001

Dr. Krishna Gopal Sharma
Department of History and Indian Culture
Rajasthan University,
JAIPUR – 320 001(Raj)

Dr. R.C. Sharma,
National Museum, Janpath
NEW DELHI – 110011
Mr. R.P. Sharma,
Institute of Archaeology,
24, Tilak marg,
NEW DELHI – 110 002

Mr. Sarovar Shende
National Museum
Janpath
NEW DELHI – 110011

Mr. Sharad Kant Sharma,
Neelambar Prachiya Vidya Peeth
24, Gangwal Bagh
JAIPUR – 302 004 (Raj)

Mr. S.R. Sharma,
Village & P.O. PAHARGARH
District Morena (M P)

Prof. T.C. Sharma
C/o R.D. Choudhary
State Museum
GUWAHATI, Assam

T.R. Sharma,
C/o Dr. V.V. Dixit
7 B, Ashey hall
DEHRA DUN – 248 001 (UP)

Shri Vikash Chandra Sharma,
Archaeological Survey of India,
Janpath, NEW DELHI – 110 011

Dr. Malti Shendge
1603 Sadashiv Peth
PUNE – 411 030 (Mah)

Dr. Vasant Shinde
Department of Archaeology
Deccan College,
PUNE – 411 006 (Mah)

Mr. R.V. Shivasharma
Archaeological Survey of India
1/91113/30/1/C
Dayanand Nagar, Vidya Nagar
HYDERABAD – 500 044 (AP)

Shri K.B. Shivataraka
Deptt of AI. H & Archaeeology,
St. Mary Syrian Colleege,
BRAHMAVARA–576 213
Karnataka

Prof. K.M. Shrimali,
155, Vaishali, Pitampura
DELHI – 110 034

Dr. Pradeep Kumar Shukla,
Studio Manoj
Parkota Hills
SAGAR – 470 002 (MP)

Dr. A.R. Sidiqui
National Museum,
Janpath,NEW DELHI – 110 001

Shri W.H. Siddqui,
Director
Raza Libarary
RAMPUR (UP)

Dr. Abhay Kumar Singh
35/A-7A Asthana Marg,
Rampur Bagh
Bareilly – 243 001 (UP)

Dr. A.K. Singh
Deptt. of Ancient, History &
Archaeology, Jiwaji University
GWALIOR (MP)

Dr. Amrendra Kumar Singh
Department of Ancient Indian History
A.P.S. University
REWA (MP)

Dr. Arvind Kumar Singh
SOS in Ancient Indian History &
Archaeology
Jiwaji University
GWALIOR – 474 011 (MP)

Mr. Arvind Kumar Singh,
Vill. Rangauli, BHARACCHA
District Varanasi – 232101 (UP)

Dr. Ashok Kumar Singh
C/o Prof. P. Singh
New E/3 Jodhpur Colony
B.H.U. Campus
VARANASI – 221 005 (UP)

Dr. Bhagwan Singh
J3/227, DDA Flats
Kalkaji
NEW DELHI – 110 047

Dr. Birendra Pratap Singh
Kabir Chaura
C23/15, Ayodhya Bhawan
VARANASI (UP)

Dr. Bhupendra Pal Singh
Block 19, Flat 4
Kabir Nagar Colony
VARANASI – 221 001

Mr. Girish Chandra Singh
21, Aram Bagh Colony
Kayam Khera, Motinagar
LUCKNOW (UP)

Mr. O.K. Singh
Director Department of Archaeology
and Museums
Imphal, MANIPUR

Prof. Purshottam Singh,
New E/3 Jodhpur Colony
B.H.U. Campus
VARANASI – 221005

Dr. R.C.P. Singh
Department of A.I.H. and Asian Studies
Magadh University
BODH GAYA (Bihar)

Mr. Ravi Pratap Singh,
Chandra Bhawan,
Alajatapur
GORAKHPUR (UP)

Dr. S.B. Singh
Department of A.I.H.C. and Archaeology
Kurukshetra University
KURUKSHETRA (Har)

Shri Sanjib Kumar Singh
National Museum
Janpath, NEW DELHI – 110 011

Prof. U.V. Singh
Departmeent of A.I.H.C. & Archaeology
Kurukshetra University,
KURUSKSHETRA (Hary)

Dr. Y.B. Singh,
Department of History
Jammu University,
JAMMU – 180 001 (J & K)

Mr. A.K. Sinha,

Archaeological Survey of India,
Janpath, NEW DELHI – 110 011

Mr. B.K. Sinha,
Excavation Branch
Archaeological Survey of India
Vivekanand Marg,
BHUBANESHWAR – 751 002, Orissa

Prof. B.P. Sinha,
68, Pataliputra Colony,
PATNA (Beh)

Mr. Niraj Kumar Sinha
Archaeological Survey of India
Excavation Branch
Vivekanand Marg,
BHUWANESHWAR – 751 002

Dr. Prakash Sinha,
2, Malaviya Nagar
George Town
ALLAHABAD (UP)

Prof. W.G. Solhelm II
Department of Anthropology
University of Hawaii
2550 Campus Road
HONOLULU – 96822 U.S.A.,

Dr. Sipra Som
E 3/224 Arera Colony
BHOPAL – 462 016 (MP)

Prof. B.L.K. Somyajulu
Physical Research Laboratory
Navrangpura
AHMEDABAD – 380 009 (Guj)

Dr. V.H. Sonawane
Department of Ancient History &
Archaeology
M.S. University Baroda
VADODARA – 390 002 (Guj)

Dr. K. Srinivasulu
Oriental College
PRODDATUR – 516 360 (AP)

Mr. P.S. Sriraman
Archaeological Survey of India,
No. 364, 16th Main,
35th Cross, 4th T Block
Jayanagar
BANGALORE – 47 (Karnataka)

Shri A.K. Srivastava
National Research Lab. for
Cultural Property
E/3 Aliganj,LUCKNOW (UP)

Mr. J.P. Srivastava
178, Pharma Apartments
Plot No. 88
Near Patparganj Bus Depot
NEW DELHI – 110 092

Mr. K.C. Srivastava
'Gokul', H. No. N-11/58, M-11-C
Mohalla Ranipur, P.O., Bazardiya
VARANASI (UP)

Dr. K.M. Srivastava,
142, Venus Apartment
Near Indira Enclave,
Rohtak Road,
NEW DELHI – 110 041

Mr. S.K. Srivastava
Archaeological Museum
Gurukul Kangari University,
HARIDWAR (UP)

Dr. V.C. Srivastava
Department of A.I.H.C. & Archaeology
Banaras Hindu University
VARANASI – 221 005 (UP)

Dr. K.K. Subbayya
Deptt. of Ancient Indian History
Culture and Archaeology,
Mysore University
Manasa Gangotri,
MYSORE (Karnataka)

Prof. A. Sundara
'Saundarya Sri'
Bharati Nagara
DHARWAD–580 001 (Karnataka)

Shri L.B. Swarnakar
Mrs. R.K. Prasad
AG1/103A, Vikaspuri
NEW DELHI

Prof. Taddei
Oriental Institute
Unviersity of Nables
NAPLES, Italy

Shri R.C. Thakur
68/D 10,Rohini, Sector VII
DELHI – 110 085

Capt. Raghubir Singh Thakur
Security Officer,
Archaeological Survey of India,
Bibi ka Makbara
AURANGABAD – 431004, (Mah)

Dr. M.J. Thanki
8/3 Government Officers Colony
Meghani Nagar
AHMEDABAD – 380 016 (Guj)

Shri B.K. Thapar,
342, DDA Flats, Hauz Khas,
NEW DELHI – 110 016

Prof. Romila Thapar
School of Historical Studies
Jawaharlal Nehru University
NEW DELHI – 110 067

Prof. K.K. Thaplayal
Department of A.I.H.C. & Archaeology
Lucknow University
LUCKNOW (UP)

Dr. Raj Kumar Tiwari
D-62, Street No.4
Laxmi nagar,
DELHI – 110092

Dr. Raksh Tiwari,
Department of Archaeology
Roshanadaula Kothi
Kaisarbagh,
LUCKNOW (UP)

Dr. V.K. Tiwari
Archaeological Museum
NALANDA – 803 111 (Bihar)

Prof. P.K. Tiwari,
2/435 Vivekanand II
Gomati Nagar
LUCKNOW – 226 016 (UP)

Prof. Maurizio Tosi
ISMEO,
ROME, Italy

Dr. D.N. Tripathi
20, Hirapur Colony
GORAKHPUR – 273 009 (UP)

Mr. Alok Tripathi
Mama Ka Bazar
Kashkar
GWALIOR – 470 001 (MP)

Prof. L.K. Tripathi
Department of A.I.H.C. & Archaeology
Banaras Hindu University,
VARANASI – 221 005 (UP)

Dr. Vibha Tripathi
B 31/35-22, Sankat Mochan Colony
VARANASI – 221 005 (UP)

Dr. Sila Tripati
Marine Archaeology Centre
National Institute of Oceanography
Dona Paula
GOA – 403 004

Mr. P.K. Trivedi,
Archaeological Survey of India
D-49, Subhash Marg, C-Scheme
JAIPUR – 302 001 (Raj)

Mr. G.S. Tyagi
C/o AGE (I), Amla
P.O. AMLA–460 553
Dist. Betul (M P)

Dr. V.D. Tyagi,
D.S. College
ALIGARH (UP)

Dr. Usha Bhende
Near E.S.I. Dispensary
Station Road
DHARWAR – 580 001 (Karnataka)

Prof. R.K. Varma
"Samarpana", 18/C, Hastings Road
ALLAHABAD (UP)

Dr. B.S. Verma
J-124 Kankarbagh Colony
PATNA – 800 020 (Bihar)

Dr. Vidula Jaiswal
Deptt. of Ancient History &
Archaeology,
BHU, VARANASI (U.P.)

Prof. Teisuke Yakata
Kashiwabara 15507
Hotaka Mach
NAGANO 399-83,Japan

Director
Department of Archaeology
Distt. Panchayat Building
5th Floor
AHMEDABAD – 380 001 (Guj)

DirectorDirectorate of Archaeology
and Museum
Government of Madhya Pradesh
Banganga Road,
BHOPAL (MP)

Secretary
Centre for Advanced Studies in
Indology and Museology,
C/o Birla Museum
BHOPAL (MP)

Secretary
Bihar Puravid Parishad
Patna Museum
PATNA – 800 001 (Bihar)

Director,
Patna Museum
Buddha Marg,
PATNA – 800 001 (Bihar)

Director,
Directorate of Archaeology & Museums
Vikas Bhawan
PATNA (Bihar)

Director
Institute of Sanskrit and Indological Studies
KURUKSHETRA – 132 119 (Har)

Director
Birbal Sahani Institute of Palaeobotany
LUCKNOW – 226 007 (UP)

Director
State Museum
Banarasi Bagh
LUCKNOW (UP)

Director
Tamil Nadu State Museum
Egmore, MADRAS (TN)

Librarian
Sri Sathya Sai Institute of Higher Learning
PARASHANTI NILAYAM – 515 134
Near BANGALORE, (Karnataka)

Registrar
Andhra University
WALTAIR (AP)

Italian Institute for Middle and Far East
ROME, Italy

Seminario di Archaeological Orientale
Institute Universitalis
C-NAPOLI, Italy

Director
U.P. State Archaeological Organization
Roshandaulla Kothi
Kaisar Bagh
LUCKNOW (UP)

Superintending Archaeologist
Aurangabad Circle,
Archaeological Survey of India,
Bibi ka Makbara
AURANGABAD – 431 004 (Mah)

Archaeological Officer,
U.P. State Archaeological Organization
Kandolia Road
PAURI-GARHWAL (UP)

*** Note:** It is possible that some names are missing in this list. It is also possible that some adresses are no longer current. In either case we request our readers and members to intimate us the corect address so that the same may be updated in our records

Plant Economy of Late Harappan from Hulas

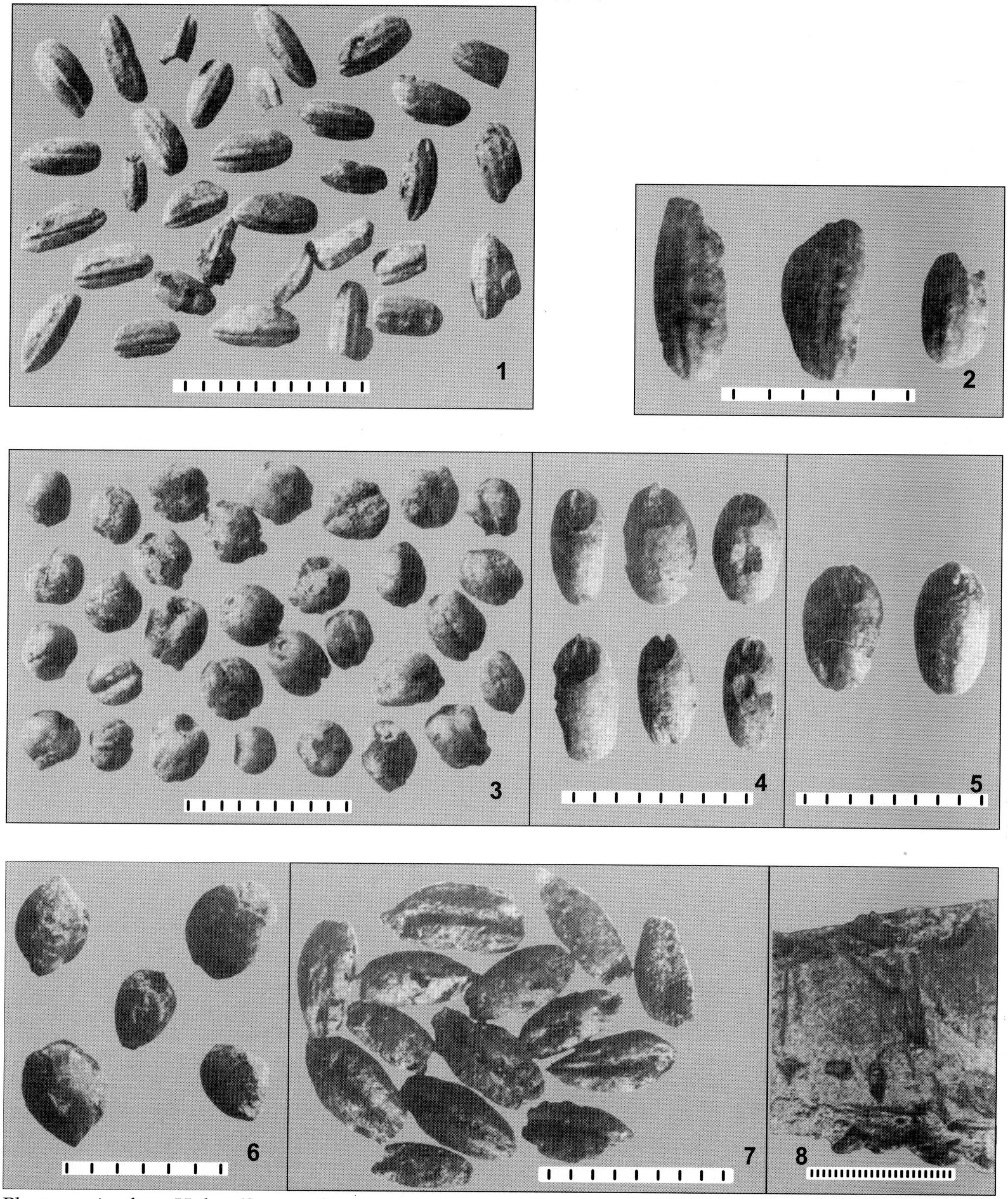

Plant remains from Hulas. (Saraswat)

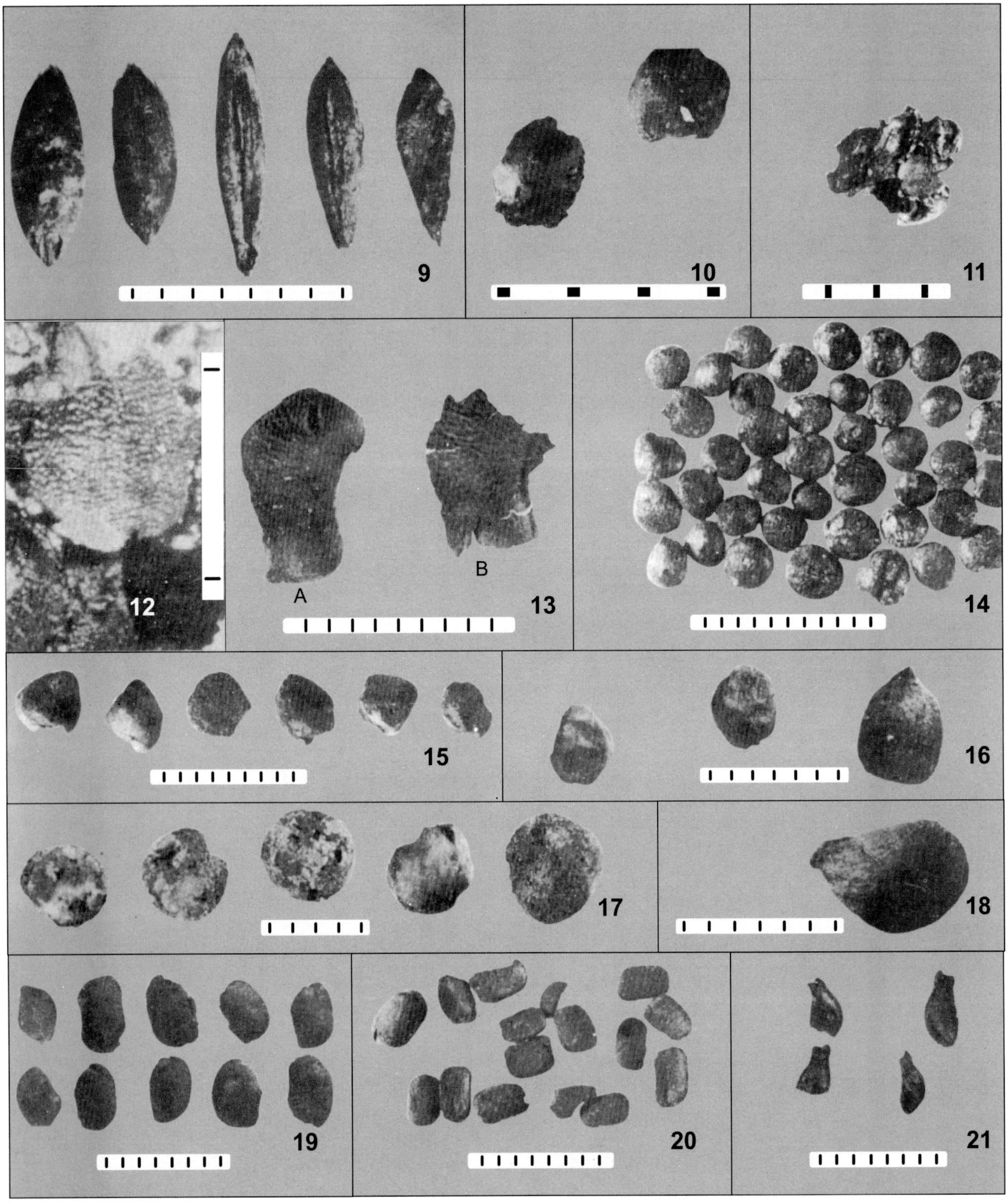

Plant remains from Hulas. (Saraswat)

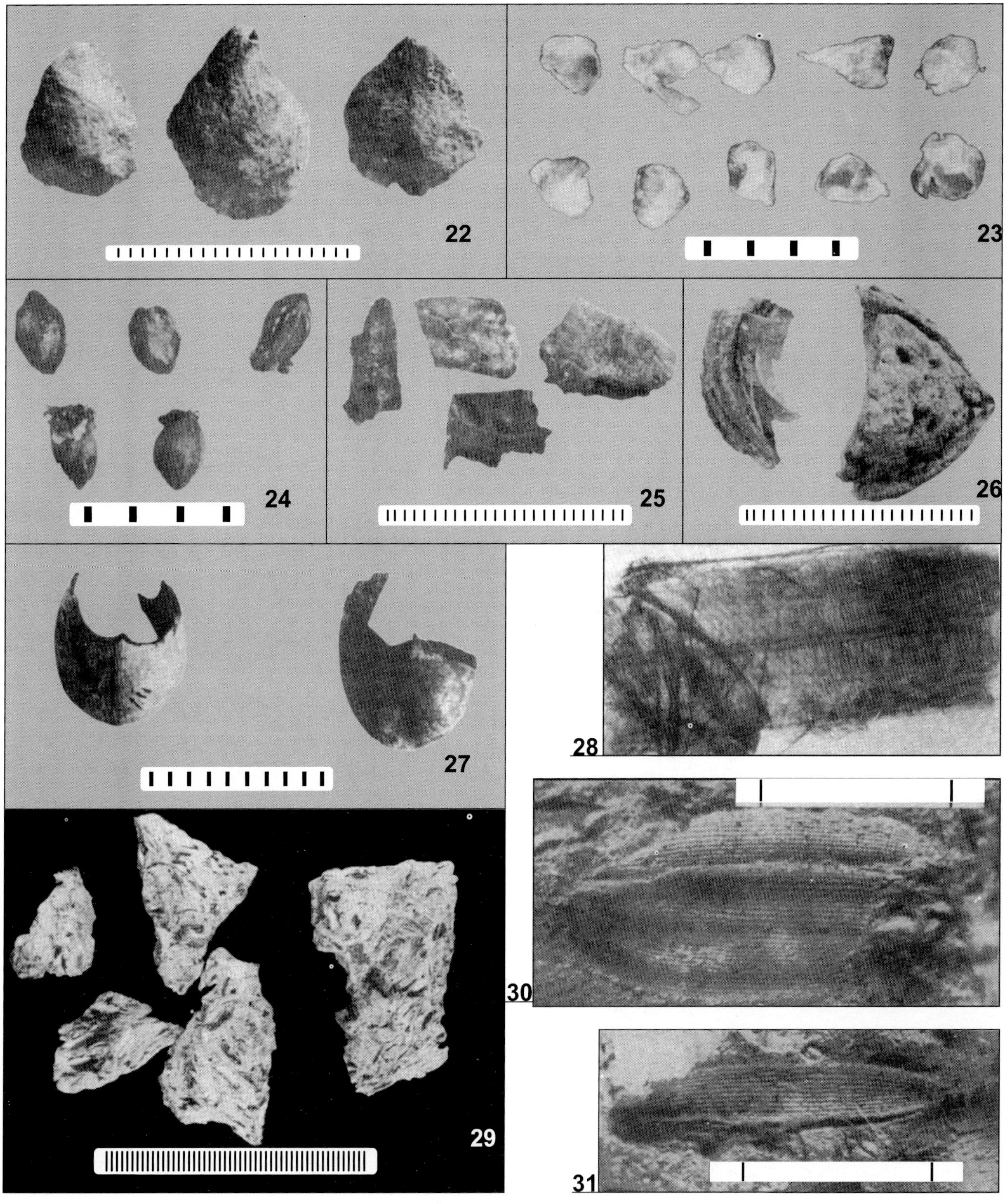

Plant remains from Hulas. (Saraswat)

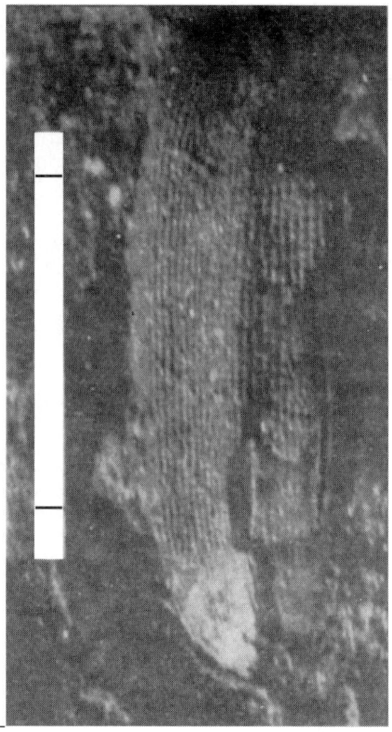
33

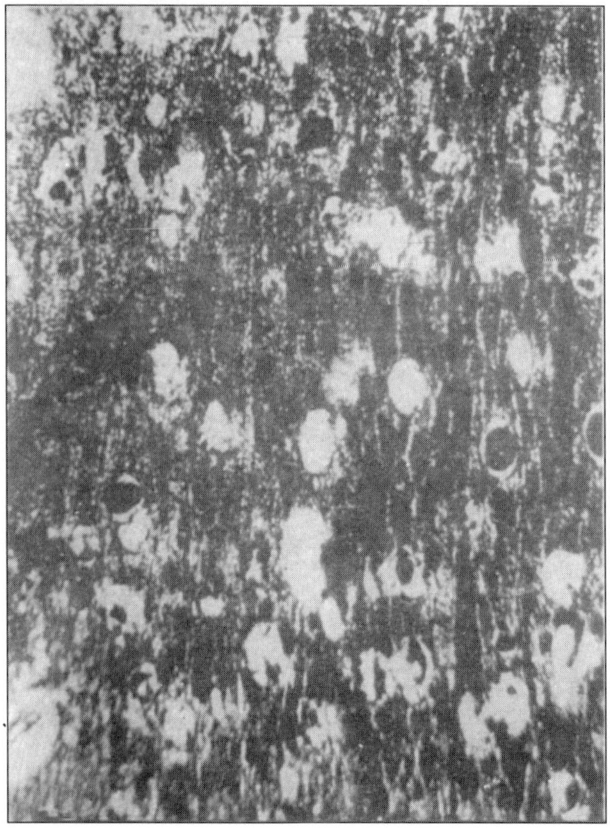
34

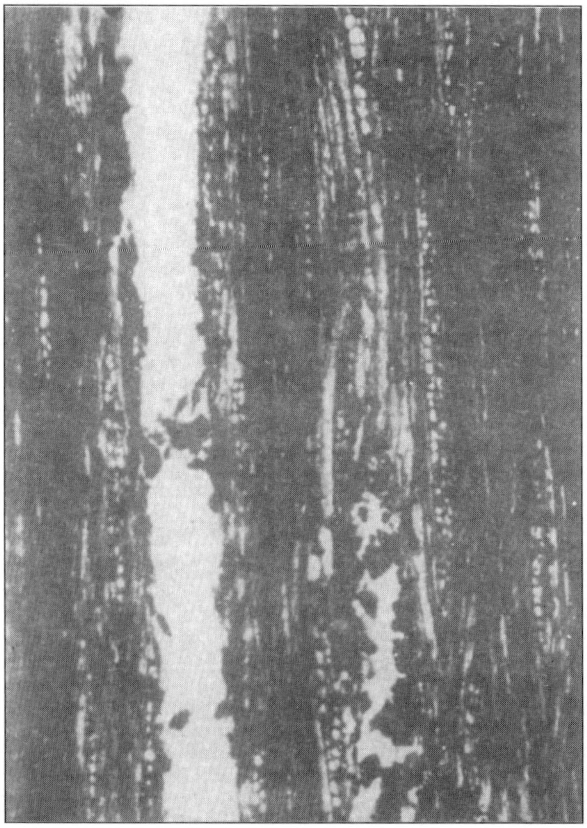
35

Plant remains from Hulas. (Saraswat)

Fig. 1. Taj Mahal : Black spots — Mosquito excreta. (Agrawal)

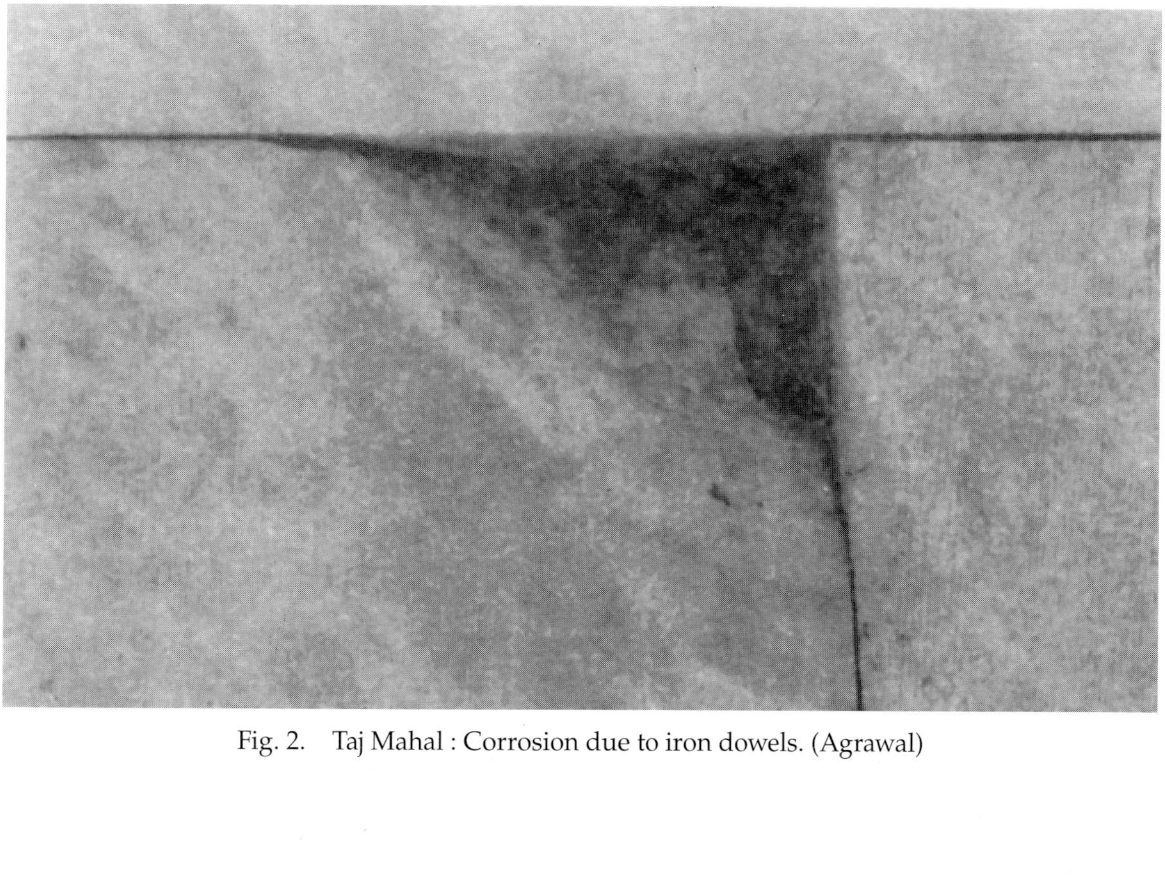

Fig. 2. Taj Mahal : Corrosion due to iron dowels. (Agrawal)

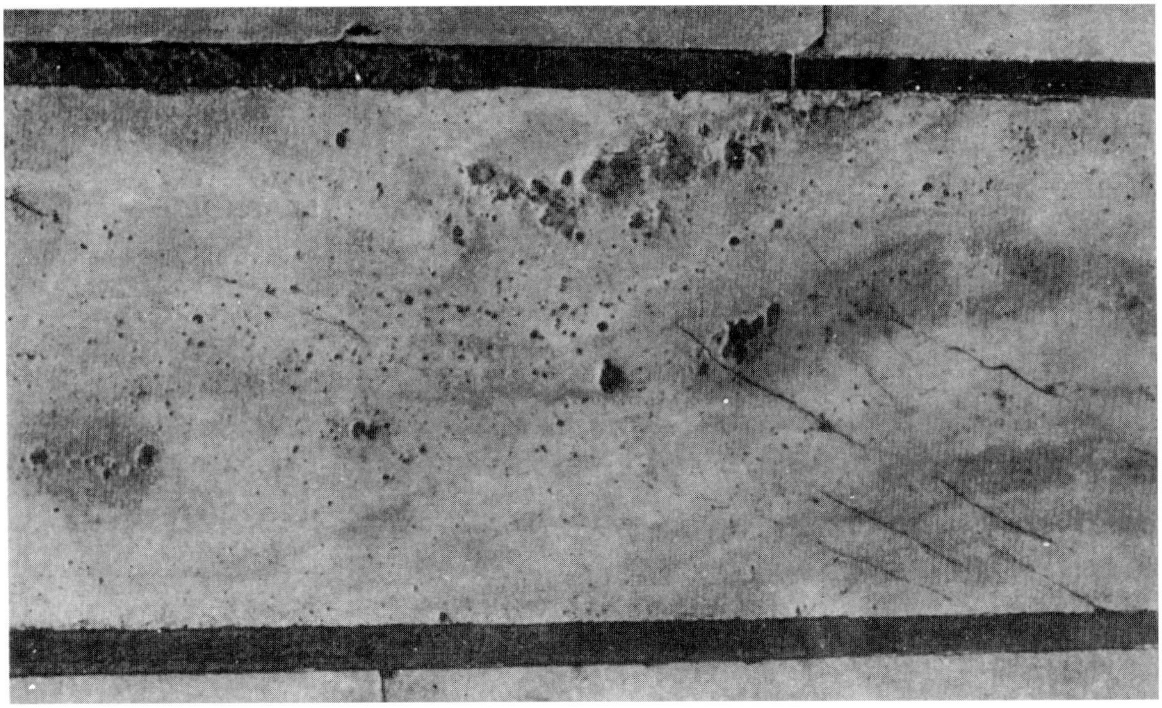

Fig. 3. Taj Mahal : Pitting in marble slabs. (Agrawal)

Fig. 4. Taj Mahal : Erosion due to water flow through spout. (Agrawal)

Ayodhyā and Rama

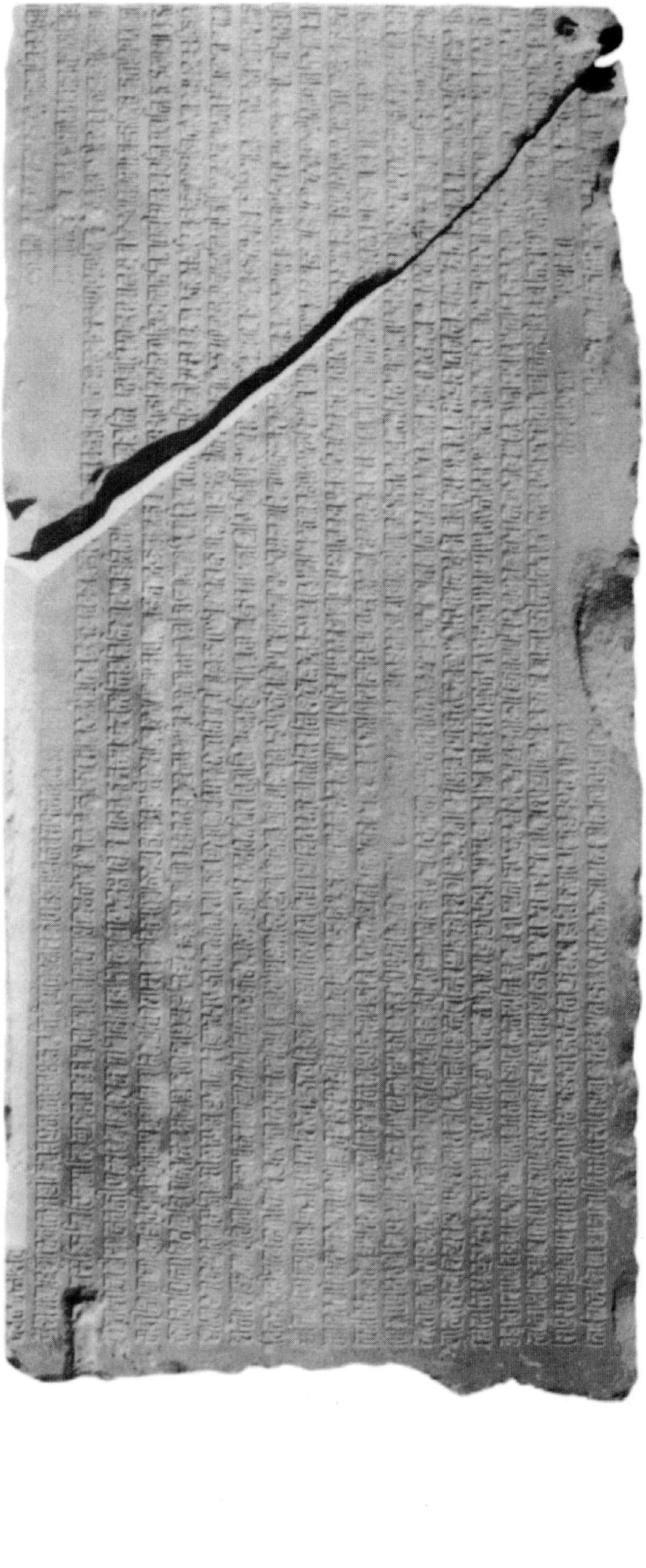

A new inscription from Ayodhya. (Shastri)

Details of the new inscription from Ayodhya. (Shastri)